BARGAINING BEYOND IMPASSE

BARGAINING BEYOND IMPASSE

Joint Resolution of
Public Sector Labor Disputes

JONATHAN BROCK
John F. Kennedy School of Government
Harvard University

AH *Auburn House Publishing Company*
Boston, Massachusetts

Library of Congress Cataloging in Publication Data

Brock, Jonathan, 1949–
    Bargaining beyond impasse.

    Includes index.
    1. Collective bargaining—Government employees—
Massachusetts.   2. Labor-management committees—
Massachusetts.   3. Labor disputes—Massachusetts.
4. Collective bargaining—Government employees—United
States.   I. Title.

HD8005.6.U53M43	331.89′0413539744	81-20652
ISBN 0-86569-110-X		AACR2

Printed in the United States of America

FOREWORD

The Commonwealth of Massachusetts Joint Labor-Management Committee for Municipal Police and Fire Fighters (JLMC) completes five years at the end of 1982. Its track record of dispute resolution without work stoppages is deserving of attention and analysis. Jon Brock's volume provides an account of the antecedents and operations of the JLMC; he also develops for practitioners and analysts alike a systematic introduction to the resolution of public sector disputes and, specifically, public safety issues. The study is timely, for these questions deeply trouble many parts of the country in a difficult budgetary and political environment.

As the catalyst involved in the generation of the JLMC, I should like to set out the essential and distinctive elements of the Committee's work that are transferrable, that are not the accident of time, place, and persons.

First, the JLMC was *created* basically by agreement and consent of the parties—the state-wide organizations of municipal management and professional firefighters and police unions. Although supported and made legitimate by statutes, JLMC was not imposed on the state-wide organizations by the hostile fiat of state law. The JLMC is *manned* by the parties, and the neutrals on the Committee are selected by them; the normal processes of state politics do not appoint the Committee members. The JLMC is *operated* by the parties with the aid of a staff of mediators responsible to the Committee members and working with them in particular cases to reach settlement and resolution of disputes. The parties thus have a fundamental responsibility for the work of the JLMC, for its results, and for adapting it to the shifting scenes of local government in Massachusetts under the continuing uncertainties and limitations on local government expenditures associated with Proposition 2½.* Finally, the state-wide parties have the *de facto* capacity to destroy the JLMC at any time by failing to cooperate. In the most fundamental sense the JLMC is their Committee, and they have a sense of responsibility for it.

Second, the experience of JLMC highlights basic problems that characterize the management side of local government negotiations—problems that have not been sufficiently analyzed or appreciated. As two case studies in this volume illustrate, the most pervasive difficulty derives from the internal divisions of local government associated with the different interests and politics among mayors, city managers, local councils, boards of selectmen, finance committees, personnel boards, town meetings, or other local government bodies, and the lawyers they hire for negotiations. Any settlement involves getting the management side of the "house" together and accommodating their internal differences and their open or suppressed conflicts. Mediation and dispute resolution across the table must first proceed within the two sides, and often with particular difficulty within the local government. These impediments to successful negotiations are often compounded by a lack of professionalism and experience with collective bargaining procedures. The internal conflicts within managements and their lack of experience, however, provide a distinctive opportunity for the management members of the JLMC to play a significant role, and the procedures of the Committee are designed to facilitate their playing such a role. They can often be more effective mediators within management and across the table with their labor counterparts than any neutral could possibly be. They often are more knowledgeable and more acceptable, can secure a more perceptive and sensitive view of the real issues, and can be more persuasive with their peers.

The labor side of local government negotiations, as Jon Brock explains, resembles private sector labor organizations, and it accordingly is more familiar to observers and practitioners. The state-level union representatives on the JLMC provide the assistance and sense of realism in negotiations that representatives of national unions often provide in local negotiations.

---

* "Proposition 2½" is a colloquial reference to a referendum question approved by 59% of Massachusetts voters in November 1980. Its primary effect is to impose a limit on state and local taxes on real estate and personal property equal to 2½% of its full and fair cash value. The voters of a city or town may raise the limitation by local vote. Proposition 2½ further provides that no law or regulation which imposes additional costs on a city or town will be effective unless the state agrees to assume the additional cost. It also repealed the provisions of state law which provided for compulsory last-best-offer interest arbitration in municipal police and fire negotiations.

Third, the JLMC was designed to provide a general forum for discussion of a wide variety of common problems between the state-wide parties in the same way that a number of national labor-management committees, without dispute-settling responsibilities, have provided a continuing forum. This volume describes such a problem-solving role for this joint committee. It is hard to exaggerate either the constructive possibilities or the avoidance of conflict on other issues to be derived from state-wide representatives seeing each other each week. In a rapidly changing political and economic climate, the establishment of a general forum for the responsible leaders of the state-wide parties is a distinctive JLMC contribution whose potential is yet to be fully achieved.

Fourth, the major unresolved issue concerning the JLMC at this juncture is the availability of a closure mechanism in a dispute over the terms of a collective bargaining agreement that cannot be resolved by the local parties or the Committee short of an order for final and binding arbitration. The passage of Proposition 2½ by referendum in November 1980 appears to have eliminated the authority of the JLMC to impose a final and binding arbitration award on a local government, although the Attorney General of the Commonwealth issued an advisory opinion on February 10, 1981 holding that the JLMC continues to have authority to order final and binding arbitration on the executive officers of a city or town but not on the legislative body requiring it to appropriate the requisite funds. In these circumstances JLMC has chosen to avoid legal confrontation; it has operated by mediation and other voluntary or non-compulsory methods and has thus far continued to resolve disputes expeditiously.

In this setting, it is significant that the greatest difficulties in achieving settlements have not come from the cities and towns with the greatest financial stringencies under Proposition 2½. There cases have been settled recognizing these extreme hardships with realism on both sides. The greatest difficulties have arisen, rather, in communities beset by personality conflicts, internal divisiveness within management and local parties, and political rivalries. Financial limitations have not been the primary source of labor-management conflict in these local communities.

This situation reinforces my view that if work stoppages are to be avoided in the public safety sector, the authority to invoke a closure mechanism is essential, even if it is utilized in only a few situations. There can be no doubt that compulsory arbitration has often tended, as it did before the JLMC in Massachusetts, to suppress the potential of collective bargaining, imaginative mediation, and other methods of voluntary settlement and to make the mandating of arbitration routine. For a stable system of collective bargaining to operate in the public-safety sector, without the legitimate resort to work stoppages, a closure mechanism is essential because some cases otherwise take so long or bargaining conduct and positions on one side or the other are so extreme—albeit technically proper—as to be explosive and destructive of responsible conduct. A closure mechanism can be utilized primarily to avoid such confrontation and to stimulate direct agreement-making.

This volume and its associated case materials were developed as a part of the larger Business and Government program in cooperation between Harvard's School of Government and Graduate School of Business Administration. The research and publication were supported by curriculum development grants from the Continental Group Foundation, Inc., Time Inc., and others whose assistance is gratefully acknowledged. Mr. Brock, a graduate of Harvard's Graduate School of Business Administration with considerable experience in the Federal Government, created a course at the Harvard School of Government on the management of people in the public sector.

The interaction of business, labor, and government in the local community has been a neglected subject of research and teaching. This volume will be welcomed as a contribution to both a better understanding of public sector collective bargaining and dispute resolution and as an introduction to the important relationships of business, labor, and government in the local community.

JOHN T. DUNLOP
March 1982

PREFACE

When I undertook study of the joint labor-management committee mechanism, I expected it to be a simple project concerning one method of dispute resolution in one state—a case study, a little analysis, and that would be that. Instead, I found myself face-to-face with very central problems in public sector collective bargaining. The results of this study, as set forth in this book, constitute a relatively sophisticated primer for and an exploration into the complexities of collective bargaining in the political and governmental realm—a world different in significant respects from collective bargaining in most private employment. Not incidentally, the book turns out to provide some help for those interested in constructing a workable and politically acceptable way to resolve contract disputes in public sector employment.

Observing hundreds of hours of deliberations, hearings, caucuses, and negotiations was a learning experience, as was interviewing scores of principals in impasse cases, talking with local politicians, discussing cases with members of the subject joint labor-management committee and staff, and co-chairing a joint committee on operational cost savings in a fiscally starved urban fire department. And I saw flesh-and-blood people earnestly trying to solve operational and labor management problems as an integral part of their personal and professional existence. I learned, in short, to temper my words with a dose of reality.

The project started out as an adjunct to my development of concepts and materials for studying the management of people in public agencies, including some current and relevant material in public labor-management relations. At about this time, as I arrived at Harvard's Kennedy School, the Massachusetts Joint Labor-Management Committee (JLMC) was just getting started. My senior colleague, Professor John T. Dunlop, was chairman of the JLMC. Knowing of my activities and interests, he introduced me to the mechanism and—prophetically—suggested that a useful book might come out of a study of it.

By way of acknowledgment, I was surprised and gratified to learn how much assistance one receives in a project like this. Ginny Spielberg's research formed the core of Chapter 2, and Bill Mattfeld's quantitative work, that of Chapter 7. Adele Langevin, now a neutral staff member of the JLMC, kindly allowed me to adapt the "Seabury" case study that she had originally done as part of her graduate work. Past and present members and staff of the Committee were generous with their time in interviews and informal discussions and in providing comments on drafts of several chapters. Paul Cody, research director of the JLMC, constantly provided cheerful, exact, and timely responses to all manner of requests for information and advice. I received helpful comments and input also from a number of colleagues, including David Lipsky, James Healy, David Kuechle, Ted Durkee, and Mark Grossman. The usual disclaimers apply.

Many people helped to type the manuscript, not because of its length, but because I rewrote it a lot. In the crunches (and there were many), Billie Lawrence and Christine Lundblad showed especial dedication and good judgment. Juliet Hills labored over the Barkfield case to refine it and lend it greater reality. Also, on the subject of rewriting, the manuscript benefitted from the editorial advice of Elydia P. Siegel.

To Lois Schwennesen I am especially indebted for persistent yet diplomatic criticism and questioning, as well as for encouragement to rip up old drafts and start again. Tolerance, it seemed, gave way to active support. In addition, Lois' research lent direct substance to the first chapter's discussion of difficulties with common means of public sector dispute resolution.

John T. Dunlop provided access to the JLMC activities and records. He also lent his expertise in labor management relations concepts and practices to the project in what seemed unlimited responses to my requests for discussion. His cooperation in both roles lent depth to my investigation and perception to the work.

On the practical side, I am grateful to the program in Business and Government at Harvard University, sponsored jointly by the Harvard Business School and the John F. Kennedy School of Government, for its financial support for this project and related work during this period.

Finally, it is my hope that the public sector, the practicing labor-management community, and students in their many forms will benefit from this work as new issues and problems are faced in the arena of public bargaining.

JONATHAN BROCK

March 1982

CONTENTS

Introduction

LESSONS FROM AN EXPERIMENT IN PUBLIC SAFETY DISPUTE RESOLUTION

In the following chapters we shall describe, analyze, and abstract principles from the study of a mechanism for resolving labor disputes. This mechanism was established in Massachusetts in 1977 to handle labor disputes in public safety. On the basis of an analysis of the Massachusetts experiment from observations through 1980, we shall identify possibilities of applying the principles underlying this experiment to other political and labor relations environments.

The mechanism that is the focus of this study is known as the Joint Labor-Management Committee (JLMC) for Municipal Police and Fire Fighters, a fourteen-member committee empowered to handle all contract disputes in the state between police or fire fighters and their respective municipalities. The Joint Labor-Management Committee was created in 1977 as a compromise, bargained between representatives of municipal management and the fire fighters when a political impasse arose over the renewal of a last-best-offer arbitration statute that had previously handled police and fire impasses.

The fourteen-member Joint Committee consists of six representatives from each of management and labor, a neutral chair, and vice-chair. Using a flexible statutory framework, the Committee has adapted or developed since its inception a large array of conventional and original tools to resolve municipal police or fire fighter disputes. The record of this joint approach has been impressive: It has reduced significantly the number of cases requiring third-party decisions and has halved the time elapsed in resolving cases referred for impasse procedures. Both management and labor have acclaimed the effect of this new procedure in improving the capacity to resolve public sector labor-management problems and in altering a previously contentious and unstable collective bargaining environment in public safety.

Early in its public labor history, Massachusetts encountered several stormy public sector labor relations episodes such as the Boston Police Strike of 1919 and the labor strife at the Watertown Arsenal in 1911.[1] The effect of these events was similar to that in other jurisdictions: Development of bargaining rights for public sector employees was held in abeyance for many years. In more recent years, however, Massachusetts has recognized—as have many other states— the rights of public employees to organize and bargain and has provided them a broad scope of bargaining rights as well as certain opportunities for impasse resolution.

The 1977 shift in dispute resolution procedures—establishment of the Joint Labor-Management Committee—is thus the latest and possibly one of the most creative steps in Massachusetts' evolution of labor legislation. Directed toward achieving labor peace and assurance of service delivery, the approach is examined in detail here so that the results of this experience can be of use to the study and growth of the theory and to the practice of public sector labor relations.

Purpose

Any apparently positive development deserves scrutiny in the effort to ease the problems inherent in providing essential public services. Those entrusted with assuring continued and improved provision of essential public services frequently analyze the practices used in the next town or another state. And, when a good solution to a familiar problem is achieved elsewhere, the possibilities for borrowing the promising method or approach ought to be examined.

This study proposes to assist that process. The joint labor-management committee approach appears to be a mechanism worth examining in that its basic structure and operating procedures are rather different from most formal dispute resolution mechanisms. This work is assembled with the expectation that study and discussion of the Massachusetts experiment in dispute resolution will (1) stimulate the identification and understanding of critical aspects of productive public sector labor-management relations and (2) result in practical application elsewhere of pertinent elements of the Massachusetts experiment.

Audience

This book attempts to provide information to both practitioners and students of public labor relations. It is for those who seek to understand how and why the Massachusetts experiment has had a positive effect on impasse resolution and labor relations in general. It is also for those who wish to abstract elements from the experiment that may be successfully adapted for use elsewhere. Through description, analysis, and synthesis of principles, this study intends to provide data and material in the conceptual and cohesive context required by both the practitioner and academic communities. It is expected that the information and analysis herein will be subjected to thoughtful discussion and trial, which are so critical to the development of practical concepts and tools in the field of public sector labor-management relations.

Scope and Limitations

Focused toward practitioners and academics in their forward-looking roles, this study is not intended to include a comprehensive review or analysis of past practices in public labor relations or even in public safety. Rather, the purpose here is to understand the workings and to study the possible broader utility of the experimental mechanism under discussion. General trends and patterns of evolution in labor relations practices are noted for the sole purpose of placing into some perspective the issues and concepts evident in the Massachusetts experiment.

This study concentrates on labor-management interaction in the joint committee forum and in bargaining relationships. It highlights institutional and interpersonal aspects of labor relations as they arise in the political world of the public sector. These aspects, occurring as they do in a political context, lend special tensions to public labor relations. These tensions create some opportunities that are exploited by the membership and structure of this joint approach to dispute resolution. Therefore, the emphasis of this work is on certain institutional and interpersonal dynamics: It is people who come to agreement. Their relationships determine the form and speed of that agreement. Accordingly we shall study the interaction between people within their institutional roles.

Finally, this study is not intended to be a quantitative record of the economic consequences to labor or management of this experiment, for calculations of settlement size and short-term impact on the municipal budget are not adequate reflections of a mechanism's value. First, it is hard to determine—independent of other factors that affect those numbers—the effect of a dispute resolution process on size of settlements. Second, such calculations, while important, do not provide a total picture of the situation; aspects such as productivity, morale, and the tenor of the ongoing manager-employee relationship are important to costs as well as to less tangible aspects of municipal operations. The numbers cited in this study, primarily in Chapter 7, therefore relate to the improvement of labor-management relationships and bargaining processes as indicated, for example, by the proportion of cases that reach arbitration or that are settled through mediation. The numbers in this regard compel attention to the qualitative effects of the experiment on bargaining and on constructive labor-management relations.

Outline

The first chapter briefly provides some perspective on how and where the Massachusetts effort is positioned in the general development of public sector labor relations practices in the United States. A brief review is made of economic pressures, structural factors, and the developing role of public sector unionism and of other dispute settlement practices. These provide a context for a discussion of current characteristics of the public sector that both requires and restricts new approaches to dispute resolution.

In a related effort to provide context and a foundation for assessing the general applicability of this experiment, Chapter 2 provides background on the labor relations dynamics and practices specific to Massachusetts which, in part, led to the formation of the Joint Labor-Management Committee. The chapter focuses on the important interaction between political and labor relations interests during the period immediately preceding development of the experimental approach in which the tense atmosphere of the period promoted a consensus for change.

Chapter 3 describes in some detail the structure and workings of the Joint Labor-Management Committee. The chapter discusses the joint committee mechanism in terms of its effort to reduce those problems encountered under last-best-offer binding arbitration and problems found generally in labor-management relationships in the public sector. Overall, the treatment is in terms of the dynamics of labor-management interactions as they relate to political and institutional structures and to the types of issues and problems arising in public sector disputes. The Committee is described in terms of its structure, the tools it uses, and the dynamics it develops, both internally and among parties to a dispute. Chapter 3 shows that although the structure of the Joint Committee was legislatively fixed by statute, its conception and implementation gave rise to a series of flexible practices and operations that evolved with experience.

Chapters 4 and 5 each present a case study of an impasse situation that the Joint Committee worked on and resolved during the early part of its existence. The studies are included as actual demonstrations of the sorts of tools the Committee was able to use in resolving the disputes described. Case examples are included to bring theory to life and to show in some detail the way in which the Joint Committee structure and methods are brought to bear on real bargaining situations. (For this reason the case studies have been used as documents in classroom discussion.) Case descriptions serve to describe Committee practices in terms of their interaction with real institutions, events, and personalities.

The case in Chapter 4 describes a municipal police dispute and efforts by the Joint Committee to resolve it. This case represents the use of some traditional mediation and arbitration techniques adapted to the committee structure and applied to the characteristics of the dispute. The case in Chapter 5 describes the approach taken by the Joint Committee in a particularly obstinate municipal dispute that had dragged on for over three years; it yielded to resolution only after use of some rather unorthodox dispute resolution techniques permitted by the committee structure and legislation. This case demonstrates both the flexibility of the committee structure and creative freedom given its membership, which permits development of new and even radical techniques that can be applied to the specific array of characteristics evidenced by a particular dispute.

Chapter 6 analyzes both cases from the standpoint of the tools used to resolve each of the disputes and the utility and relationship of those tools to the goals of the new, cooperative mechanism.

The discussion analyzes whether the situations described in the cases represent effective or ineffective applications of certain concepts underlying the JLMC and sheds some light on whether those concepts have validity in resolving public sector disputes in general. Analysis of the two cases highlights the application of tools and methods available to a joint committee and suggests why and when a tool or mechanism seems to work best and when it may be much less effective.

The seventh chapter assesses the Joint Committee's impact on impasse resolution and bargaining when measured by the objectives surrounding its establishment. It examines data related to changes in speed of settlement and degree of third-party intervention and then discusses the change in the quality of bargaining relationships—each since the inception of the joint mechanism.

Discussed in Chapter 8 are two important issues in public bargaining that a joint labor-management approach to dispute resolution may address. In particular, it examines the stability of the bargaining environment and the role of politics. Since stability of the environment and the role of politics differentiate many current public bargaining problems from those in private employment, this chapter highlights the conceptual development and practical improvements made possible by examining these two aspects of the JLMC experiment.

The ninth and final chapter seeks to abstract from the Massachusetts experiment those elements of the committee approach of relevant and practical use elsewhere. These elements are presented as general principles and considerations for designing and carrying out, in other arenas of collective bargaining, dispute resolution practices with similar results. As general principles these elements may be useful in assessing existing mechanisms as well as to restructure or create productive means of handling labor disputes in public employment and elsewhere.

Endnote

1. There are many accounts of these episodes. See, for example, Murray B. Nesbitt, *Labor Relations in the Federal Government Service* (Washington, D.C.: the Bureau of National Affairs, 1976), p. 28; or Sterling D. Spero, *Government as an Employer* (New York: Remsen Press, 1948), p. 258.

Chapter 1

THE NEED FOR NEW APPROACHES TO PUBLIC SECTOR DISPUTE SETTLEMENT

Resolution of labor disputes in the public sector has always required institutions and tools to fit the special range of problems inherent in public employment and administration. The Taylor Law and the studies preceding and following its enactment in the state of New York represent an important example of the growing recognition of special problems related to public employee labor-management disputes and in the design of mechanisms to handle them.[1] The growth in public sector labor relations in the 1960s and early 1970s led to further development of institutions and tools for dispute resolution.[2] For a variety of historical and institutional reasons, however, collective bargaining and related practices specific to public employment have not evolved to the same point as those in much of the private sector.[3] Therefore, consensus and stability concerning dispute settlement practices in the public sector have been elusive, and controversy persists. In recent years the evolution of these practices and their statutory basis has attracted the attention of neutrals, politicians, academics, and practitioners on both sides of the table.[4]

The fiscal and economic pressures of the early 1980s and the public visibility such pressures have brought to governmental operations now add impetus to the examination and adoption of tools to resolve impasses over public employment contracts. As taxpayer concern over the cost of public services heightens, more attention may become focused on labor costs and the steps taken by management to control them. The need has sharpened, therefore, for tools

1

to deal with public problems arising from fiscal limitations—tools which are consistent with the need for public safety and welfare and which take into account the role of the political process.

As taxpayers resist further increases in their tax bills and governments at all levels are forced to cut or limit expenditures, localities will be affected through reductions in tax receipts, in revenue sharing, and in local aid. The economic conditions—inflation and slow growth—that lead taxpayers to seek relief cause governments to seek ways of cutting costs.[5] These same economic conditions, moreover, cause the government employee, as a taxpayer and consumer, to seek higher wages, greater benefits and increased job security. Under such conflicting economic pressures and objectives, the possibilities are heightened for disputes between employees and the public employer.

These intense and opposing economic and budgetary pressures make the quality of the relationship between labor and management both more critical to the achievement of acceptable solutions and more difficult to develop and maintain. Labor organizations will intensify the use of existing tools and channels for affecting wages, working conditions and job security to make gains or even to maintain their current status, while management will seek, even in jurisdictions and fields in which they have not felt such pressures before, to restrain increases in labor costs. The public, however, will probably resist reductions in the level of public services.

As one example, germane to this volume, the 1980 passage of Proposition 2½ in Massachusetts promises to cause serious difficulties for the public, for public managers, and for union leaders.

Limitations on local spending or taxation now seem to be a general trend in public expectations of government. As this study goes to press, several cities and towns have proposed or implemented layoffs, and bargaining over the form and impact of these layoffs has begun in earnest. Elsewhere, contract bargaining is beginning to reflect an apparent necessity to lower labor costs or restrain its rate of growth. Wage increases smaller than expected are appearing in management proposals in exchange for somewhat vague promises of job security. And, public protests have accompanied many of the cutback proposals.[6] Long-range effects of Proposition 2½ are still unclear, since funding decisions are still being hammered out and the fiscal year in which tax rates fall will have only begun as this study goes to press.

Notwithstanding the above-mentioned current fiscal pressures, this chapter will briefly describe some of the important factors that have influenced the evolution of public labor-management relations practices. Some of the evolution is continuing simply because of relative inexperience in the public sector with formal collective bargaining and dispute settlement and because of dissatisfaction with existing systems for resolving labor disputes. Other aspects of the evolution relate to the necessity of developing tools and mechanisms appropriate to the special features of public management and employment, especially those features that most clearly set them apart from private sector labor-management relations practices. An understanding of these public-private differences and a look at the development of public sector dispute settlement practices suggest areas in which progress and experimentation are necessary and provide a backdrop against which to evaluate the Massachusetts experiment in dispute resolution.

Public and Private Sector Differences

As in any developing field, dispute resolution techniques must be invented and tried. As experience develops, changes must be made to reflect new information and situations. Much of the need for scrutiny of public bargaining and dispute settlement practices arises from this newness and ongoing maturation, and some of the pressure is due to the recent shifts that will limit—after decades of growth—government spending, services, and employment. The need is compounded by the limitations in public employment on the use of tools developed in private sector industrial relations, not all of which are entirely responsive to the different features of bargaining and disputes in the public sector.

Because of resistance to public employee bargaining, the inadequacy of private sector techniques, and the rough edges still present on many new public techniques, the labor relations environment in public jurisdictions keeps changing as new practices are introduced and tried. An important aspect in improving public sector labor-management relations, then, is to seek ways to stabilize the bargaining environment—a stability that has long since come to many segments of private employment. An equilibrium in the rules and practices governing labor-management interactions frees the parties to solve substantive problems affecting working conditions, productivity or other matters of mutual concern. A stable bargaining envi-

ronment also may permit evolution of new bargaining and dispute
resolution tools to replace disorderly, confusing, or bitter periods
of change and adjustment.

Accumulated Experience

The formal practice of public sector labor relations is generally
newer by some thirty years than private sector labor relations. Certain traditions and mechanisms of bargaining, contract administration, and methods for dispute resolution that are well understood
and widely carried out in the private business sector have not been
adopted fully in the public sector. Although public labor relations
practices borrow much from the private sector, such as basic bargaining and mediation techniques and the adaptation of arbitration
from grievance to interest disputes, many of the borrowed mechanisms do not appropriately incorporate the needs of the public,
public employment, and the peculiar problems of the parties in
public sector labor disputes.

Part of the difference in development is attributable to the historical fact that public sector unionism has lagged behind that of the
private sector. Substantial growth in public sector employment did
not really begin except in a few specialized fields until after World
War II, when government expanded at all levels. The 3.5 million
workers in state and local government in the years just following
World War II had grown to 13.1 million employees in 1979 and are
closer to 13 million today.[7] While public sector unionization was
slow in taking hold, it has grown rapidly, to the point where the
proportion of membership in public employee organizations to total
employment in the public sector is over twice that prevailing in the
private sector.[8]

Related to these developments is perhaps the most important
point explaining the lesser maturity of public labor-management
relations: Public employees generally did not begin to receive formal
collective bargaining rights until the mid-1960s. Although associations of employees had previously formed for a variety of professional
purposes and for legislative lobbying for wages and benefits, formal
collective bargaining rights had long been denied them.[9] Consequently, interest in unionization was slow in coming, and there
seemed to be little need on either side of the table for bargaining skills and relationships or for dispute resolution mechanisms.
Rather, the bargaining that occurred took place informally or as

legislative lobbying for changes in compensation or conditions of work.

Sovereignty

Philosophical and operational arguments, which were continually raised by those opposed to public employee unionism, contributed importantly to the delay. Basically, opposition focused on sovereignty and the related arguments of impropriety or impracticality of permitting public employees to participate actively in the determination of employment conditions. In addition, it was feared that such involvement could lead to practices which might disrupt public services or could distribute public resources in a manner contrary to the broad public welfare.[10]

It is widely acknowledged that the opposition to union recognition and bargaining rights weakened—particularly for the white-collar work force—in 1962 when President John F. Kennedy issued an executive order permitting federal employees to unionize and bargain collectively over working conditions.[11] At that point, as some states followed suit, unionization became far more practical and acceptable as the right to organize and bargain was established legally and formally. Prior to this time in public employment, bargaining relationships existed among blue-collar workers at a number of shipyards and military installations, and in public transit where private predecessor organizations had left a legacy of bargaining and dispute resolution practices (some of which included tripartite interest arbitration).[12] Still, most of the formal development of modern public bargaining rights and systems dates from the Kennedy Order, although relations between employee groups and legislatures and some informal bargaining with executive branch officials predate this period.[13]

Separation of Powers

Although formal authority to negotiate agreements may be vested with the public employer, the split between executive and legislative powers of the employer creates a gap in both control and responsiveness in bargaining and settlement in many jurisdictions. This division of powers permits employee groups to use channels to nonexecutive actors, actions that are uncharacteristic of private employment relations. Labor's power to do so in the public sector arises from the history of employee groups, which prior to formal bargaining rights often included a close relationship to the local legislature.

Diffused Authority. Further, since most legislatures or local elected bodies through their "power of the purse" must approve contract financing, the authority for contract settlement lies in a vague and changing dimension somewhere between the executive and legislative branches of government. This vagueness can add to management's confusion and inability to agree internally before negotiating with the union, which in turn can result in disorganization, lack of strategy, and inappropriate bargaining tactics, and, thus, in an unstable relationship and environment.

Informal Lobbying. To effect changes in wages and working conditions during the period when employee unions and associations were denied collective bargaining rights, many public employee groups developed relatively close ties with their local legislative bodies which determined matters of compensation through the legislative process.[14] This range of activities was a response to the lack of face-to-face bargaining and the prohibition of strikes or other means to influence management concerning terms of employment. For similar reasons, public employee unions have been strong proponents in the legislative arena of civil service protection. In many jurisdictions, as a result of this history, a stable, long-standing relationship exists between public employee organizations and their respective legislatures—a relationship which has remained strong even where the process for determination of wages and working conditions has shifted largely to the collective bargaining arena.

However, even where bargaining itself takes place between the union and the executive branch employer, the structural elements and parameters of collective bargaining (such as mandatory, permissive, and prohibited subjects of bargaining, neutral bodies, and methods for dispute resolution) are still determined largely through the legislative process, generally at the state level. Therefore, employee groups usually continue through their legislative relations to influence actively the laws governing public bargaining. Executive management typically does not have a working relationship with its legislative counterpart to provide a similar means of furthering management's interests on these matters. In public employment, among other factors, management's history, tenure, and perspective are frequently too limited to encourage successful engagement in such activity.

Multiple Managers. The split between executive and legislative power makes the employer a two-headed bargainer (at a minimum). It is difficult for this split personality to successfully adopt the expectations and techniques of bargaining and dispute settlement that assist the typically more unified and single-minded employer in the private sector. With authority for management divided between the executive and legislative branches of government and with the additional splintering of management power among staff and line managers, civil service rules, and personnel officers, confusion not usually found in private employment can be added to most public bargaining relations.

While private unions frequently require ratification of a settlement reached at the table (as do many public unions), private management less commonly requires this formal an approval, especially from a group that was not at the table. While multi-employer bargaining and some other situations may require a formal process of accommodation on the management side, management ratification is present in virtually every public bargaining situation. The less common need for such mandatory ratification on the management side in the private sector has left public employee labor relations with little to borrow. As a result, techniques for smoothly introducing this management ratification feature into public bargaining and dispute resolution practices have yet to be worked out and widely used.

Decisions cannot be made at the bargaining table if the management representative lacks sufficient authority to make or carry out a decision.[15] In many instances, therefore, the employee group involved will choose to exercise its relationships or prerogatives with the legislative actors who are not at the table. Often, management has no equivalent tradition or means to counterbalance this route to the legislature. The political dimension of many executive-legislative relationships can also complicate the legislative ratification of a bargained settlement.

Elections

The election and political appointment of decisionmakers on the management side is another obvious difference from private employment. The pressure of elections and electoral considerations affect the continuity and experience of management decisionmakers (both legislative and executive) in bargaining and may also influence management's priorities and positions on issues during bargaining. Frequently, the activism of employee groups in local politics complicates matters. A strong electoral relationship between employee groups and legislators may similarly affect bargaining postures through the interplay between the executive and legislative branches of management.

Turnover.   The elective and political aspects of the management side can cause frequent turnover among management negotiators and/or policymakers. When such turnover is a factor, the management side bargaining agent may have little experience and the bargaining relationship suffers from lack of continuity; often complicating the ability to settle, to improve the tenor or structure of the relationship, or to make progress in improving work practices or contract administration.

In general, electoral turnover of executive and legislative officials can make it difficult to achieve the continuity on the management side that would permit learning of collective bargaining techniques and development of all-important informal relationships with the principals on the labor side. Even where the negotiator may be a career civil servant, frequently the decision making or policy setting resides, as many would argue it should, with elected officials whose tenure may be short and who may not have in mind the past or future of the bargaining or employment relationship.

Electoral Considerations.   A mayor running for reelection who is also negotiating (or making the decisions) may have primary interests that are unrelated to the employment relationship under discussion but that may affect management behavior at the table. The union's position in the election may be a factor. On the legislative side, inexperience, lack of continuity, or political considerations may characterize an entire city council or board of aldermen. The result is a predictable ratification battle each contract period between council members or with a mayor or manager. The turnover caused by elections and other political considerations can affect the ability to build internal management relationships just as short management tenure affects building a productive labor-management relationship.

The Management Structure

Civil service rules in the public sector complicate an already difficult environment for making policy decisions. The laws and regulations governing civil service employment complicate efforts to alter work practices and restructure service delivery. Civil service regulations

have evolved that restrict managerial prerogatives in job classification, hiring, employee transfer, layoffs, and so forth with the stated objective of protecting workers' rights. Public employee unions frequently are committed to these concepts (often they or their forebearers were instrumental in passing civil service legislation) and they may be unwilling to trade any of these perceived gains for greater management flexibility in dealing with fiscal and organizational problems. Furthermore, on those occasions when both sides desire to alter a practice, civil service rules may conflict and prevent action. (For example, a community wishing to preserve previous minority employment gains during a layoff may be precluded from doing so by civil service seniority provisions, even though the labor-management contract could otherwise be amended.) Civil service rules thus add dimensions of structural rigidity and complexity to human resource decisions that are rarely equaled in private employment.

Management and union leaders, of course, may not focus equally on personnel and labor relations matters. Union leaders whose duties focus primarily on labor-management relations tend to be singularly well versed in personnel rules and the practices of collective bargaining. In contrast, managers, mayors and other municipal representatives lack experience in these matters and have a wider spectrum of constituents to whom they must answer. Labor-management relations are usually only one of many duties and issues on public managers' minds—one in which they are frequently untutored or uninterested prior to the expiration of a contract.

Public and private managers may not have the same incentives influencing their behavior in labor-management matters. Because of stresses within the public management structure and relationships between management levels and institutions, it is particularly difficult simply to borrow private sector practices and apply them to the management side; the organizational structure and pressures facing the decisionmakers are not analogous. Public management inherently lacks the constancy and anchors that are possible in organizations with greater stability in their goals and in which economics has fewer competitors as factors in decision making. Also, the ideology that prevails among public managers frequently tends to reflect the traditional view of sovereignty: that bilateral bargaining is not an appropriate way to allocate an important portion of public resources.

The Labor Structure

On the labor side, however, the greater degree of similarity between public and private unions as institutions with similar interests suggests a closer interchange of techniques and traditions. It also suggests a far greater commitment to bargaining as a means of determining wages and working conditions. Through the hierarchy and networks in regional and national labor organizations, there are more opportunities for communication among public union leaders and between public and private union leaders than among and between their management counterparts. The fact that many private unions now organize in the public sector and that public unions are often affiliated with private unions at the national level leads naturally to more exchange in this arena. This exchange, combined with the continuity and frequently sophisticated political knowledge and relationships of the union side, can result in a marked disparity in the capacity of the two sides to bargain or resolve disputes constructively. (On the other hand, in jurisdictions where public bargaining is very new, where it is nonexistent, or where management is especially practiced at labor relations, the management side in fact may be far stronger than this general discussion suggests.)

The imbalances discussed here are not intended to suggest that management has less access to the necessary tools of labor relations and personnel management but to point out that structural factors affecting managment's priorities and skills may tend to limit management's interest in obtaining and sharpening these tools. Many municipalities have successfully sought to strengthen their internal ability to handle labor relations by establishing procedures and modes of communication and by clearly fixing responsibility for bargaining. In general, however, public management has a structure and features that predispose it to instability and uncertainty in the bargaining relationship, particularly if perceptions of practices used in the private sector unduly influence the parties' expectations of the process.

Sovereignty, Settlement, and Strikes

Probably the most obvious and oft-cited example of public-private differences in dispute resolution is the general prohibition of strikes in public employment. The lack of, or avoidance of, the strike in public employment is frequently articulated as the imperative for creating alternative mechanisms for resolving public sector labor disputes.[16]

In private employment, the strike (and strike threat) is a fundamental tool to force settlement of an outstanding contract dispute. In the public sector, where both the stakes and traditions are different and where short- and long-term economic considerations are less likely to be foremost in the employer's mind, the strike or threat thereof may have a different degree of utility than it does to private employee organizations. However, where services perceived as essential are threatened by a strike, legal or not, the community—and sometimes the public employee—finds it important to avoid a strike. The problem becomes even more critical when safety, sanitation, or other services deemed essential are threatened.[17] Interestingly, in the public sector the lack of the strike may be advantageous, even to the union side, for strikes can cost a public employee union political support in the community.

The need to preserve sovereignty has been invoked frequently as a reason to keep the right to strike from public employees. Perceptions of essential public services are related to notions of protecting the public welfare and maintaining the sovereignty of the people. According to the argument, it is within the state's authority to determine the allocation of public resources and the type and level of public services to be offered. This general political philosophy is frequently extended to suggest that the exercise of public employee bargaining rights, in the manner practiced in the private sector to determine wages and working conditions, would infringe on the sovereignty of the state and would leave the public welfare improperly to the influence of a single group's interest.[18] This argument inhibited granting of bargaining rights; once bargaining rights were granted the argument was aimed more specifically against the right to strike. Indeed few states grant public employees even a limited right to strike.

Whether proper or improper, the difference between the public bargaining environment and that in which the strike is permissible has helped to cause a search for settlement-forcing tools appropriate to the public sector and its special needs.

Without a mechanism for forcing closure, however, public management may lack incentive for settling an outstanding contract dispute, if for no other reason than simply to save the money that would otherwise be part of a pay increase. Management may conclude that the matter can be settled later, perhaps at greater convenience; that some political controversy may be avoided; that the interest costs on wages not paid out may be saved; or that retroactive wage increases may not be required when settlement finally comes.

Refusing to settle a contract dispute that would result in increased costs, particularly in times of fiscal stringency, is frequently a very attractive and sometimes politically necessary position for a local public executive. Yet, however attractive or unavoidable such a position may seem, the lack of good-faith bargaining will have consequences on future responsiveness of employees and on the quality of services that ultimately emerge from the dispute.

The Search for Impasse Procedures

Strikes by public safety workers have occurred in spite of negative public opinion and legal prohibition. While many of those strikes occur in communities where dispute resolution procedures have not become established and accepted,[19] the evidence is a bit unclear as to whether the existence or lack of such alternative procedures best avoids strikes. The answer probably lies in the particular tenor of labor-management relations, the types of alternative mechanisms available, and how well the procedures fit the problems to be resolved. The continuation of illegal work stoppages graphically illustrates that strike prohibitions per se are not solutions and that some constructive alternative is needed for handling disputes.

Increased Bargaining

Before the development of widespread bargaining rights and disputes over their exercise, the need for and consequent development of dispute resolution mechanisms languished. During the late 1960s and early 1970s, however, as the opposition to public employee bargaining began to weaken, laws were introduced with increasing frequency and scope. Development of dispute resolution practices lagged behind these developments.

The timing and method of initial acquisition and current form of public employee bargaining rights vary among states as much as the historic and cultural roots of the regions vary. For example, the local governments in some states are now required by law to bargain with employee organizations, whereas public employees in other

Table 1-1　Availability of Bargaining Rights for 50 States, New York City, and the District of Columbia, in 1969 and 1979

	1969	1979
Public employer required to bargain in at least one service category.	15	38
Employer permitted but not required in at least one service category.	13	0
Public bargaining prohibited in all service categories.	7	3
No provisions.	17	11

Source: *Summary of Public Sector Labor Relations Policies,* 1969 and 1979 editions. U.S. Department of Labor, Labor-Management Services Administration.

states where bargaining is forbidden by statute, case law, or attorney general opinions continue to rely on informal lobbying. However, ever-increasing numbers of public employees are acquiring and using bargaining rights in the United States as a whole. As of May 1979 thirty-six states, the District of Columbia, and New York City had legislative provisions for collective bargaining for at least some of their public employees—well over twice the number of the previous decade (see Table 1-1).[20]

Dispute Resolution

As bargaining rights were introducd and expanded, most bargaining laws provided—at best—limited capacity to resolve disputes, especially contract disputes. With limited possibility of gaining the legal right to strike and dissatisfaction with the capacity of available procedures to force settlement, public employee unions in some states and in an occasional local jurisdiction sought other means—usually legislative—to equalize the relative power of the two sides in the process of seeking or resisting settlement.

　　Opposition to the strike left public bargaining with nothing to borrow directly from the private sector, after which most of the regulatory structure of public bargaining seems to have been borrowed. In states where attempts were made to add some dispute resolution capacity, various forms of mediation, fact-finding, and, later, arbitration were added.[21] Frequently, only the former two existed, leaving the final decision still in the hands of the employer, a position that still left the union feeling unequal as a bargaining partner. So even with additions of mediation and fact-finding, without some way of actually forcing final settlement, the advantage seemed to lie with management, which frequently had less interest in bargaining and settlement than did labor.

A closure mechanism favored by many public unions was for third-party binding arbitration of interest disputes. Such provisions appeared in several states in the late 1960s. The passage of binding arbitration statutes, predominantly to resolve disputes concerning public safety employees, can be largely viewed as a result of labor's efforts to equalize bargaining power in a relationship in which the right to strike was usually absent. (Only in seven of nineteen states are employment categories other than police and fire given the right of mandatory and binding arbitration. And in only one state where mandatory and binding arbitration exists are police or fire fighters excluded.)

The arbitration of interest disputes where arbitration laws have been enacted to force parties to settle outstanding contract disputes involves a neutral third party empowered to resolve disputes under prescribed procedures. Under some statutes the third party's decision is final and binding, while under others arbitration is only advisory. Several variants of arbitration (including conventional arbitration, package last-best-offer, and issue-by-issue last-best-offer arbitration) have been tried with various degrees of success and satisfaction and have to date been the subject of a number of studies.

Legal strikes are still uncommon in public employment. Still, worker days of idleness due to strikes have increased dramatically in the public sector since the mid-1960s, generally reflecting the growing need for dispute settlement practices as organizing and bargaining rights have increased. Table 1-2 summarizes this trend.[22]

Varied State Approaches to Dispute Settlement

As each state has authority to establish its own policies and procedures for handling labor-management relations, each has developed (or avoided) a set of impasse procedures, just as each has developed its own form of bargaining rights and administration thereof. No clear trend is apparent in the success of one form of dispute settlement over another; rather, different systems work differently in different states.[23]

In 1969 only a few states had legislative provisions for binding arbitration in interest disputes. By 1975 about half the states with bargaining rights has some such provisions, four of which mandated

Table 1-2   Public Sector Work Stoppages (workers and days idle in thousands)

Year	Total		
	Number of stoppages	*Workers involved*	*Days idle during year*
1958	15	1.7	7.5
1959	25	2.0	10.5
1960	36	28.6	58.4
1961	28	6.6	15.3
1962	28	31.1	79.1
1963	29	4.8	15.4
1964	41	22.7	70.8
1965	42	11.9	146.0
1966	142	105.0	455.0
1967	181	132.0	1,250.0
1968	254	201.8	2,545.2
1969	411	160.0	745.7
1970	412	333.5	2,023.2
1971	329	152.6	901.4
1972	375	142.1	1,257.3
1973	387	196.4	2,303.9
1974	384	160.7	1,404.2
1975	478	318.5	2,204.4
1976	378	180.7	1,690.7
1977	413	170.2	1,765.7
1978	481	193.7	1,706.7
1979	593	254.1	2,982.5

Source: U.S. Department of Labor, Bureau of Labor Statistics, 1979.

binding arbitration and the remainder authorized its use on volun- tary bases.[24] In 1979 nineteen states had some form of mandatory arbitration, and many others provided for voluntary arbitration[25].

In some states the strike has become available as a means of resolving contract disputes. As of mid-1979, eight states provided a limited right to strike for public employees. With individual varia- tions, five of these states (Alaska, Minnesota, Montana, Oregon, and Pennsylvania) provided a limited right to strike that excluded police, fire, and/or other "essential" employees after certain specified im- passe procedures were exhausted. Vermont and Wisconsin excluded state employees but permitted all categories of municipal employees with the right to strike following prescribed impasse procedures. Only Hawaii allowed strikes as the ultimate recourse for all public employees, but again only after impasse procedures had been complied with (fire fighters were required to go to arbitration).[26] In general, strikes by public employees—especially public safety employees—are almost always prohibited.

Problems with Arbitration

With a wider range of application and recent experience with interest arbitration, a number of common issues or limitations have surfaced with regard to arbitration practices. These common issues appear to be (1) preservation of sovereignty versus delegation of authority to the arbitrator, (2) limitations on the arbitrator's scope of authority, (3) ensuring neutrality of the third party and the arbitration process, and (4) the desire to maximize collective bargaining and negotiation activities between the parties.

Sovereignty and the Public Interest. Delegation of power to determine the outcome of contract disputes from a duly-elected, representative public body to an appointed arbitrator or panel has raised a number of questions about sovereignty that are related to earlier arguments against bargaining rights.

In 1979 both the Minnesota and New Jersey Supreme Courts, and in 1980 the Michigan Supreme Court, upheld each state's interest arbitration statute which had been challenged on grounds (among others) that they constituted an illegal delegation of legislative authority to nonaccountable nonelected arbitrators. These and other opinions have been divided,[27] however, reflecting the view that keeping the dispute settlement process accountable to the public remains an important element of public sector dispute resolution.

The political and ideological desire to retain sovereignty or accountability for the popular government runs through many attempts at designing dispute resolution mechanisms. One method that some states use to ensure accountability is simply to preserve for elected officials the final authority to determine the outcome of disputed settlements. As of 1979 in New Hampshire and Kansas, for instance, the state legislature maintains this responsibility, and in Nebraska the governor makes the determination.[28] Another method of maintaining public control over dispute resolution has arisen in Texas, where according to the statute then prevailing (H.B. 185, Sec. 1 et seq. [1973]) police and fire fighters have standing to bargain and may request mediation and arbitration only on passage of local referenda. Only nine cities to date have passed such referenda, which are essentially mechanisms by which the public itself is a

party to settlement in wages, hours, and working conditions. Florida
has used another method of providing public accountability. Collective bargaining negotiations are to be open to the public, and if an
impasse persists beyond mediation and fact-finding, the matter is
brought to the legislature to be considered at a public hearing.[29]

Most of these systems, which seek to safeguard sovereignty and
public accountability for distributing public resources, represent a
significant departure from bargaining principles common to private
labor-management relations and which are the basis of other aspects
of public sector bargaining relationships, such as contract negotiation and methods of unit determination. The contrast of these
sovereignty-conscious systems with those that offer arbitration as a
closure mechanism allows one to see the continuing, unresolved
tension between the principles of sovereignty and dispute resolution
through a third-party settlement. Even where arbitration is available, this tension frequently persists between management and
labor and makes the success and acceptance of arbitration problem-
atic.

Scope of Arbitrator's Authority.   Where an arbitrator is empowered to resolve disputes, the scope of the third party's power to
mandate a settlement has been legislatively limited in some states.
These limitations represent an attempt to preserve public accountability and prevent undue encroachment on the power of the elected
representative. Related concerns have resulted in passage in seven-
teen states of legislative criteria and standards to which arbitrators
must adhere.[30] These criteria, while useful guidelines, frequently
suffer from two drawbacks: (1) they are difficult to measure or assess
(such as "ability to pay"), and (2) they may prevent consideration of
issues important to resolving the underlying causes of the dispute.
For example, pay parity with another town or service group may be
of critical importance to resolving a dispute. In New Hampshire and
other states, this issue has been declared by statute to be beyond the
scope of the arbitrator. In contrast, pay parity may be considered by
an arbitrator in eleven states, although its definition varies a great
deal.

Many different problems arise with each dispute and cannot all be
anticipated by legislators considering impasse resolution statutes.
Development of statutes and procedures flexible enough both to
address the wide variety of anticipated disputes and, yet, to not
overstep the bounds of practicality and public accountability has
proven to be elusive.

Neutrality.   Although an arbitrator or panel is responsible to the parties in dispute and is accordingly expected to operate independently of other influences, some jurisdictions have been charged with imposing, through the appointment of the arbitrator, a political viewpoint or otherwise improperly influencing the direction of settlement. This problem is seen particularly in states that mandate arbitration when one or both parties do not voluntarily agree to the process or when one appointed official appoints the arbitrator. The parties' perception of the arbitrator's neutrality will strongly influence their acceptance of his or her judgment or the system for dispute settlement.

Arbitration versus Bargaining.   Binding arbitration was expected to encourage closure and force municipalities that would otherwise have less incentive to settle either to bargain seriously and seek settlement or to have the issue settled by an outside party. The last-best-offer form of arbitration was intended to increase that incentive, and some literature on the subject suggests that the fear of a disruptive and negative settlement would lead both parties to bargain seriously.[31]

A great deal of discussion concerns whether final and binding arbitration stimulates or "chills" collective bargaining and negotiations. There is general consensus in the field, however, that the greater the involvement of the parties in settling the dispute, the more acceptable the outcome and the better the long-term relationships and eventual reduction in number of impasses.[32] To this end, a substantial number of states (Connecticut, Iowa, Maine, Washington, Wisconsin, to name a few) require that a series of procedures, including mediation and fact-finding, be undertaken prior to arbitration.[33] But, this has not in all cases worked to minimize the use of arbitration procedures.

Arbitration in Massachusetts

In 1973 Massachusetts joined what was then a handful of states in providing binding and compulsory arbitration for resolving police and fire fighter contract disputes. Like many other states, it provided for mediation and fact-finding services to help resolve disputes prior to invoking arbitration. The legislation came largely as a result of lobbying by the fire fighters, who sought arbitration as a way of finally providing closure to disputes that, even with mediation and fact-finding, still remained open. The package last-best-offer (LBO) form of arbitration was adopted in Massachusetts. Under this approach the arbitrator must choose the settlement package presented either by labor or the one presented by management.

The advent of arbitration frustrated management probably as much as the early impasse arrangements frustrated labor. Reflecting management concerns elsewhere, the state-level management organizations resisted and subsequently sought to alter the arbitration arrangements under which a third party made the decision regarding wages and working conditions. The third party's power to choose a settlement seemed particularly unsavory since the employer—not the third party—had to pay the settlement costs. Reflecting their fiscal responsibilities, pride, and philosophical principles, municipal authorities were loathe to have an outsider tell them how to spend their money. The third party did not have the perspective of an insider on the real problems, nor would the third party have to live with the effects of the settlement on day-to-day services and labor-management relations.

After passage of the LBO statute and after early experiences with it, management resisted its application by frequent court challenges, by legislative maneuvering to alter the statute, and through its bargaining behavior. Dissatisfaction with this dispute settlement arrangement also led to political divisions at the state level since Massachusetts legislators tended to side with either labor or management in the highly polarized discussions over the 1977 renewal of the statute that authorized last-best-offer arbitration.

Although the fire fighters and police continued to support LBO, its results were disturbing in a number of respects. First, under the procedures in the impasse statute, the length of time between declaration of an impasse and its resolution averaged six to seven months. Those disputes that were arbitrated took an average of fifteen months to be settled, often damaging bargaining relationships in the process and leaving operational and relationship problems unresolved. Second, more than half of the declared impasses were settled by arbitration, suggesting the "chilling" or "narcotic" effect of the procedures on actual bargaining. Third, a great deal of bitterness characterized individual bargaining relationships, and issues frequently would fester over several bargaining rounds. Fourth, the interventions and attempts by management to undermine, alter, or otherwise resist the statute created a further impediment to bargaining as parties awaited the outcome of legal and legislative battles instead of bargaining.

The existence of a mechanism satisfactory to both sides, then, was yet to be found. Missing was a solution that took into account management's need for fiscal control, labor's need for resolution, and the need of both sides to solve mutual problems. So, the evolution of public bargaining tools continued in Massachusetts.

Massachusetts Experiments with a New Mechanism

Changing the system once again in 1977, after three years of bitterness over binding arbitration, state level management and labor (and their supporters in the legislature) came together to create a different mechanism they hoped would better serve the purposes of collective bargaining and the provision of municipal services. They hoped that by resolving disputes through joint and equal representation of both parties, the new mechanism would also take into account the kinds of politics that affect each side. It created a forum in which the public welfare and resource allocation issues inherent in a given dispute could receive attention equal to that given employee interests.

Under the sovereignty principle, only elected officials with fiscal responsibility and accountable to the public could properly allocate public resources to wages. However, wage determination through bargaining is of critical importance to public unions. If both sets of considerations and values could be accommodated, both sides could be relatively satisfied and the fruitless political and philosophical debate could be quelled.

In creating a new dispute resolution mechanism, Massachusetts labor and management leaders attempted to deal with the conflicting methods of determining wages and working conditions reflected in the debate between sovereignty and bargaining.

A Continuing Evolution

The necessity for impasse mechanisms different from those common to private employment becomes clear when the pressures and institutions in public labor relations are examined. The resistance to a strike option, differences in management structure and experience, the issue of sovereignty, and the strong influence of legislative and elective politics all are important elements in developing and operating dispute resolution systems in the public sector. Overall, efforts undertaken to resolve disputes have not yet achieved satisfactory results, as indicated by growing numbers of work slowdowns and stoppages, continuing court actions, and other expressions of dissatisfaction.

Thus, many governmental entities need improved handling of labor-management disputes and would benefit by a strengthening of their ability to solve service delivery and fiscal problems related to employment costs and conditions. To the extent that improved collective bargaining and labor-management cooperation are important to achieving public sector purposes and to the extent that many current mechanisms are unsatisfactory in this regard, it seems useful to examine the now-unique experience in Massachusetts for aspects that resolve important philosophical and operational problems and that may be exportable. Extraction of useful principles may benefit thereby the study and practice of public sector labor relations.

Endnotes

1. See for example, *Final Report*, State of New York, Governor's Committee on Public Employee Relations, March 31, 1966; *Interim Report*, State of New York, Governor's Committee on Public Employee Relations, June 1968.
2. See for example, Nesbitt, *Labor Relations;* and James L. Stern, Charles M. Rehmus, J. Joseph Lowenberg, Hirschel Kasper, Barbara D. Dennis, *Final Offer Arbitration: The Effects on Public Safety Employee Bargaining* (Lexington, Massachusetts: Lexington Books, 1975).
3. For a description of many of these reasons, see Benjamin Aaron, Joseph R. Grodin, James L. Stern, eds., *Public Sector Bargaining*, Industrial Relations Research Association Series (Washington, D.C.: The Bureau of National Affairs, 1979), especially Chapters 1, 2, and 6.
4. For a recent review of many of these issues see Myron Lieberman, *Public Sector Bargaining: A Policy Reappraisal* (Lexington, Massachusetts: Lexington Books, 1980). For an excellent discussion of issues and developments in the evaluation of public bargaining, see B.V.H. Schneider, "Public Sector Labor Legislation: An Evolutionary Analysis," in Benjamin Aaron *et al.*, *Public Sector Bargaining*, Chapters 5 and 7.
5. For a discussion of such scrutiny see Selma Mushkin, ed., *Proposition 13 and Its Consequences for Public Management* (1979); and Lieberman, *Public Sector Bargaining: A Policy Reappraisal*, pp. 158–162.
6. For an example, see *Boston Globe*, April 10, 1979, p. 1. See also, Rebecca Black, "The Employment/Wage Trade Off: Union Response to 2½," *Impact 2½*, No. 8, August 15, 1981, Proposition 2½ Monitoring Project and the Lincoln Institute of Land Policy, Cambridge, Massachusetts.
7. *Handbook of Labor Statistics* (U.S. Department of Labor, Bureau of Labor Statistics, December 1980), p. 201.

8. *Ibid.* and *Statistical Abstract of the United States* (U.S. Department of Commerce, Bureau of the Census).

9. See Nesbitt, *Labor Relations*, Chapter 1; Lieberman, *Public Sector Bargaining*, Chapter 2; Jack Stieber, *Public Employee Unionism: Structure, Growth Policy* (Washington, D.C.: The Brookings Institute, 1973).

10. There are many discussions of sovereignty and bargaining rights and the subsequent weakening of opposition. For one such discussion, see Sterling Spero, *Government as an Employer*; or Harry H. Wellington and Ralph K. Winter, Jr., "The Limits of Collective Bargaining in Public Employment," *The Yale Law Journal*, Vol. 78.

11. For one discussion, see Nesbitt, *Labor Relations in the Federal Government Service*, Chapter 1.

12. See Nesbitt, and Emerson P. Schmidt, *Industrial Relations in Urban Transportation* (University of Minnesota, 1937).

13. *Ibid.*

14. See for example, Derek C. Bok and John T. Dunlop, *Labor and the American Community* (New York: Simon and Schuster, 1970), pp. 316–17.

15. On the relationship of negotiator and decisionmaker in bargaining, see Sumner H. Slichter, James J. Healy, and E. Robert Livernash, *The Impact of Collective Bargaining on Management* (Washington, D.C.: The Brookings Institute, 1960), p. 926.

16. For a review of the issues and analysis of the strike issue and some alternative closure devices, see Thomas A. Kochan, "The Dynamics of Dispute Resolution in the Public Sector," in Aaron *et al.*, *Public Sector Bargaining*.

17. See for example Stern *et al.*, *Final Offer*, p. 1; or Bok and Dunlop, *Community*, p. 331.

18. See for example, Wilson R. Hart, *Collective Bargaining in the Federal Civil Service* (New York: Harper and Brothers, 1961), p. 250. There are numerous discussions of the sovereignty question in connection with public employer bargaining and dispute settlement.

19. Seven cities in which such strikes occurred in 1979 are: Anderson, Indiana; Cleveland, Dayton, and Toledo, Ohio; Louisville, Kentucky; New Orleans, Louisiana; and Wichita, Kansas. More recently was the Kansas City, Missouri, fire fighters strike. See Kochan, "Dynamics of Dispute Resolution," pp. 160–163, on the effect of dispute resolution techniques on strike activity in public safety.

20. Compiled from *Summary of Public Sector Labor Relations Policies*, U.S. Department of Labor, Labor-Management Services Administration, 1979. For information on public safety employee bargaining history, see also H. A. Juris and K. B. Hutchison, "The Legal Status of Municipal Police Employee Organization," *Industrial and Labor Relations Review* April 1970, p. 352.

21. Schneider, "Public Sector Labor Legislation, An Evolutionary Analysis."

22. Adapted from *Work Stoppages in Government, 1979* (U.S. Department of Labor, Bureau of Labor Statistics, March 1981, Report 629). In particular, note Table 6, page 8: "Work Stoppages by Major Issue, All Industries and Government, 1978 and 1979." For more detail on strikes, including a breakdown of state and local government statistics, see Table 1, page 4.

23. A useful comparison among three different LBO statutes and their utility and limitations in the state of adoption can be found in Stern *et al.*, *Final Offer Arbitration*. See also Kochan, "Dynamics of Dispute Resolution"; and "Review of Michigan's Compulsory Arbitration Act Public Act 312 of 1969" Department of Labor and Department of Management and Budget, State of Michigan, May 21, 1979; Thomas A. Kochan, Mordekai Mironi, Ronald G. Ehrenberg, Jean Baderschneider, and Todd Jick, *Dispute Resolution Under Fact Finding and Arbitration: An Empirical Analysis* (New York: American Arbitration Association, 1979), a study of the effects of New York's compulsory arbitration law. See also Arvid Anderson, chairman, Office of Collective Bargaining, City of New York "Interest Arbitration: Still the Better Way," speech before the CERL Employment Relations Forum, Tampa, Florida, December 5, 1980, pp. 15 and 16.

24. Joseph R. Grodin, "Political Aspects of Public Sector Interest Arbitration," *California Law Review* 62, No. 3, May 1976.

25. *Summary of Public Sector Labor Relations Policies.*

26. *Ibid.* Interestingly, of the three states with the general right to strike, only Pennsylvania had an unusually high number (73) of work stoppages in 1979. (Montana had 6 and Hawaii, 2.)

27. *City of Richfield* v. *IAFF,* Local 1215 and State of Minnesota, 1979–1980, PBC 36,501 (Minn. Sup. Ct. 1979); *New Jersey State Policemen's Benevolent Association, Local 29* v. *Town of Irvington,* 88 N.J. 271, 403 A.2d 473 (1979); Michigan Superior Court 1988 re Michigan Comp. Laws 423.233 (1978). See also Grodin "Political Aspects," p. 683.

28. *Labor Relations Yearbook, 1979* (Washington, D.C.: Bureau of National Affairs, 1980). Also, *Journal of Collective Negotiations in the Public Sector*, 9, No. 2, 1980, Harvy Kershen, ed. Baywood Publishing Co.

29. *Labor Relations Yearbook, 1979*, p. 123.

30. *Summary of Public Sector Labor Relations Policies,* 1979.

31. See Carl M. Stevens, "Is Compulsory Arbitration Compatible with Collective Bargaining?" Industrial Relations, Vol. 5, No. 2 (February 1966); or A. J. Geare, "Final Offer Arbitration: A Critical Examination of the Theory," *The Journal of Industrial Relations*, December 1978; or Anderson, "Interest Arbitration"; or William D. Robitzek, "Final Offer Arbitration and the Labor Management Posse: Heading Off Municipal Disputes at the Impasse," *Boston University Law Review* 59:105; or Stern *et al.*, *Final Offer Arbitration*; and Daniel G. Gallagher and Richard Pegnetta, "Impasse Resolution Under the Iowa Multi-Step Procedures," *Industrial and Labor Relations Review*, Vol. 32, No. 3 (April 1979). Robitzek's "Final Offer Arbitration" is a useful summary of the early experience of the Massachusetts Joint Labor-Management Committee.

32. Peter Feuille, "Final Offer Arbitration and the Chilling Affect," *Industrial Relations* 14, 302 (October 1975); Kochan *et al.*, *Dispute Resolution Under Factfinding and Arbitration*, especially p. 179.

33. *Summary of Public Sector Labor Relations Policies,* 1979.

Chapter 2

THE BITTER ROOTS OF A JOINT COMMITTEE APPROACH

An understanding of the labor relations practices and environment and the political history in Massachusetts that gave rise to a joint committee is important in assessing the transferability of this approach to dispute resolution in other occupations and jurisdictions.

Historical Tension

Genesis of the Joint Labor-Management Committee

Binding and compulsory arbitration had been available in Massachusetts since 1974 to settle labor disputes between police or fire fighters and their respective municipalities. The mechanism that replaced the general use of binding arbitration was a joint labor-management committee, composed of six management and six labor representatives and chaired by a neutral. This committee was empowered to exercise jurisdiction over, and resolve, any police or fire labor dispute, and was given a flexible mandate to do so using a variety of tools. The Joint Labor-Management Committee for Municipal Police and Fire Fighters first took shape in an agreement of September 1977 by representatives of the Professional Fire Fighters of Massachusetts, affiliated with the AFL-CIO (the fire fighters also represented the police interests), and the Massachusetts League of Cities and Towns.

This chapter depends significantly on energetic and careful research by Virginia Spielberg at the completion of her studies for a Master's in Public Policy degree at the John F. Kennedy School of Government, Harvard University. I am grateful for her perseverance and help.

The agreement was a product of a drawn-out public political dispute, played out in the state legislature, in the press, and in the governor's office. After significant controversy over renewal of the old binding arbitration statute in the spring and summer, quiet negotiation and compromise on a new mechanism took place in the fall of 1977. The last-best-offer binding arbitration law was favored by labor and just as strongly opposed by the municipal association. Arbitration settlements under the statute, which legally had to be funded by the local government legislative body, were cited frequently by municipal authorities as just another uncontrollable cost imposed on them by a state-level statute and administrative mechanism.

The compromise on a new statute was reached with the private mediative and design assistance of John T. Dunlop, Lamont University Professor at Harvard University and a former Secretary of Labor. With his substantive input and his mediator's interest in the accommodation of warring parties, an agreement took shape that ended the bitterness and feuding that had dominated discussion of the subject for most of the year. The agreement provided for a two-year experiment that would use the process to which both sides had acceded (and, indeed, helped to design) and in which representatives of both sides would participate. The mechanism that was intended to create agreement between parties to a dispute was itself a product of agreement.

A September 19, 1977 memorandum between the parties was translated into statutory language and a bill passed by both houses of the state legislature. It was signed into law by the governor, with neither the executive nor legislative branches making a significant change or public complaint. These actions ended a year of intense political dispute and closed the door on at least three years of conflict over employee welfare considerations versus local control of government costs.

Evolution of Public Employee Bargaining in Massachusetts

The Joint Labor-Management Committee in Massachusetts represents a new step in what had been an ongoing development of mechanisms for conflict resolution in the state. Although, since the early twentieth century, fire fighters and police have belonged to associations that might be characterized as unions, they only formally received the right to organize for collective bargaining purposes in Massachusetts in 1965 and 1966. The difficulties in securing this right dates from the early history of public sector unionism in the state. In 1919, when Boston's Police Commissioner Curtis refused to recognize the newly formed police union and fired twelve members of the force for being union members, 1,500 of the 1,900 police went out in the now famous Boston Police Strike. Four days of looting and riots followed in which a million dollars worth of property damage was done and three people killed. The reaction to the crime and violence was increased anti-union sentiment. Governor Calvin Coolidge called out the National Guard to restore order, fired the strikers, and in the process destroyed the union. Both Coolidge and President Wilson denounced police unions, and the American Federation of Labor (AFL) revoked all of the charters to police groups it had given out earlier that year.[1] (That AFL charter was only restored to Massachusetts in 1979.) While fire fighters retained their union's charter from the AFL and the police formed benevolent, self-help associations after 1919, the specter of the Boston Police Strike has loomed in the minds of government officials and the public as a reminder of the vital nature of the protective services. It also has served union leaders as a reminder of the public reaction to strikes of public safety employees.

As a consequence of the anti-union sentiment in the wake of the strike, the efforts of public employees in Massachusetts to win bargaining rights received far slower response than did similar efforts in the private sector. In 1937, two years after the federal Wagner Act (the National Labor Relations Act) gave collective bargaining rights to private sector employees involved in interstate commerce, Massachusetts passed the "Baby Wagner Act" (Chapter 105A of the General Laws of Massachusetts). This act completed the extension of bargaining rights to private sector employees within Massachusetts.

At that time, the Massachusetts Labor Relations Commission (LRC) was established to administer the state labor relations statutes. An executive commission reporting to the governor and modeled after the National Labor Relations Board, the LRC is authorized to determine appropriate bargaining units and to supervise elections to determine the exclusive bargaining representative for a group of employees. The LRC also is empowered to adjudicate complaints of unfair (prohibited) labor practices by either party and can issue a cease and desist order for the prohibited practice and take actions to enforce its order.

Not until 1958, however, were public employees in Massachusetts granted the right to join unions (Chapter 149, Section 178D of the general laws). At that time, they were permitted only to "present proposals" to their employers regarding wages and working conditions. Collective bargaining rights were first given to state employees in 1964 (Chapter 149, Section 178D) when they were permitted to bargain over working conditions, but not wages. In 1965 all municipal employees in Massachusetts except police were given the right to bargain over wages, hours, and terms and conditions of employment; police were given the right in 1966.

Interest Dispute Resolution Becomes Part of Massachusetts Public Labor Relations

In 1965 formal dispute resolution techniques for public employment were delineated for the first time in Massachusetts. If, after a reasonable period of negotiations, or sixty days before the municipal budget was ready, there still was no agreement between the parties, either party could petition the already-existing Board of Conciliation and Arbitration (BCA) to initiate fact-finding.

Established in 1886 to promote the peaceful settlement of disputes in the private sector, the BCA is within the state's Department of Labor and Industries, within the Secretariat of Manpower Affairs. It is a tripartite board, composed of one representative from each of management, labor, and the public. All three members are appointed by the governor and serve coterminously with the governor, who also appoints one of the three to chair the Board. The chairperson is executive director of the BCA and an associate commissioner of the Department of Labor and Industries.

The Board has three areas of responsibility: mediation, fact-finding, and arbitration. Its mediation services are available to both public and private sector parties, whereas fact-finding is a public sector action only and is used as a means of resolving interest disputes that cannot be resolved through the usual mediation techniques. Between 1974 and 1980 the BCA was authorized to offer interest arbitration service in the public sector only in police and fire fighter disputes. It also provides grievance arbitration services to both the public and private sectors.[2]

Lack of Finality in Dispute Resolution

Before 1974, if mediation and fact-finding did not resolve the problem, there was no way to break the impasse in the legal absence of a strike threat. Contract disputes could—and frequently did—remain open for years. Therefore public employees in Massachusetts wanted stronger tools to bring closure on disputes and prevent management from foot-dragging. Public safety employees wanted either the right to strike or binding arbitration. The right to strike was forbidden in Massachusetts, as in some thirty-two other states.[3] Although the right to strike was discussed during the period leading to the 1974 binding arbitration law, in general the leaders of municipal management, represented at the state level by the Massachusetts League of Cities and Towns, were unwilling to entertain the thought.

Perhaps for different reasons, the more sophisticated public employee groups were also not overly interested in the right to strike, since a strike, even if legal, could seriously impair public support for a union. It was feared that police and fire fighters particularly would be criticized, given the public perceptions of their duties and the consequences to the public of a strike by these groups. Similarly, public officials had a special interest in settling police and fire contracts expeditiously to avoid the possibility of an interruption in these services.

Massachusetts Adopts LBO . . .

In 1973 the Massachusetts legislature rewrote and codified its entire collective bargaining statute (Chapter 150E, Massachusetts General Laws, replacing Chapter 149, Sections 178D through N). Chapter 150E provided all public employees, both state and local, with full bargaining rights. As part of that recodification, for a three-year trial period between 1974 and 1977, municipal police and fire employees were given the right to call for last-best-offer binding arbitration to resolve interest disputes.

The original bill calling for final and binding arbitration for police and fire fighters was presented in the legislature on March 27, 1973. The hearing on this bill, held by the Senate Committee on Transportation, had to be moved to a large auditorium because over 1,000 uniformed fire fighters showed up to be in the audience. The main group supporting the bill was the Massachusetts Professional Fire Fighters Association, and introduction and passage of the bill is generally attributed to the political strength of the fire fighters. Opposed to the bill were municipal leaders (mayors and selectmen), the Massachusetts Taxpayers Foundation, the Massachusetts League of Cities and Towns, and the *Boston Globe* (which ultimately became a lukewarm supporter of the idea).[4]

As the previous chapter notes, the move to include last-best-offer arbitration for police and fire fighters in the 1973 revisions was reflective of a growing attitude among public employees nationally, but especially among public safety employees, that mediation services or fact-finding were not sufficient in many instances to force closure and end contract disputes. In the mid-1960s the notion of applying arbitration techniques to public sector interest disputes came under wide discussion. The idea was borrowed, it seemed, from some combination of private sector grievance experience and foreign (largely British Commonwealth) public sector practice.[5] Also considered was the tradition of tripartite arbitration of contract disputes common to some private urban transit contracts that stayed with those units after coming under municipal ownership.[6] In general, final and binding arbitration of interest disputes was sought as a means to ensure that disputes would, indeed, come to an end in a timely fashion, and it was expected that the parties would be encouraged to bargain seriously. At that time the final offer form of arbitration was adopted in a number of states—for example, Pennsylvania (1968), Michigan (1969), and Wisconsin (1972)—to deal with certain classes of public sector impasses.[7]

The final offer form of arbitration differs from conventional arbitration in that the arbitrator may not fashion the award in accordance with his or her view of the situation but must choose between the final positions of the parties and award one of those positions. The specific form of final-offer arbitration differs among the states on such matters as the timing of the final submission, possibilities for mediation following submission, and separation of economic from other issues. In one common form, the arbitrator is permitted to choose either party's position on an issue-by-issue basis. In others, the arbitrator is permitted to choose only the package offered by one side or the other. Massachusetts adopted the latter form.

In general the concept underlying last-best-offer binding arbitration, infrequently articulated, is that the threat of having to accept for settlement the position tendered by the other side would be so repugnant that it would force the parties to seek to accommodate their differences. In this way, if it did not cause the parties to reach full accommodation through the bargaining process, it would force more reasonable last offers.[8]

After using a creative analytic scheme involving probabilities and a form of game theory, Professor Howard Raiffa of the Kennedy School of Government and the Harvard Business School has suggested that, in fact, the thinking behind last-best-offer forms of settlement is inaccurate. The incentives are much greater for the parties to present more outlandish demands in the last-best-offer package process than to submit responsible, possibly middle-of-the-road proposals, as much conventional labor relations wisdom suggests. Interestingly, in Raiffa's analysis, parties that are un-schooled as well as those who learn how the game works are equally likely to submit outrageous offers. Should both parties do so, the likelihood diminishes of a settlement that would contribute to labor peace and thereby to a bargaining relationship that would facilitate problem solving.[9] If Raiffa has properly modeled bargaining behavior, it may be that last-best-offer arbitration should be accorded at least a second, more critical round of scrutiny.

. . . But Not Without A Legislative Battle

Binding arbitration did not easily pass in Massachusetts. On September 19, 1973, the comprehensive Public Employees Collective Bargaining Bill (S1771) passed by the Massachusetts legislature did not include last-best-offer arbitration for police and fire fighters. The fire fighters initiated a separate bill that called for final and binding arbitration (H1086), which was passed by the legislature but vetoed by Governor Sargent. The State House of Representatives failed to override that veto by one vote on October 16, 1973. However, in June 1974, the legislature successfully enacted a bill providing last-best-offer final arbitration for police and fire fighters in Massachusetts.[10]

Arguments in Support of Arbitration

During that period five main arguments for binding arbitration were advanced by supporters of the bill. First, police and fire fighters were not allowed to strike in Massachusetts, so no dispute resolution techniques existed if bargaining, mediation, and fact-finding failed. The argument was that the balance of power between the parties in negotiations was unequal since employees could not strike; a public employer was under less pressure to resolve a dispute; employers frequently saved money by delaying the wage increase; and often it was politically advantageous to oppose a wage increase. A municipality legally could ignore a fact finder's recommendation. Also, a municipal legislature could refuse to appropriate the funds for a contract that had been agreed to. Finally, serious negotiations might be delayed until after the municipal budget was set, thereby making it even more difficult to get ratification of a subsequent agreement.

A second argument was that final and binding arbitration would improve the collective bargaining process. It was the hope of the proponents of last-best offer arbitration to "squeeze unreasonable ideas out of each side's proposal by the threat of awarding the decision to the other side. In short, the taxpayers end up with the lesser of two evils."[11] The statute was constructed such that before arbitration proceedings could begin, all other mediation and fact-finding—and unfair labor practice—proceedings would have to be completed in an attempt to assure that the parties had bargained in good faith to that point. Fire and police spokesmen argued that the new arbitration law would not even affect those cities and towns that bargained in good faith.

Third, the bill required construction of the arbitration panel itself in a manner that would allow each party to choose an arbitrator; then the two arbitrators would choose a third. The arbitration panel was given ten criteria, listed in the statute, with which to judge the amount the final offers received. These criteria included the expected financial impact of an award on the municipality and its ability to pay.[12]

As a fourth major argument, proponents of arbitration stated that police and fire fighters must be paid a decent wage in order for them to provide the best services, and that lingering disputes and the uncertainty and poor relations attached to unsettled contracts harmed the delivery of those services.

Finally, as the *Boston Globe* editorialized in October 1973, the final arbitration decision was only a three-year trial experiment. If the procedure didn't work, the right could be rescinded in 1977.

Arguments Against Arbitration

Opponents of final-offer arbitration for police and fire fighters used three main arguments. First, municipal leaders argued that police and fire fighters would raise costs by using binding arbitration to establish wage parity with officers in other towns, forcing local leaders to raise taxes. They argued further that the Montreal strike experience might be repeated in Massachusetts cities and towns. (Montreal police struck in 1969 because a large wage increase the arbitrators had given them was still not enough to give them parity with Toronto.)

The second argument against final and binding arbitration was the fear that locally elected officials would lose control of the municipal budget. In the bill before the legislature, the decision of the arbitrators, who were not popularly elected, would be binding on the elected officials and local legislative body, not to mention the taxpayers.

Finally, arguing that true collective bargaining would be destroyed, opponents believed that final and binding arbitration would give fire fighters and police the greater bargaining power. Local officials worried that public employees would always hold out for arbitration and not participate in meaningful collective bargaining. Although arbitration could assure that a settlement was reached without a work stoppage, it might not encourage serious, intensive good-faith bargaining. Moreover, it was argued that an outside arbitrator might not have an appreciation of a city's financial capabilities, of the management problems, or of the particular labor-management relationship or work setting. Thus, it was argued, an arbitrator might well make an award less suited to the work setting and to labor relations in general than one hammered out by the parties themselves. The arbitrated award might seem manifestly unfair and inappropriate to either party, who, finding the solution distasteful, would be frequently motivated to come to the table next time seeking to get even. It was predicted that this combination of discouragement to bargaining and possibilities for distasteful or inappropriate settlement would exacerbate unstable labor relations and result in operational and bargaining difficulties.[13]

Arbitration Is Tried

After all the public controversy and legislative maneuvering, Massachusetts adopted the last-best-offer form of arbitration after its 1973 work on its overall collective bargaining statutes. In that law, the Board of Conciliation and Arbitration was required to provide last-best-offer arbitration on the package of issues still in dispute if mediation and fact-finding did not yield a settlement after a specified period of time.

Last-best-offer arbitration was first used in Arlington, Massachusetts. The *Boston Globe* reported on January 26, 1975, that in the Arlington case the parties did not try to settle contract differences before going to impasse proceedings. Rather, after only perfunctory bargaining, they turned to fact-finding and then to arbitration. According to the *Globe*, the nonbinding fact-finding report came out in August 1974 recommending a 10.71 percent wage increase for the fire fighters, to keep pace with fire fighters' wages in nine other communities to which Arlington was frequently compared. The city had offered 8 percent, which was apparently in line with the increase offered to the rest of Arlington's municipal workers. Following failed mediation and after fact-finding, the union petitioned the Board of Conciliation and Arbitration for last-best-offer arbitration, and on January 6, 1975, the arbitrator received each party's last-best-offer: On the wage issue, the town proposed an 8 percent wage increase, and a 10.7 percent increase was sought by the fire fighters.

The arbitrator chose the union's offer, noting that he was impressed by the union's willingness to come down to the fact finder's recommendations. The City of Arlington claimed that the arbitrator had not adequately considered its ability to pay nor were the interests and welfare of the community considered. The city also claimed that, since the Arlington police had settled for an 8 percent wage increase, this fire fighters' settlement would hurt police morale. Other cities and towns became concerned. The City of Arlington challenged the constitutionality of the Massachusetts arbitration statute in court, but in 1976 the Massachusetts Supreme Judicial Court upheld the constitutionality of the statute (*Town of Arlington* v. *BCA*, 352 NE2d 914, 921 [1976]).

The Mechanics of Massachusetts LBO

To contrast the new mechanism with its predecessor, it is worth describing briefly the process through which all disputes were settled prior to 1978. The last-best-offer process of arbitration was set up as an adjunct to the mediation and fact-finding process already on the books, and the sequence of procedures was rather clearly if not rigidly defined. The mediation and fact-finding processes previously represented the full range of options available for dispute resolution. Under those procedures, which were continued, either party could petition the Board of Conciliation and Arbitration for determination of the existence of a bargaining impasse. The Board had ten days within which to make a determination of an impasse; otherwise an impasse was assumed to exist. The statute required that a mediator be appointed by the Board within five days of impasse determination to work with the parties. The parties also had the option of choosing a mediator on their own. In either case, the mediator was given twenty days within which to resolve the dispute.

If mediation failed, either or both parties could petition the Board for the commencement of fact-finding procedures under which a fact finder would investigate the issues in dispute and would have thirty days to produce a set of recommendations. The fact-finding process is an investigatory process wherein the fact finder assesses the positions of the parties and seeks to recommend an appropriate settlement. Frequently the fact finder's recommendations were agreed to by the parties as the basis of a settlement or later, under arbitration, often formed the basis of the arbitrator's award.

The Board was empowered to appoint the fact finder, or the parties on their own could agree to a fact finder. The statute gave the fact finder the authority to mediate during the period of his or her charge of the case. The statute permitted any of the time deadlines described above to be altered at the request of the parties.[14] Because of complaints regarding time delays, a 1975 amendment to the law gave the parties the right to waive fact-finding and go directly to arbitration.

Under the 1974 statute, arbitration proceedings could begin if after thirty days following issuance of the fact finder's report the parties had still not settled the dispute. Arbitration proceedings began only once the Board of Conciliation and Arbitration made a determination to send the parties to arbitration. In addition to the thirty-day requirement, arbitration proceedings could not begin if there were outstanding unfair labor practice charges dated prior to the date of the fact finder's report. (A governor's task force in 1976 found that charges were often being filed simply to stall the process, but noted that amendments to the law in 1975 appeared to have lessened the potential for frivolous charges to hold up the proceedings.)[15]

If the parties had not agreed on the fact finder's report and no prohibited practice charges interfered, the Board would notify the parties, who each would then select a member of the arbitration panel from lists provided by the Board, who, in turn, would jointly select a neutral chairperson. If there was no agreement on a chairperson, the Board would appoint the chair. The parties also had the option to be heard by a single arbitrator selected by the Board. The statute required that a hearing begin within ten days after the chairperson was appointed and that the hearing must then be completed within forty days. At the close of the hearing each party would submit to the arbitrator or panel its last-best-offer on each of the issues in dispute. Within ten days, unless the parties had waived fact-finding, the arbitrator or panel would select either the package presented by one of the parties or the fact finder's recommendations. An opinion explaining the selection of the final offer for the award was due from the arbitrator within thirty days of the end of the proceedings. The law provided that the parties could reach a settlement at any point during the arbitration process prior to issuance of the award.

The award was intended to be final and binding on both parties; however, a legal remedy was available through the state Superior Court to enforce the award. Although a large number of awards were reported to have been challenged, as was the Arlington award, an award was not subject to any other review and, unlike a negotiated settlement, was not subject to funding approval by the affected municipal legislature. Unless successfully challenged in the court (or ignored by the municipality until enforcement was sought by the union), the award, by law, had to be funded.[16]

The last-best-offer mechanism generated a great deal of controversy during its first three years, and a major political battle began to take shape as the June 30, 1977 expiration date of the statute drew near.

Objections to Last-Best-Offer

The *Boston Globe* reported that of the fifty cases that went to last-best-offer arbitration in that three-year period, the union position was chosen in twenty-nine settlements. Some opponents of the law claimed that, since the union "won" more than half the time, unions tended to wait for the arbitrator's decision rather than to bargain in good faith. Thus, some critics blamed the increase in declared impasses over the three-year period on the new law, which they saw as encouraging impasse and arbitration, although others saw inflation and the cities' fiscal problems as paramount causes of impasses.

Critics also argued that last-best-offer arbitration for police and fire fighters encouraged other public employees to adjust their demands to whatever the police and fire fighters received. This action would place local governments in a predicament known as "whipsawing"—that is, if the police or fire fighters got a big settlement one year as a result of the last-best-offer selection, the other municipal unions might seek it the next year, as the Arlington case suggested. Conversely, if another union in the town got a larger than usual increase, an arbitrator in a police or fire case might reason that equity demanded an award of a similar amount in a police or fire arbitration.[17]

Labor Relations as a Political Issue

The Sloan Report

During the period of political debate, on May 17, 1977 a report was published entitled, "The Impact of Final Offer Arbitration in Massachusetts: An Analysis of Police and Fire Fighter Collective Bargaining." The report, referred to as the "Sloan Report" because it was published through the Sloan School of Management at the Massachusetts Institute of Technology, analyzed the economic impact of the final-offer-arbitration statute and sought to assess its effect on the collective bargaining process of public safety employees and municipal employers. The authors worked from economic and settlement data for Massachusetts police and fire fighters from fiscal years 1972 through 1977 and used teachers as a comparison group. The major conclusions included the following:

1. The number of impasses for police, fire fighters, and teachers had gone up during the period that final and binding arbitration had been in existence. There were 371 impasses before and 630 after final arbitration went into effect.
2. Most of the increase in the number of impasses were police/fire impasses: Before the law, 45 percent of impasses were for police and fire fighters, and afterward, 57 percent.

Several explanations were offered for these findings. First, the report suggested that the bargaining environment was different in 1975–1976 than in 1972–1974. For example, there were greater fiscal constraints on cities and towns in the later period, giving them less room to bargain. Inflation was also higher in the later period, which, the report reasoned, would increase the demands of the unions. Also, the wage settlements in 1971–1973 were affected by the federal wage and price control program in effect at the time. The unions, it posited, probably were bargaining for catch-up wages after the program ended. Therefore, the difference in bargaining climate, it was suggested, probably caused an increase in the number of impasses, more so than the change in laws.

The Sloan Report also offered the theory that the new dispute resolution technique by its mere existence may have prompted its own use—that is, the unions may, according to the report's reasoning, have wanted to try out arbitration because it was new. The study cited the drop in the number of cases ending in final-offer awards after 1975 as evidence to support this theory.

In addition, it stated that the results "will not lend support to the notion that the addition of final-offer arbitration to the array of impasse procedures available to Massachusetts police and fire fighters had a positively significant effect on the salary levels they were able to achieve in negotiations. At the same time we can conclude that safety employee bargaining units within the Commonwealth have come to rely more heavily on outside parties in the settlement of their contract disputes. Whether this latter finding is the result of the availability of the impasse procedures or the difficult economic situation of the last few years is uncertain."[18]

So, the study did not find, in its analysis of the data, that the existence of binding arbitration had any deleterious effect on the results of collective bargaining in public safety. The study, however, did not address the effects of the practice on bargaining relationships, bargaining behavior, or the bargaining climate.

The Massachusetts Municipal Association denounced the study and its timing, whereas the fire fighters welcomed it. In fact the Sloan Report was quite limited in its conclusions since it interpreted only certain available quantitative data. Its effect, moreover, was exaggerated because it appeared at the height of a controversy that encompassed a broad range of political and labor relations questions. The study did not address the bitterness that was widely reported in bargaining relationships at local levels and made no mention of the very polarized political atmosphere in evidence between the parties at the state level. This bitterness affected the lobbying activities of labor and management and ultimately the legislative behavior of elected lawmakers seeking to respond to these two usually conflicting constituencies. This atmosphere was reflected in the type of bargaining behavior counseled by state-level labor and management to their local counterparts and in the mutual antipathy of state-level labor and management officials.

Management Opposition: Study by the League of Cities and Towns

As in previous discussions of the binding arbitration statute, local officials complained bitterly about having a third party make important and costly decisions for them, particularly when that third party might be largely unfamiliar with the local situation and would not have to live with the consequences of the decision. The Massachusetts League of Cities and Towns, speaking for municipal managements across the state, was very much opposed to the renewal of binding arbitration. During the 1977 battle, the League sought ways to prevent its renewal, largely through their efforts in gaining the governor's support. In 1973 they had been relatively inactive on the issue, even though the idea of third-party decisions affecting their budgets and control over working conditions was anathema. At that time the state's municipal management forces were not yet organized to deal on legislative issues of this sort. However, in 1977 a more active League led to a strategy intended to oppose the renewal of the statute.

This more organized effort, representing management interest, cited the results of binding arbitration. A study by Paul C. Somers for the League concluded that "outcomes unduly favored unions" and noted that the last-best-offer by the union was chosen approximately twice as often as was management's. (The report did not analyze or address, however, whether or not this finding reflected objective circumstances, arbitrator prejudice, or the type of offers management typically had been tendering.) The study by the Massachusetts League of Cities and Towns concluded that the awards were not all that "inequitable," but that "the process was not generally accepted, . . . the economic impact has been unduly excessive, . . . the average case took over one year to complete, . . . the arbitration step, itself, did not appear effective at inducing settlements and . . . final offer . . . has increased reliance on third-party procedures. These findings lead me to conclude that the final offer system in Massachusetts has not worked well during its first two years, July 1, 1974, through June 30, 1976."[19]

Finally, the process of impasse, mediation, fact-finding, and last-best-offer arbitration was taking around fifteen months to complete in those cases that required arbitration. By the time one agreement had been reached, it was often nearly time to negotiate the next agreement. In some cases, two contract deadlines had come and gone. These elongated, formalistic, and contentious procedures were costing unions and municipalities thousands of dollars in direct legal fees and were harming relationships between the parties. The Director of the Massachusetts League of Cities and Towns, Kennedy Shaw, declared that the trial period of last-best-offer arbitration in Massachusetts had been "disastrous," not even helping the unions. The League felt that the legislation should be permitted to die in 1977.[20]

The Governor's Task Force and the Governor

Not everyone found fault with the 1974 arbitration statute, as we saw in the Sloan Report. Also, in the winter of 1975, the Department of Labor and Industries had organized the Governor's Task Force on Impasse Procedures at the request of interested legislators. The task force was composed of representatives of labor, management, and neutral organizations; its mandate was to "explore . . . Massachusetts' experience under Chapter 150E and G4 and Chapter 1078 [the new arbitration laws]." The task force was convened at this time to "look back over the first eighteen months of the law's life and to look ahead to July 1977, when the final-offer-arbitration provisions will expire unless extended by the legislature."

Two of the major issues in the task force report referred to problems that had required alterations in the statute. First, the task force found that cases took longer to be closed than the legislation's prescribed time limits, part of the reason being the length of the selection process for both fact finders and arbitrators. The task force lauded the change in the Board of Conciliation and Arbitration (BCA) policy that sought to limit the number of candidates the parties could choose from in an effort to shorten the time spent in selection. Second, the task force noted the change in the "retroactivity" policy. Retroactivity of an award had been limited initially to the beginning of the fiscal year most recently begun. Municipalities could thereby try to delay arbitration so that the arbitrator's decision did not occur until the beginning of a new fiscal year, thus severely limiting the length and cost of retroactivity of a new contract. This problem was solved by emergency legislation allowing retroactivity of an award to the date of expiration of the last contract.

However, the task force concluded that evidence was insufficient to examine how the new law encouraged collective bargaining and

whether it brought more disputes to resolution at the bargaining table. They stated it "premature to properly evaluate the law's success in either fiscal year." The majority of the task force agreed that the effects of the new law would not be evident for a few years, and, therefore, they strongly recommended a two-year extension of the law when it expired in 1977.[21]

Governor Michael Dukakis was not as enthusiastic as the governor's task force. The governor had taken a position against final and binding arbitration, noting that, in the face of the state's fiscal problems, local aid by the state to municipalities was on the decline, making the municipalities' already high costs of government even more difficult to meet. In keeping with his policy to avoid imposition of further financial requirements on local governments, he announced publicly his opposition before the Massachusetts Mayor's Association on May 8, 1977. Dukakis had based his position on his pledge to help financially pressed municipalities and on his belief that he could work the parties toward a compromise statute. In his speech Dukakis suggested a compromise bill that would allow for binding arbitration only if the community were determined by the Massachusetts Labor Relations Commission not to have bargained in good faith. (T. Dustin Alward, president of the Massachusetts Professional Fire Fighters, had commented that the "one problem with the State Labor Relations Commission is that it takes over a year to decide anything."[22]) Dukakis's statement came several days after the Public Service Committee of the Massachusetts legislature voted (with a few alterations) an extension of the law.

Labor Influence

Reflecting their continued interest in the existence of binding arbitration, the fire fighters played the primary role in lobbying for renewal of the statute. The police unions, perhaps partially as a result of the riots of 1919, as a rule were less well organized politically in Massachusetts. Perhaps their smaller and more splintered organizational base and shorter recent history in the state have combined to render them less politically active than their fire fighter brethren. Still, one observer noted: "No one manipulates the Massachusetts House and Senate with greater ease than the state police and fire fighters. The legislators have been doing their bidding for years."[23] In particular, however, it is the fire fighters who are singled out as one of the most formidable political and lobbying forces in the state.

The Legislative Fight

While the Massachusetts League of Cities and Towns, the primary group representing municipalities, had won the support of the governor against the bill, they could not muster legislative support equal to that of the labor side. In Massachusetts, municipal managers, although faced with the need for fiscal responsibility—especially in view of New York City's financial problems and public sentiments regarding California's Proposition 13—simply did not have the structure, continuity, political resources, or vote delivery power that public employee unions had. Here again, the role of politics in forming public sector labor policy and in the structure of public bargaining relationships critically affected the parameters of labor relations that were set.

The Senate overwhelmingly passed its bill to extend arbitration (without a trace of the governor's compromise), and the House was expected to pass it. Binding arbitration, as the *Globe* pointed out, was "an issue of both symbolism and substance for unions and management."[24] According to some observers, Dukakis felt that time was on his side because he could refuse to sign the bill. (The then-current law expired on June 30, 1977.) In this event, it was reasoned that unions and management would have to work out a compromise: unions, to avoid losing binding arbitration altogether, and management, to avoid two more years of arbitration in its current form.

As expected the House passed the bill on May 31, 1977, and on June 5 Governor Dukakis sent to the legislature a bill with amendments to broaden management rights and to limit the scope of arbitration so that matters of managerial policy would not be subject to arbitration. As promised, this bill included a provision requiring the Labor Relations Commission to rule that the municipality had not bargained in good faith before a dispute could go to final-offer arbitration.

On July 23, the legislature overwhelmingly approved its own bill on arbitration and defeated Dukakis's compromise measures. Dukakis promptly vetoed the bill, and four days later the legislature overrode Dukakis's veto 26 to 10 in the Senate and 166 to 59 in the House. This eleventh-hour reprieve was called a "testimony to the political clout of the police and fire fighters."[25]

Genesis of the Joint Labor-Management Committee

The Parties Bargain

Three days earlier, representatives of the Massachusetts League of Cities and Towns and the Massachusetts Professional Fire Fighters had met—reportedly for the first time during this particular round of political argument—to negotiate on the arbitration bill, seeking a compromise between the two versions that they might mutually urge on the governor and the legislature.

The fire fighters' willingness to compromise appears to have resulted from a series of actions begun by the Massachusetts League of Cities and Towns. During this late summer period in 1977 the League had commissioned a public opinion poll by a local political consultant—who also had close ties to the labor movement—to gauge public feelings on binding arbitration for police and fire fighters. The results were described by the pollster as "schizoid." Nevertheless, the League saw the results as sufficiently favorable to go ahead with a petition drive to force reconsideration of the bill either by the legislature or by a public referendum. The poll showed that although 97 percent of the public trusted fire fighters, 90 percent of those surveyed thought that the public should have an opportunity to vote on public employees raises.[26] As one prominent public union leader said privately, "We knew that if public employee raises were dependent upon a popular vote, no public employee in the state would get a raise until 1988!"

With these results—and the law in effect—the Massachusetts League of Cities and Towns and the Governor's Local Advisory Committee (made up of local government officials) began to organize a petition drive to get a referendum concerning the arbitration issue onto the November 1978 ballot. The municipal organizations did not have a good track record with referenda; earlier they had been unable to collect the 50,000 signatures needed to obtain a referendum on repealing the laws giving school committees fiscal autonomy. However, the current Massachusetts League was regarded as a more professional and better organized group, and there was reported to be a unanimity among municipal governments against binding arbitration.

In August 1977 the League began organizing a petition drive for October–November 1977 to collect the 50,000 signatures necessary to put the binding arbitration issue on the ballot. Once these signatures were collected, the legislature had until May 3, 1978 to reconsider the arbitration law. If the legislature rejected the petition, the League had to collect only 10,000 more signatures by June 8, 1978 to put the initiative on the November ballot.

The League chose not to go straight to the people with a binding referendum (if it had 55,000 signatures, the initiative was automatically on the ballot) because the League hoped to work the issue out with the legislature. This strategy reflected the League's serious concern over its ability to collect enough signatures. However, the labor side did not know the specifics of the progress of the drive, but was aware of the polls.

Seeking Accommodation

By accounts of the principals, a number of meetings had taken place between the municipal group and fire fighters through the summer to try to reach a compromise, but these efforts were inconclusive. In August the group began to look for a mediator since both saw something to lose should the other side carry the issue. The name that came up was that of John T. Dunlop, an experienced mediator and arbitrator. Dunlop was nearby at Harvard University where he was a professor and former Dean of the Faculty of Arts and Sciences.

Several of the parties to the Fire Fighter-League talks knew people who knew Dunlop, and, in the manner of the byzantine world of Massachusetts politics and labor relations, the city manager of Cambridge, Massachusetts (where Harvard is located) was asked to call Dunlop. City Manager Sullivan asked Dunlop if he would meet with some representatives of the fire fighters' union and the Massachusetts League of Cities and Towns regarding a problem, but he did not state the subject of the meeting.

Dunlop agreed to see them and invited them to lunch on August 30, 1977 on the campus of the Harvard Business School. The League of Cities and Towns was represented by its executive director, Kennedy Shaw, and Demetrios Moschos, assistant city manager of Worcester, Massachusetts. The Fire Fighters were represented by T. Dustin Alward, president of the Professional Fire Fighters of Massachusetts, Martin Pierce, regional vice-president of the International Association of Professional Fire Fighters, and J. J. Jennings, legislative agent of the Professional Fire Fighters of Massachusetts. At that meeting, they explained briefly the background and the legislative battle that had just taken place. Among the factors were the governor's position, the existence of the petition drive, the Fire Fighters' strength in the legislature, and the fact that legislators were in a position of choosing between their loyalty to their constituency (taxpayers and municipalities—many under financial pressure) and their own considerable political loyalty to the fire fighters.

After hearing them out on the problem, Dunlop arranged to see the representatives of each side separately. Impressed that they had themselves sought to work it out, and seeing room for compromise, Dunlop fashioned a written compromise solution over the Labor Day weekend and presented it to the groups separately in a general form.

Consensus on a Mechanism

Dunlop's draft agreement provided for a joint committee of labor and management officials, to which the two groups had assented. On September 19th a memorandum was agreed to, and on September 28th it was turned into legislative language by the parties themselves, whereupon the petition drive was terminated. The agreement also left intact the binding arbitration machinery, but gave the Joint Labor-Management Committee preeminent jurisdiction over any impasse in public safety.

For the most part, this form of joint labor and management interaction comes out of certain experiences in private sector labor relations. In particular it reflects Dunlop's experience in such matters as the Construction Industry Stabilization Committee of 1969–1974, which was widely credited with slowing wage increases in the construction industry and otherwise stabilizing labor relations in that industry. [27]

The document was taken to the state legislature and the governor as a joint proposal by the two sides, relying largely on the legislative skills of the Fire Fighters, the League's alliance with the governor, and the desire of all the politicians (executive and legislative) in question to find a graceful way out of the dilemma. Before the document was taken to the governor and the legislature, Dunlop, seeking to maintain the mutuality and trust that was at least tentatively established between the previously warring sides, exacted a promise from the two sides that no changes in the document would be permitted unless both sides agreed to the change. The proposed bill was described separately to the governor, to the president of the

Senate, and to the speaker of the House. Seeing the two sides in agreement on a mechanism they thought workable, these important political figures quickly agreed and resolved the political dilemma created by the intense battling for votes in the legislature and the problem of subsequent election support. It left the governor with a compromise rather than an overridden veto. Despite the fact that it was not his compromise, he was pleased to see an alternative to arbitration that would seek responsible and constructive dispute resolution.

The fire fighters had been in touch with the police unions and at this point began to include them actively in the process. The delay in police involvement caused some resentment. Nevertheless, the Boston Police Association in particular—for this and other historical reasons—was the only significant group in the state that formally opposed the compromise legislation.

The parties also were persuaded by Dunlop to see to it that prior to enactment those agencies that comprised the existing labor relations machinery (the Labor Relations Commission and the Board of Conciliation and Arbitration) be briefed on the agreement and its probable effect on their operations. The compromise would significantly affect the workings of the BCA, for over half their business was reported to be related to the last-best-offer statute and its various dispute resolution procedures. Although the compromise bill left the BCA intact, it effectively and purposefully rescinded most of its independence and influence over public safety dispute resolution. However, continuation of some BCA functions—such as initial receipt of impasse petitions and mediation—would require a constructive working relationship with the new Joint Labor-Management Committee. Reportedly, the briefing of the head of the BCA was handled badly, and relations with the BCA and the JLMC were difficult until leadership of the BCA changed several years later.

Political Ratification

In any event, the legislators were willing to process the bill as it had been agreed to, although there was reportedly some resentment that the parties resisted legislatively initiated changes. The bill passed nearly untouched, and the governor signed it, giving the new Joint Labor-Management Committee broad power to resolve the police and fire fighter disputes and a way to avoid binding arbitration.[28]

The political process in this instance was, in fact, a labor-management accord, and it produced a mechanism that began with the support of both parties. Those parties now also had an important stake in the outcome.[29]

Features of the Compromise

The Joint Labor-Management Committee was empowered to take jurisdiction in any dispute over a police or fire fighter contract, whether or not they were petitioned by the parties for such jurisdiction. Through a variety of informal mechanisms as well as formal procedures, the Committee was to seek to mediate as much as possible and was given the power to arbitrate in those instances in which a mediated solution was not possible. If it chose to arbitrate, it was not restricted to last-best-offer arbitration, but could employ conventional arbitration techniques.[30]

Just how the Committee would settle disputes had yet to be determined. Over the next several years a series of techniques would be developed in response to the problems the Committee found. A large array of tools and techniques subsequently evolved and the factors that account for their existence and success have their roots in the fit between the structure of the Committee, its state and local interconnections, the political system of government, and the realities of the labor relations environment. The next chapter describes the basic tools that have evolved and analyzes the political, interpersonal, and labor relations dynamics that cause them to operate as they do.

Summary

The parties were driven together by a history of bitterness and dissatisfaction—and the uncertain outcome of management's petition drive. Their joint discussions formed a mechanism that accommodated their own differences and permitted—indeed forced—their representatives in the political process to enact impasse legislation that accurately reflected the joint interest of both labor and management. Never before in the state's public bargaining history had the form of impasse resolution given each side equivalent weight in the eyes of the other. Past statutes were considered inadequate by one side or the other, if not considered a process dominated by the other side in creation and operation. This time it was different.

The specifics of the process by which disputes would be settled had yet to be worked out; however, those who had requested and designed the new structure and who knew intimately both the history and current needs of the environment would be those who would develop and be entrusted to see to the results of the new process. Furthermore, by establishing a voluntary committee the parties would be directly accountable for the results not just to the public but both to each other and to their respective labor and management communities.

Emerging from the history of dissatisfaction and imbalance and the more recent history of bitterness and near continuation of perceived imbalance, those interests that engineered the compromises—those between labor and management and their political allies and within the labor and management communities—would be able to try their hand at building a new way to resolve public sector disputes. To the two sides it was a matter of self-interest. By studying the results of that self-interest—enlightened or not—we can examine some fundamental principles of labor relations in a governmental and political context.

Endnotes

1. For one description of the Boston Police Strike see Richard Ray, "Police Strike Boston in 1919," *Boston Globe*, September 16, 1969, p. 22.
2. For a general summary and description of public employee bargaining in Massachusetts see John Burke, ed., *A Guide to the Massachusetts Public Employee Bargaining Law*, third Ed., prepared for the Massachusetts Labor Relations Commission, Institute for Governmental Services, University of Massachusetts, 1978; and "Rules and Regulations of the Board of Conciliation and Arbitration," the Commonwealth of Massachusetts, Executive Office of Manpower Affairs, 1978.
3. *Summary of Public Sector Labor Relations Policies*, 1976, U.S. Department of Labor, Labor Management Services Administration.
4. *Boston Evening Globe*, March 27, 1973, and March 28, 1973.
5. See Stern *et al.*, *Final Offer Arbitration*; Geare, "Final Offer Arbitration"; Stevens, "Is Compulsory Arbitration Compatible with Collective Bargaining?"
6. Schmidt, *Industrial Relations in Urban Transportation*.
7. See Stern *et al.*, *Final Offer Arbitration*.
8. See for example, Stevens, "Is Compulsory Arbitration Compatible with Collective Bargaining?"

9. Conversations with Professor Howard Raiffa, Harvard University, 1979, 1980.
10. *Boston Globe*, September 20, 1973, October 16, 1973; *Boston Sunday Globe*, June 23, 1974.
11. *Boston Globe*, September 16, 1973.
12. See "Rules and Regulations," the Commonwealth of Massachusetts.
13. These pro and con arguments were made by labor, management, and legislative individuals. See *Boston Globe*, October 12, 1973, for a presentation of two points of view.
14. See Burke *et al.*, *A Guide to the Massachusetts Public Employee Bargain Law*; and "Rules and Regulations."
15. Massachusetts Department of Labor and Industries, "Interim Report of the Governor's Task Force on Chapter 150E and Impasse Procedures," September 20, 1976, p. 1.
16. Massachusetts General Laws, Chapter 150E.
17. *Boston Globe*, November 11, 1976, p. 3.
18. David B. Lipsky, Thomas A. Barocci, with William Suojanen, *The Impact of Final Offer Arbitration in Massachusetts: An Analysis of Police and Firefighter Collective Bargaining*, May 17, 1977.
19. Paul Somers, "An Evaluation of Final Offer Arbitration in Massachusetts" Personnel and Labor Relations Bulletin, Massachusetts League of Cities and Towns, November 1976, p. 28.
20. *Boston Globe*, November 11, 1976, p. 3.
21. "Interim Report of the Governor's Task Force."
22. *Boston Globe*, April 9, 1977, p. 1.
23. *Boston Globe*, August 29, 1977, p. 15.
24. *Boston Globe*, May 30, 1977, p. 3.
25. *Boston Globe*, June 28, 1977, p. 1.
26. Interview with poll manager, December, 1979.
27. For a discussion of the Construction Industry Stabilization Committee see D. Quinn Mills, *Government Labor and Inflation: Wage Stabilization in the United States* (University of Chicago Press, 1976).
28. For public reports of the compromise see *Boston Globe*, October 4, 1977, October 18, 1977, November 16, 1977.
29. The foregoing discussion concerning the development of the JLMC compromise comes from a series of interviews or discussions with the principals involved.
30. Massachusetts General Laws, Outside Section 4A, Joint Labor-Management Committee, as established by Chapter 730 of the Acts of 1977.

Chapter 3

STRUCTURE AND OPERATIONS OF THE JOINT LABOR-MANAGEMENT COMMITTEE

Although the joint labor-management committee approach to resolving public safety impasses was generated in Massachusetts, the most interesting aspect of the experiment is the prospect of a more general application of its principles to the resolution of public sector disputes. In this chapter, these arrangements for dispute resolution are described from the standpoint of commonly applied principles of labor relations and labor relations dynamics and in the context of the specialized public sector environment that was discussed in Chapter 1.

Although public debate over extension of the last-best-offer statutes for settling police and fire disputes was dominated by polarized positions and bitter rhetoric, each side had concerns that were considerably more complex than their public positions indicated. It was not simply a matter of unions wanting the highest possible settlements and management wanting to retain all authority to determine labor costs; rather, both sides desired to improve the bargaining process to bring about more constructive and expeditious settlements to contribute to the welfare of union members and to the delivery of fire fighting and police services. Although, in the absence of an alternative, the police and fire groups had been strongly in support of the last-best-offer legislation, they had had experience and foresaw problems with the type of collective bargaining and bargaining environment that resulted from the use of last-best-offer arbitration. In the absence of an alternative device to force settlement of disputes, however, the labor side firmly supported renewal.

51

The objectives that surfaced during private discussions between the parties which led to the legislative compromise are the concepts that come to govern the structure and operations of the Joint Labor-Management Committee. A brief discussion of these objectives (examined in Chapter 7) will greatly help to explain the tools that have been employed and their utility as dispute settlement tools in contexts other than Massachusetts public safety.

Commitment to Collective Bargaining

Increasing Collective Bargaining

In general the new mechanism was intended to encourage bargaining and minimize third-party involvement. The 1977 statute that created the Joint Labor-Management Committee mandated the Committee to employ a wide range of settlement tools. As part of the compromise, the statute also left on the books the last-best-offer form of arbitration begun under the 1973 statute, but gave the Joint Labor-Management Committee the right to assert primary jurisdiction in any police or fire dispute, effectively empowering the Committee to prevent a dispute from going to last-best-offer arbitration. The Committee itself was empowered to arbitrate disputes and could, in fact, choose to employ the last-best-offer form of arbitration. However, it quickly became Committee policy to use arbitration only as a last resort, after all efforts and tools to encourage collective bargaining were exhausted.

Direct Bargaining, Practicality, and Acceptability

The emphasis on free collective bargaining has its roots in the dissatisfaction surrounding the perceived negative effects on bargaining of the last-best-offer statute. This emphasis is reflected in the stated objectives of the Committee.

The primary objective in designing a new means of resolving disputes was to make settlements more a result of a collective process in which the parties themselves, rather than an outsider, would make the trade-offs among the issues. The LBO process had put the parties into a sort of lottery, or roll-of-the-dice posture, with only one winner. The unhappy party frequently sought redress either at the next contract round, or by other means, with redress or resentment destabilizing the relationship in the interim. The intent of the new process was to encourage outcomes more practical and satisfactory to all than in last-best-offer arbitration. The "either-or" choice made it more difficult to carry on subsequent labor-management relationships and administer the contract. Unless the last-best-offers of the parties were relatively close, the LBO process seemed to produce destabilizing outcomes, even though the proximate dispute was settled.

Both sides in the compromise wished to see labor-management disputes settled by direct bargaining between the parties rather than through arbitration or other third-party decisions or interference. More practical settlements formed by the parties themselves and acceptable to both sides would be more likely to come about through direct bargaining than through third-party decisions. By direct bargaining, the parties who make the decisions are those who are most familiar with the issues and who have to live with the product of the settlement process.

More Mediation and Less Uncertainty

To facilitate an increase in the amount of direct bargaining that was taking place, the designers of the Joint Labor-Management Committee hoped to create a mechanism that would avoid arbitration and decision making by anyone other than the parties. They were determined to mediate in ways and on levels that had not been tried under the pre-1978 dispute settlement procedures of the Board of Conciliation and Arbitration.

A need was also perceived for third-party (mediators and arbitrators) familiarity with settlement patterns and relationships elsewhere in the state. It was clear to the founders that disputes were not solely a result of internal factors, but were often also related to relativities in wages and working conditions to nearby or related municipalities or to other workers in the same jurisdiction. A negotiator or third party with perspective in such matters is more likely to be a strong and effective factor in the negotiation process.[1]

By keeping the parties talking and narrowing their differences through mediation, it was expected that problems could be resolved in a more practical manner. Also, ongoing—frequently mediated—dialogue between the parties on the issues could avoid another problem; in choosing to leave the decision to an arbitrator or avoiding mutual contact, each side ran the risk of being surprised or embarrassed by the outcome. If the parties were in regular contact, if information was being exchanged directly (or through the mediator) while positions were changing through the negotiating process, surprises could be avoided. They hoped to lessen the likelihood of surprises and embarrassment detrimental to the bargaining relationship by fostering the sort of information exchange that occurred through direct bargaining and mediation but which did not occur frequently in last-best-offer arbitration.

Structural Change to Promote Problem Solving

Rather than simply receiving an edicted solution to the immediate dispute, the originators of the JLMC felt that the parties and the community would benefit from a mechanism that would help them, first, better structure their collective bargaining relationship and, second, resolve substantive problems concerning working conditions or the delivery of services. Without attention to such fundamental problems, the real source of the dispute could emerge again and again.

The group that produced the compromise felt that both the limitations of the existing LBO statute and the limitations of the existing bureaucracy prevented constructive problem solving from taking place. Often, collective bargaining relationships or outcomes will not improve without some fundamental alterations in the structure of the bargaining relationship, the actors involved, or the methods used. The resolution of difficult disputes by arbitration proceedings which focused only on the settlements of individual cases did not provide a means to influence or correct fundamental structural problems in the bargaining process or relationship. A more flexible mechanism might find ways to help the parties to interact more successfully in the future. Under the last-best-offer statute, only the issues in dispute could command the interest of the arbitrator and parties involved. Without a mandate or a means for considering preventative medicine for the future, discussion would stop with those issues.

The new mechanism, therefore, was designed to preclude confinement to the issues on the table if other matters obstructed the bargaining relationship or resolution of more basic issues contributing to the problem on the table. The Committee, frequently through informal means, would seek to deal with these underlying structural matters.

The capacity for structural changes to deal with issues of service delivery were also important to the management group among JLMC founders. They felt that in a period of fiscal stringency, alterations in productivity or work-force distribution might be important objectives for a city or town government. Over the longer term there might well be a need to respond to changed demand for types or volume of police or fire services or a need to change management priorities and practices. To explore and accommodate such change would require two-party discussion in a broad context of labor and management concerns; certainly, if such alterations were not part of the last-best-offer package, it could not be chosen by the arbitrators. Recognizing this lack, a more flexible mechanism was sought to allow some response to these broader and longer term concerns.

Local Responsibility for Settlement

In addition to the effect on the settlement of specific issues in dispute, direct negotiations were viewed as a process that would contribute toward developing an atmosphere of communication and trust by causing the parties to deal directly, discuss their interests, and resolve their differences. An improved relationship between the parties would aid in resolving and preventing problems during the term of the contract and in future negotiations, whereas disputes settled by third parties in arbitration or in negotiations handled primarily by attorneys or other agents were considered less likely to improve day-to-day operational or later bargaining interactions between the parties themselves. With the relationship building that would accompany JLMC-promoted joint discussions, and the improvement in communications and trust that might also effect mutual understanding of political, organizational, and substantive needs and constraints, it was expected that subsequent negotiation would be less likely to end in dispute—and again require third-party decisions.

The existing system leading to last-best-offer arbitration did not, in the view of management and labor representatives forming the new mechanism, impose on the parties responsibility for bargaining or for settlements. Rather, it permitted an escape valve whereby either party could declare an impasse at an early stage, effectively "kicking the dispute upstairs" where it would be decided. The increase in impasses in the years since the LBO statute first went into effect suggested the tendency, through this process, to give the Board of

Conciliation and Arbitration and other outside parties the responsibility for settlement, often resulting in a settlement resented by one of the parties.

In addition, it was believed that an increase in direct bargaining would more likely consider the views of publicly elected officials with fiscal responsibility than would third-party settlements; an important objection of cities and towns to LBO and arbitration generally was that arbitrators were not fiscally or otherwise responsible for the settlements. Since the LBO statute required that localities fund arbitration awards, this matter was of serious concern. (One observer noted that, between 1974 and 1977, it seemed as though all Massachusetts police and fire fighter disputes were settled by someone from New York, "always from New York, who took the next shuttle out of town.") The group of Committee founders, therefore, agreed that arbitration would not be considered until all possible tools, mediation efforts, and joint bargaining took place. With this policy, local definition of issues, bargaining parameters, and settlement would be encouraged.

Reduced Time and Contention

Importantly, both the union and municipal parties to the discussions resulting in the JLMC compromise wanted to achieve rapid settlements. Under the 1974 procedure, in some cities and towns policemen and fire fighters had been working without new contracts for up to three years, and their wages remained unadjusted. Labor and management representatives to the compromise were concerned that long and contentious formal proceedings would continue to harm the development of bargaining relationships and the day-to-day management of the safety service. During arbitration or litigation, relations rarely improved and usually deteriorated, and the quality of service and morale of the work force was often said to have suffered. In the interest of fairness and efficiency, both sides sought, in designing a new process, to shorten the length of time necessary to settle disputes. If the contention and bitterness that arose during this process could be reduced, the compromisers thought, more constructive labor-management relationships might be formed and more constructive and expeditious settlements might be possible in the future.

Less Litigation and Reduced Costs

Based on experience with LBO, both sides were also interested in reducing the costs of the settlement process. Attorneys' fees and arbitrator costs mounted for both sides in the elongated, legalistic, and frequently litigious 1974 process. The cost was especially burdensome to smaller towns and bargaining units, where in some cases legal costs exceeded the money difference between the sides. Savings could be reaped, it seemed, by reducing the time required to reach settlement as well as by obviating the use of a complicated quasi-judicial proceeding.

In these and other respects, the new 1977 statute and mechanism were designed to improve bargaining, reduce contention, and gain more desirable substantive and structural outcomes. The parties to the compromise hoped that the practices they were proposing would bring to bear more responsible leadership and greater expertise in the settlement of disputes than was possible under the LBO statute and practices that had evolved with it.

Structure of the Joint Labor-Management Committee

The structure of the mechanism and some of the practices that evolved are sketched in the statute and procedural rules of the Committee. The Committee refined its practices still further as its experience with resolving cases accumulated and as policy discussions progressed within the group. The remainder of this chapter will describe the structure and operations of the Joint Labor-Management Committee, which features are critical to the results obtained by the experiment. The description highlights the labor-relations dynamics that result from the joint structure as it is applied to dispute resolution.

Joint Membership and the Appointment Procedure

The membership and appointment procedures are central to the operations of the Committee in resolving disputes. The membership was established to balance labor and management representation. When the JLMC was established under a statute effective January 1, 1978, it was composed of thirteen members, including a chairperson. Under the statute effective July 1, 1979, a vice-chairperson, who votes only in the absence of the chairperson and acts in the chairperson's place only when authorized, was added to the original membership. The remainder of the Committee is made up of six management members and six labor members (and their nonvoting alternates). Among the six management members are a variety of municipal affiliations. For example, in 1979 the JLMC consisted of a mayor, a former selectman and officer of the Massachusetts Selectman's Association, a town manager, an assistant city manager, a city labor relations director, and a former town finance committee member.

The six labor seats were equally represented by the police and fire fighters, largely union officers. In the first years of the Committee's operation, the three fire fighters included the president and two senior officers of the Professional Fire Fighters of Massachusetts, which is affiliated with the International Association of Fire Fighters, AFL–CIO. The International Brotherhood of Police Officers (IBPO), affiliated with the National Association of Government Employees, and the Massachusetts Police Association were both represented among the three police seats on the Committee; initially, the IBPO held two of the seats and the Massachusetts Police Association, one. This seat arrangement was to alternate each year between the two police organizations.

Nominations for the six management seats on the Committee, according to the statute, are made by the gubernatorially appointed Local Government Advisory Committee. Nominations for the labor seats come from the International Brotherhood of Police Officers, the Massachusetts Police Association, and the Professional Fire Fighters Association of Massachusetts. The statute requires that the governor appoint to the Committee the nominees proposed by these organizations. The chairperson and vice-chairperson are nominated by the Committee and presented to the governor, who is required by law to make the appointment. Members can be removed only for malfeasance and similar actions.[2]

Voluntary Service

Members of the Committee serve without compensation, although the chairperson is paid on a per diem basis. Voluntary service is intended to affect the dynamics of the mechanism to encourage settlement between the parties. This provision of the statute is purposeful in that both sides wished to avoid what they described as "bureaucratic tendencies" ascribed to the existing state agency in dispute resolution (the Board of Conciliation and Arbitration). Rather than create or modify a full-time bureaucracy, those designing the Joint Committee sought to set up a mechanism that they thought would more directly encourage and assist settlements to be reached through collective bargaining. In addition, rather than alter the rules under which the BCA worked, voluntary service in a separate agency by people with a professional interest in settlement rather than in conflict was conceived as an alternative to the Board, which was an institution whose operations and staff were seen by the parties as fraught with bureaucratic inertia.

Seeking to alter the contentious character of labor relations in the state, the designers shaped the statute to change the operating rules and mechanism by which disputes would be settled to one emphasizing informal accommodation rather than competitive legal proceedings. To accomplish these intentions, the Committee was established as an independent and volunteer agency. Unpaid members, maintaining their institutional affiliations to labor or management, would more likely promote settlements that reflected the needs of each side and would be more likely to seek expeditious resolution. Because they would have their full-time jobs to attend to, they would have a natural interest in rapid resolution and in helping the parties to resolve the dispute themselves, if not this time, the next time around.

Membership, Bargaining, and Public Policy

As will be discussed later, many of the Committee's activities in resolving contract disputes rely on its ability to establish credibility and to gain the trust of the parties. Thus, the Committee members' professional affiliations and personal relationships with municipal and local labor leaders are important. Similarly, the ability of Committee members to understand the issues in dispute allows the Committee an advantage not ordinarily shared by arbitrators or mediators. Because of the members' backgrounds, the Committee as a neutral can understand fire fighting safety or manning issues as would a fire fighter; on the other side, it can also understand the implications of a shrinking tax base as would a city manager or comptroller. This substantive expertise of the membership provides one tool to encourage the parties to bargain seriously, largely by relying on expert members to turn aside unreasonable or preposterous proposals.

The network of professional and personal contacts of the membership enables constructive Committee involvement in disputes. For example, through these contacts, the Committee may learn of potential disputes before they have become official impasses or before positions harden. Once the Committee is involved in settling a dispute, these contacts and the members' expertise may enable it to discover more easily and rapidly the real issues and bargaining positions, thus allowing, through mediation or other means, a more rapid settlement.

Since the membership has expertise and a range of contacts and familiarity with local and regional conditions, extensive "education" of the neutral (i.e., Committee) is not required concerning the technical or political issues or about the relationship of the parties. In addition, the Committee, through informal contacts and through its formal involvement, will have information not easily or ordinarily available to an arbitrator brought in one case at a time, particularly one from outside the area. A more knowledgeable neutral is ordinarily desirable, and the Committee's approach is structured to strengthen that aspect of bargaining assistance.

The personal and professional contacts of Committee members can enforce an internal discipline on the activities of individual Committee members. Close contact with a party to a particular dispute or to the member's labor or management constituency also influences Committee members to represent the interest of their constituents in the Committee's deliberations. Simultaneously the member will be seeking to maintain institutional neutrality and standing in his or her own community. Members are thereby encouraged to facilitate direct bargaining and to seek settlements acceptable to the parties. This aspect of the joint composition of the Committee tends to create a dynamic that encourages acceptable settlements reached through bargaining.

A volunteer agency is not without its practical difficulties. Union officials normally spend a large proportion of their time on labor-management matters. Despite the significant amount of time taken up by Committee business, such use of time falls within their generally understood range of responsibilities. It is less common for municipal managers and legislators to spend a large proportion of their time on labor-management responsibilities; mayors and city managers, for example, typically have a range of responsibilities in which labor relations is perceived as only one. Municipalities are required by law to grant employees who are Committee members time away from their normal responsibilities to carry on Committee business, whether that be formal meetings of the Committee or other activities such as mediation and monitoring of negotiations.[3]

The stipulation of voluntary service by Committee members was intended (1) to avoid the unintended formation of a new bureaucracy, (2) to maintain each Committee member's motivation to reflect in policy matters or in particular disputes the interests of their constituencies or counterparts, and (3) to maintain the member's primary interest in the promotion of prompt and constructive settlements and structural reform in labor-management relations.

Relationship to Other Institutions

In forming a new mechanism to deal with labor-management disputes, it is important to consider the legal and political relationship of the new mechanism to other, existing bureaucracies with power or standing in labor dispute resolution. Competition or jurisdictional confusion between agencies is unlikely to contribute to labor peace and may confuse, anger, or bring about undue attention to bureaucratic rivalries. Because of initial carelessness in developing the relationship between the Board of Conciliation and Arbitration and the Joint Labor-Management Committee, at least some such stresses evolved. Since a large proportion of the Board's work was in public sector dispute settlement, it is not surprising that tension arose. The operational difficulty arose because some parties, preferring arbitration, attempted or threatened to resist Committee jurisdiction and go directly to the Board to seek a "better" deal. Cooperation between such agencies may be used to prevent "forum shopping" or nonconstructive use of related legal channels—and also to prevent wasteful jurisdictional battles of the bureaucratic sort. Similarly, cooperation among agencies with influence over labor policy can avoid inconsistency in application of standards and resolution of disputes or complaints that might otherwise contribute to a poorer labor-management environment, difficulty of settlement, or to a lack of respect for the available mechanisms.

Officially, the Committee exercises its powers independent of other state agencies. Although formally within the Department of Labor and Industries, the Committee members and chairperson are appointed directly by the governor and are not subject in any way to the authority of the Secretary of Labor and Industries or any of the Secretary's subordinates. This is consistent with aspects of the Committee's structure and statute that seek to make it independent of political control, but the Committee does have an important formal and, as a result of efforts by all three agencies, informal relationship with the Board of Conciliation and Arbitration and with the Massachusetts Labor Relations Commission.[4]

The JLMC statute specifies that "the Committee shall have oversight responsibility for all collective bargaining negotiations involving municipal police officers and fire fighters,"[5] allowing it to become involved at any time in the course of a dispute or potential dispute, even if the Board has official jurisdiction. (The statute effective July 1, 1979, which amended slightly the 1977 statute, gave the JLMC original jurisdiction over all cases. As a result, notification of impasse is now filed with the Committee rather than the Board as it had been originally under the 1974 LBO statute and the 1977 statute, which established the Committee.) The law specifies a thirty-day period during which the JLMC must act to assert its jurisdictions. If it does not, jurisdiction falls to the BCA and its normal procedures, although the Committee can reassert jurisdiction by notifying the board of its intent.

A less formal part of the Committee's relationship to the Board, but one that has played a role in dispute resolution, concerns the use of mediators and arbitrators employed by the Board to settle disputes under the JLMC's jurisdiction. This use has been intended to avoid duplicative staffing between the agencies and to productively use available talent. Increasingly, a better working relationship between the Committee and the Board is resulting in information exchange on specific disputes and policies and on resource sharing. In addition the Committee has occasionally determined that the proceedings of the Board may be more appropriate for solving certain disputes or for dealing with the initial stages of mediation. On one occasion, in its first three years, the Committee sent a case to the Board for last-best-offer arbitration, although it normally eschews such proceedings.

Budget and Staff

Since the fiscal year that began July 1, 1979, the JLMC appears as a separate line item in the budget of the Commonwealth of Massachusetts. It does not receive funding from any other agency, although in practice the cooperative use of the resources of the BCA supplements the Committee's activities. In 1979, the Committee's budget was $150,000, and for fiscal 1981 it was $408,155. In the same two years, the BCA had a budget of $330,808 and $381,000, respectively.

The Committee has the statutory authority to hire such staff as it finds necessary to conduct its business, subject to the availability of funds. Surely, a variety of staffing arrangements would have been possible. The Committee, as it formed, chose to have two full-time senior staff representatives—one representing labor, the other management. Later, in 1979, additional staff known as field investigators were hired to work with the senior staff. In addition, the Committee hired at the outset a research director and a secretary/administrative assistant, whose role has since expanded to relieve the substantive staff of administrative duties. Periodically, other temporary employees are hired for specific cases or projects.

After a few years of experience, the JLMC seemed to hit upon a formula that seems now rather stable. First, the administrative and substantive activities are separated and the neutrality of the administrative activities protected. Second, the substantive activities of the staff are closely tied to Committee priorities. Third, a strong administrative person tracks the work flow and manages the administrative details of the office. These administrative functions are key to the operations of the group, to its effectiveness and timeliness, and to the resultant perceptions of outside parties of the group's efficacy and neutrality.

The two senior staff members jointly manage the neutral field investigators, and the neutral chair, or vice chair, meets occasionally with the staff to discuss professional problems and techniques. The presence of all staff members at Committee meetings helps keep them aware of priorities and policy decisions and keeps them part of the overall endeavor.

Periodically, other temporary employees are hired for specific cases or projects. The research director is responsible for, among other duties, compiling statistical information for internal management and policy purposes and for developing a data base that would permit comparison of wages, benefits, and other contract provisions among bargaining units in the state. Such data provided by a neutral source were intended for use in mediation or arbitration to more directly compare the size and scope of settlements and to avoid comparisons that might result in extreme bargaining positions or in destabilizing wage patterns within or among communities.

The Role of Staff Expertise

The senior staff representatives perform a variety of tasks—including mediation, assessment of bargaining situations, drafting arbitration awards, and making recommendations to the Committee—that require sophisticated knowledge of labor-management relations and collective bargaining and an ability to get along with and win the trust of the parties. While the senior staff members serve as neutrals, the selection of two senior persons, one from each of the two communities at interest, represented a conscious decision not to have a neutral professional staff in a traditional sense, but one parallel with the Committee itself, to try and guarantee a fair and neutral outcome through the representation of both points of view. It was also hoped that easier access to the real issues in dispute would be facilitated as trust and understanding would be more rapidly forthcoming between a party in dispute and a neutral with a similar substantive background or experience.

The senior staff serve as the "eyes and ears" of the Committee and, by their relative seniority and stature in the labor or management community, are intended to perform duties otherwise reserved for Committee members. The activities of the senior staff can, therefore, act as critical supplement to the scarce time of volunteer Committee members.

In many respects, the senior staff performs interchangeably with full-fledged members of the Committee, although staff members are not permitted to vote on case or policy issues. Also, because they are to work as neutrals, they are not intended to be influenced as greatly by their respective constituencies. This condition is enhanced by their full-time Committee employment. The distinction between members and senior staff is, however, important in maintaining policy control and final decisions by voluntary, appointed principals. Operationally, the distinction permits the existence of two levels, rather than one, of senior people to help resolve disputes. The staff is empowered, at the direction of the Committee, to investigate and analyze situations and to mediate or employ other tools to promote what one staff member has termed "the joy of settlement." Skilled senior people are important to the Committee's operation in assisting the Committee principals in making informed judgments and in independently handling and settling disputes.

Under the revised statute (1979) and the budget related to it, the Committee has hired as neutrals a number of less experienced staff members. People in this group have less substantive background relating to either the labor or management side. When an impasse petition is received, the neutral staff members generally are those asked to make the assessment prior to a Committee decision on whether it will take jurisdiction.

The specific duties of the staff people have changed and evolved as the Committee has operated. When the JLMC becomes involved or interested in a case, formally or informally, the Committee generally requests that one of the staff assess the situation and report on it. Such assessment might take place over the phone or in person, depending on the staff member's familiarity with the persons or situation. Often staff members directed to informally assess a situation find themselves involved unwittingly in mediation when they arrive to assess a conflict.

The insight and judgment of the senior staff members has become a major tool of the Committee in determining a formal or informal action regarding a case. Although their role was initially somewhat unclear, as time went on these staff members, at the Committee's discretion, increasingly became involved in assessing, mediating, and advising the Committee on actions and in drafting and making recommendations on arbitration awards. Because staff members work full time—in contrast to the Committee members—the staff's activities expanded by an important amount the quantity of casework that the Committee could handle. And because Committee members volunteered their time, it seemed necessary to use full-time paid staff to buttress the Committee members' own activities. The Committee hoped to attract top-quality staff in part by its ability to pay salaries commensurate with the sort of talent they required. The 1977 statute specified that the Committee's hiring would be outside most civil service screening and classification requirements although affirmative action hiring practices are observed.

To handle cases expeditiously, it is crucial that volunteer Committee member time be used efficiently when it is available. Therefore, the ability of the staff to perform competent assessments and to assist in mediative efforts is an important ingredient in the Committee's productivity. Since Committee members themselves cannot ordinarily take the time to learn case details in sufficient depth to make proper assessments, they must depend significantly on staff judgments regarding the status and possible methods of handling the case. To be sure, the staff recommendation is often challenged, but

Figure 3–1   A Partial Hierarchy of Tools in Alternate Methods of Dispute Settlement

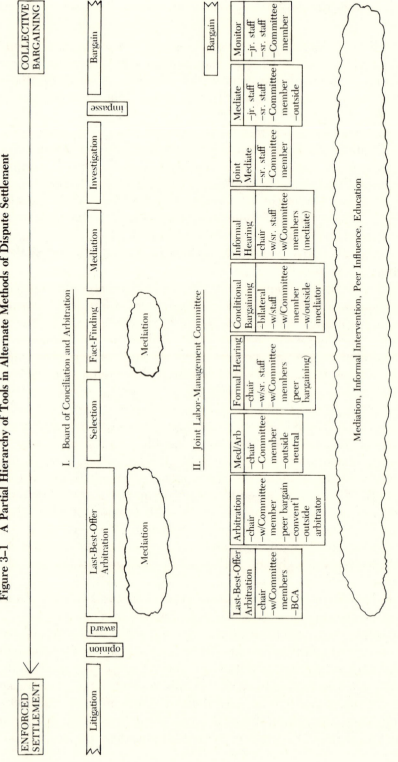

"outside" = independent neutral assigned by Joint Labor-Management Committee   "BCA" = mediators from the Board of Conciliation and Arbitration oral reports furnished by the staff provide the substance for Committee discussion and judgment.

Minimizing Third-Party Involvement

Figure 3-1 illustrates the differences in philosophy and flexibility between the old last-best-offer and arbitration process and the process made possible by the joint committee approach. The process illustrated in the top of the figure is that followed in the last-best-offer arbitration and related impasse procedures. It runs along the continuum from bargaining (on the right) through mediation and fact finding to arbitration, and finally to litigation. (Prior to 1978 the majority of impasse cases were settled by the use of arbitration or litigation.) The lower portion of the diagram depicts the Joint Committee's process as it is described here, with bargaining at the right, arbitration at the left. The variety of tools and methods of application available to the Committee is suggested by the greater number of boxes and the variants on each tool indicated by the descriptions within each box. Even arbitration as practiced by the Committee falls further along the continuum toward bargaining because of the forms of arbitration that are employed.

The Committee's dispute settlement activities can be placed along a continuum, as represented in Figure 3-1. At the right-hand extreme the parties have maximal participation and independence to settle their own disputes in a climate of free collective bargaining. At the left, increasing intervention by other parties is evident. In moving toward the left, the Committee may employ a variety of steps that increase the degree of assistance or intervention in the process. The process of seeking settlements may move along the continuum as impasses are reached, or tools may be selected anywhere along the continuum as the situation warrants. Finally, but rarely, the Committee may find settlement to require the participation of a third party in arbitration (at the far left end of the spectrum). Under the Committee, tools of settlement and levels of involvement and intervention can be tailored to the type of dispute, the issues, the personalities, or the structure of the labor-management relationship in question. In contrast, the BCA proceedings necessarily began at the right and proceeded in sequence to the left, frequently finishing far to the left end of the continuum.

As practiced, Joint Committee arbitration typically has elements of bargaining and local determination uncharacteristic of the system depicted in the top of the diagram. More than anything, the Joint

Labor-Management Committee founders sought to promote settlement outcomes resulting from bargaining. Committee activities and
tools minimize the movement away from features of bargaining that
tends to occur as third parties enter disputes. Most disputes handled
under the new system are settled toward the "collective bargaining"
end of the spectrum.

Seeking the "Joy of Settlement"

Impasses Are Not What They Seem

As is the intention of most impasse procedures, mediation and other
Committee-induced negotiations frequently take place after official
declaration of an impasse. In contrast to the rigid steps of the predecessor mechanism, the flexibility allowed under the statute and
practices of the JLMC provides an opportunity to turn a formal
impasse into the beginning of serious attempts at settlement between the parties rather than an acknowledgment that bargaining
cannot succeed.

Figure 3-1 shows in each of the boxes in the bottom part of the
diagram some examples of Committee tools. Ordinarily, first to be
tried is simple encouragement to bargain or monitoring of direct
negotiation, then conventional mediation, then a form of more complex or "higher level" mediation, possibly utilizing increasingly
senior people. Next are informal hearings with mediation or perhaps
bargaining between Committee members on behalf of the parties.
Finally, and only after failing in these other attempts, a third party
may be called on to impose a settlement.

A Hierarchy of Tools

At each stage of its involvement in a dispute the Committee seeks to
reopen discussion, remove obstacles, and provide an environment of
hope or a threat of unwelcome intervention. It seeks to settle a
dispute as closely as possible to the collective bargaining portion of
the spectrum shown in Figure 3-1. Mechanisms are involved and
invented to maximize the possibility of resolution through direct
collective bargaining. Only as successive impasses are reached does
the Committee move along the continuum in Figure 3-1 from direct
bargaining toward a third-party settlement. Similarly, most of the
tools, especially at the early stages, can be applied by successively

senior levels of personnel: by junior staff, senior staff, Committee members, or later by the chair or an outside neutral without involving a more interventionist tool.

The Committee has adopted and invented a number of tools (methods of dealing with disputes and internal procedures) that seek to avoid third-party involvement or influence, whether that be in the form of an arbitrator or even a judge. Unlike the several tools available to the BCA, the Committee tools, although they may follow the order in Figure 3-1, do not have to be applied in any particular order and can be applied as the situation warrants. The order in which they are drawn in Figure 3-1 represents increased third-party involvement in the settlement process as one moves from right to left. The Committee will start as far to the right (towards collective bargaining) as the situation seems to allow.

Largely, these tools have evolved as the Committee's philosophy and objectives have been applied to the patterns of encountered problems. As its primary tool, within the constraints of a particular dispute, the Joint Committee always seeks to maximize the degree of direct bargaining between the parties, pushing as far as it can toward agreement through that means. Sometimes direct bargaining, so encouraged, leads to settlement; other times it only serves to narrow the range of issues or, perhaps, to highlight problems of personality or posturing that are affecting the progress of negotiations. In such cases, more complex and, frequently informal means of Committee involvement are applied.

Tools to Fit the Problem

Over time a hierarchy and general order seem to have evolved in which these tools are applied that depend on the nature of the dispute and perceived difficulty of settlement. Early in the Committee's existence it typically sought to mediate or to monitor each dispute informally and then apply successive degrees of involvement and influence. With experience, however, an informal set of criteria have developed that determines the first appropriate Committee action to resolve a dispute. This Committee decision is largely based on the staff assessment and other information, if any, available through informal channels. For example, a dispute that arises from some relatively straightforward differences on issues might be assigned to a staff mediator, whereas a dispute involving a very complex substantive question might be referred to a Committee member or a particular staff member possessing expertise in the matter. Or, if a complicated personality conflict is seen, a Committee member (or two) with some connection to one of the parties might be assigned to mediate. Thus, the portion of Figure 3-1 showing the Committee's operations has under each of its tools a hierarchy of actors who may invoke the tool, depending on the circumstance. Assessment may be done by anyone from a field investigator to a Committee member. Mediation can involve the same range of actors or may involve a mediator from the BCA or an outside mediator, as Figure 3-1 suggests.

If the differences involve political questions, a Committee member who is a mayor or otherwise experienced in politics might be assigned to help. If the parties are especially far apart as a result of suspicion or mistrust, the use of two mediators, one from a labor and one from a management background, might be used. Many combinations are possible, and the Committee has sought increasingly to tailor its involvement to each situation as it perceives it. The case studies in the following two chapters depict both the selection of tools to fit the dispute and the hierarchy of increasing involvement of outside parties and decision makers as the disputes resist efforts at settlement through more direct bargaining.

The processes that have evolved and the order in which they are employed are reflective of this desire to maximize agreement and move the parties as far as possible by means of direct bargaining or mediation. Failing at this, the practicality and acceptability expected from direct bargaining are sought by using some more complex tools and thereby avoid moving the dispute directly to arbitration or other interventions.

Varied Forms of Mediation

The Committee generally starts off with minimal intervention, simply gathering information informally to see whether mediation or other assistance is or may be necessary. At this stage the Committee often decides that its involvement is not necessary or beneficial and may simply allow bargaining to take its course. Typically, Committee members are not directly involved at this early stage, although special knowledge or beneficial ties to the parties may suggest some form of informal involvement by a Committee member. Occasionally, a Committee member may be in a position to provide some momentum by personal intervention, should the issues and personality factors seem amenable to such involvement.

More often, the Committee will begin its involvement by providing a relatively conventional type of mediation in a form that, in its judgment, would be most useful. For example, the Committee might request that the Board of Conciliation and Arbitration send from its staff a mediator who is known to be acceptable to the parties or otherwise well suited to the problem. As might be expected, it had been reported that the presence of BCA mediators not well regarded by the parties contributed more to disharmony than to agreement. Use of BCA mediators has worked out increasingly well as the relationship between the two agencies has improved.

As another example, on occasion the Board has provided to the Committee the names of retired mediators residing in the western part of Massachusetts who have been used intermittently to resolve disputes in the western region, thus saving travel time from Boston and other costs. Because a person in that area can more easily meet with the parties as the situation demands, resolution may be expedited as momentum toward settlement is maintained. Even these small courtesies between the Board and the Committee have contributed to labor peace.

In addition to the use of BCA mediators, the Joint Committee will from time to time assign an independent mediator to handle the dispute. In general, outside mediators will be used where Committee involvement is not expected to be a necessity or where the skills or stature of a particular mediator seem to fit the situation. The relatively small permanent staff, combined with the flexibility to bring in mediation talent more tailored to the problem, permits a broader range of assistance than would a larger staff.

The form of mediation applied depends greatly on the judgment of the Committee as to which sort of arrangement is most likely to resolve the problems in question satisfactorily. For example, if the Committee expects that a case will ultimately require deeper involvement of Committee member expertise or resources, it will often begin mediation with its own staff rather than with outside mediators in order to keep "in-house" the information. Hence, the information may be more easily accessed later should Committee members become involved or one of several forms of Committee arbitration be required.

The most common form of Committee activity is staff mediation, although sometimes "assessment" or observation, perhaps with some limited advice to the parties, defines the extent of involvement. In addition to mediation by neutral staff, frequently either the senior labor staff representative or the senior management staff representative will mediate as a single neutral, a tactic that has worked rather well under the umbrella of Committee neutrality.

"Joint" or "tandem" mediation is used where the situation is too sensitive to accept the neutrality of a single senior staff representative or where mistrust between the parties dictates the need for a confidant of each side. It is a time-consuming technique, where both the senior management and labor staff members participate as a "two-headed" mediator. Using this technique, each side talks separately to its counterpart and the two staff members come together to seek progress or agreement. The technique works to assist settlement because it affords more open and forthcoming interaction between persons possessing mutual acquaintanceship or expertise (labor or management, police or fire fighting). As a result, each of the joint mediators may obtain more quickly a deeper understanding of the problems on each side of the dispute. The technique seems especially useful in situations with significant mistrust between parties or where inexperience or a past problem with third parties has soured the parties on external involvement. Because of the substantive and interpersonal communication that is engendered by joint mediation, more information may be available to the mediation team than might be gleaned by a single, traditionally neutral mediator in the same situation. (The case study in Chapter 4 demonstrates the use of joint mediation, and Chapter 6 analyzes it further.) While this technique has been used most frequently at the senior staff level, it has also been used with a Committee member from each side. Typically, this sort of Committee-level assignment would arise if the dispute is deemed unlikely to be—or has not been—responsive to staff level involvement, or if political or other external problems obstruct settlement. Most of the time, however, Committee member involvement is "saved" for a later point, as described in the following section and in the case study in Chapter 5.

Informal Hearings, Renewed Mediation, and Avoidance of Arbitration

Ordinarily, mediation in one of its staff-level or external forms would continue until the dispute was resolved or until it reached a "new" impasse. If not resolved, when the staff made its weekly report to the Committee, a discussion over next steps would ensue. In that discussion, a further impetus to bargaining ordinarily would be sought, usually moving to some level of Committee involvement and often a bit away on the Figure 3-1 continuum from unfettered direct bargaining toward third-party involvement. A more typical point in the process for informal intervention by a Committee member comes after staff efforts at mediation; very likely, one or two Committee members would become involved as mediators. This form of Committee involvement occurs most commonly if a staff member becomes "used up" with respect to credibility, where they can no longer make progress, or when the mediation process otherwise stalls.

If both informal Committee-level intervention and mediation is unsuccessful or "used up," the Committee frequently will seek to break that impasse by moving to techniques that intervene more formally and intensively in the direct bargaining process. Generally, at this stage they will call for an informal hearing, although some limited use of fact-finding has recently been made. The Committee may decide to have a dispute go from staff mediation directly to a hearing if the members believe that a hearing will be the most conducive format to further accommodation by the parties. As we shall describe in the next section, the hearing format has a number of forms and purposes.

Whether at the hearing stage or an earlier point, the involvement of Committee members usually leads to a range of other devices not typically available through the staff; various formal and informal involvements and interactions may be used, as may informal individual or group meetings among various combinations of the parties and Committee members and staff. As the string of options runs out or as the number of outstanding issues and range of disagreement narrows as far as seems possible, a formal hearing may then take place where arbitration may be used in one of several forms to resolve the dispute.

Hearings as a Tool for Mediation and Bargaining

The informal or preliminary hearing comes about after the Committee has discussed the case and concluded that further direct negotiations or mediation will not be fruitful without some additional impetus. Sometimes a case is brought in for a hearing soon after the Committee becomes involved. More often, however, an informal hearing will be called after other efforts—usually staff-level mediation—have, in the Committee's judgment, gone as far as possible or have been frustrated in narrowing the differences. The informal hearings are referred to as "hearings on the issues." (Since a case is referred to an outside mediator because the Committee expects resolution, it would be rare for such a case to come in for a hearing.)

The practice of a preliminary hearing has evolved as another step between bargaining and more direct third-party intervention. Optimally, it would create a deadline or an aura of uncertainty regarding the outcome that would cause the parties themselves to settle. As an event with the imprimatur and personal involvement of the chairperson or vice-chairperson, it is used as a tool to break the impasse by further defining or narrowing the issues. It does so by creating a change in the process—one with significant uncertainty, perhaps the implied threat of arbitration—that frequently influences the willingness of one or both parties to disclose information or alter a position. Apart from the changed forum, the additional, new neutrals may allow the parties to respond to the different skills, perspective, or stature represented by the chair or by other members of the Committee or staff who may be present. If the case later goes to arbitration, this hearing serves to provide further background on the issues or personalities to the members or chair of the panel.

Informal hearings are routinely scheduled for individual cases that the Committee has decided to move out of a normal mediation process. These generally are held at the Committee's headquarters and are typically attended by the chairperson or vice-chairperson and one each of the labor (police or fire fighters, depending on the case) and the management Committee members, sitting as a panel. Often, the two senior staff members will sit in as part of the panel in place of Committee members. This same panel will often serve as the arbitration panel should the matter be arbitrated by the Committee; if any of the panel are "used up" at this stage, others will substitute for them in later proceedings. However, as members of a panel, staff members always serve in an "assessor" capacity and cannot vote should the matter be arbitrated. The assessor role involves advising the chairperson or vice-chairperson (whichever is hearing the case) on the substance of the problem, the personality factors, and the history of the dispute. Also, through their continuing involvement in the dispute, the presence of the staff or Committee members provides the parties with a familiar channel; it polices the parties' honesty and avoids the necessity of completely reestablishing each party's relationship with the neutral. In contrast, under the LBO process the appointment of an arbitrator frequently required that new relationships be built and education of the neutral begin anew on the issues and positions of the parties. Assessors can often serve these functions and thereby free Committee members for disputes where they are explicitly needed or can make a special contribution.

Ideally, the chairman and other members of the panel will be briefed prior to the hearing by the staff regarding the issues in dispute, positions of the parties, and areas of agreement and disagreement. Often information on the true position of the parties, the role of personalities, and history of the relationship is part of an extremely informal briefing that precedes the hearing. The hearing is made more effective by the transmission of this information to the panel, who then need not waste time on background questions. With that background already in mind, the panel will listen to and ask questions of the parties or may meet separately with the parties to probe for possible areas of agreement under these new circumstances—that is, mediate.

As with many uses of fact-finding and other such proceedings, the Committee tries to promote collective bargaining and settlement between the parties themselves; thus, informal hearings usually result in further mediation or other forms of negotiation, sometimes on the spot. Often, at these hearings, the labor and management disputants meet in separate rooms with their Committee or staff counterparts of the panel in a form of joint mediation. When such mediation takes place, the labor and management panel members will meet together with the chairperson periodically during the session to compare areas of potential agreement, going back and forth with proposals and counterproposals, much like standard one-person mediation. The chairperson might also meet with the parties individually, depending on the circumstances. Joint mediation at the Committee level is employed fairly often when a dispute reaches this stage of the process in order to utilize the relatively closer relationship, trust, and capacity to educate and persuade that often can be developed between representatives of each party.

Frequently, the informal hearing and related mediation processes result in agreement; generally, they at least narrow the number of issues and the range of differences. In the latter circumstance the parties may be asked to continue bargaining under specified conditions, usually a range of issues agreed to between them at the hearing or stipulated by the Committee. In one case it appeared from discussion at the hearing that progress had ceased because the mayor and a key aide had stopped attending bargaining sessions. Informal discussion suggested that agreement might be reached if the union saw the decisionmakers at the table and received assurances on some matters under discussion. The Committee "ordered" the parties—using the peer network afforded by its membership and the flexibility and oversight in the statute—to negotiate for a period with the mayor and his aide present. This approach subsequently resulted in settlement. In most instances such "conditional" bargaining is carried on with some continued involvement by Committee staff or members as mediators or assessors.

Occasionally, further negotiating progress is deemed unlikely and the remainder (or the bulk of) the preliminary or informal hearing is devoted to choosing a process for resolving the dispute; at a minimum, the session seeks to gain agreement on procedures to resolve the dispute. For example, the panel might suggest that the parties agree to a specific form of arbitration on the remaining issues. The arbitration may be conventional issue-by-issue, last-best-offer, or a package last-best-offer arbitration, depending on the situation and the parties' proclivities. Nevertheless, if the Committee sees possibilities for further mediation, it will so proceed and will not consider arbitration until such further mediation reaches yet another impasse.

Formal Hearings and Arbitration

If arbitration is deemed the only possibility for settlement and is agreed on, a new hearing date may be set. The arbitration panel may be the same as the hearing panel unless they are "used up" or it is otherwise unadvisable. The panel may consist of the chairperson or vice-chairperson plus one Committee member from each side. Alternatively, a single arbitrator may deal with the case, who may be the chairperson, vice-chairperson, or an outside arbitrator appointed by the Committee. When calling in an outside arbitrator the Committee may specify certain restrictions in the form of arbitration, the issues to be arbitrated, a time frame, or instructions for mediation prior to arbitration. In general, referral to arbitration—internal to the Committee or external—will come only after other less intrusive remedies have been applied and the differences narrowed. Until the end of 1980 the Committee also had the option of returning jurisdiction to the Board of Conciliation and Arbitration to continue through the LBO process.

Peer Bargaining: Bargaining by Proxy

If there appears to be room for a settlement at a formal hearing, the joint mediation process may begin again with the labor and management (Committee member) panelists working as mediators, much as might have occurred at the informal hearing, with the help of the chairperson. If this form of joint mediation fails, the panelists generally discuss the matter and seek to come to agreement themselves on a settlement. This especially interesting device is called "peer bargaining." If possible, they will gain the assent of their respective sides and produce a settlement. If not, they may go back and forth with each other, with their respective sides (or, perhaps, each visiting the other's side) to try to mold an agreement. If they fail to bring the parties to agreement, the two Committee principals will (sometimes at, sometimes subsequent to the hearing) continue to bargain between themselves to produce an agreement. Here again, they will generally go back to their respective sides to seek approval. Once the panel reaches agreement, the Committee will issue an arbitration award if efforts to gain agreement by the parties have failed.

The features of this process reflect the Committee's objectives to further collective bargaining and promote more realistic and acceptable settlements. Because the panel contains a management and a labor representative who are both knowledgeable about and responsible to their respective parties, continued bargaining takes place within the panel by virtue of this constituent selection and appointment. Also, the panelists usually have had confidential or informal discussions with their respective parties, and they therefore know, and feel somewhat bound by, the true interests and positions of the parties. At the same time, the members' institutional loyalty to the Committee and its mandate for settlement and the personal/professional relationship with other Committee members provide greater incentive and ability for settlement than exists between the parties. Personality or political difficulties that often plague bargaining are removed when discussion of the matter takes place between Committee members. The substantive interests of the parties are very much in the forefront of the volunteer Committee members' minds, for the matters left in the debate are the substantive issues.

While this second-order, or peer, bargaining between Committee members is not direct bargaining, arbitration carried out this way is

intended to come closer to a bargained result than would simple
arbitration; the interests of the parties continue to be represented
and settlements expedited. It is interesting in this regard to observe
that the arbitration may be, but is less frequently, handled by the
chairperson or vice-chairperson as a single arbitrator. The panel
form is preferred because the Committee believes that the result of
give-and-take by appointed representatives of labor and management is more in the public interest and in the joint interest of the
parties than would be an arbitration award by a single individual or
panel with less stake in the outcome or less familiarity with this or
related situations. An appointed representative of the management
side, representing the fiscal responsibilities of the municipality, will
have been influential in the settlement rather than leaving the settlement to an outside neutral, an important measure bowing to the
principle of sovereignty. Only once in a peer bargaining situation has
the chairperson actually had to arbitrate an issue that the panelists
could not agree on.

Agreement as Award

Frequently, an arbitrator or the labor and management panel members reach a settlement that is acceptable to the parties and is agreed
to in private but that may not be publicly acknowledged—perhaps
because of the political considerations of one side or the other.
Under these circumstances, the Committee will issue an arbitration
award. Still, the fact that agreement has been reached makes it
possible for easier contract administration and subsequent day-to-day
and bargaining interactions. Occasionally, however, the result of
peer bargaining or other forms of arbitration are not acceptable to
one or both parties, and the award is simply issued simultaneously to
both parties.

Other Interventions

Attempts at Long-Term Reform

The JLMC is especially interested in facilitating settlements that
contribute to constructive labor-management relations in the future.
Occasionally, as part of a settlement, the arbitration award will contain restructured contract language, particularly in instances where

parties have not been experienced in contract interpretation and administration and where preexisting contract language may raise problems in administration, open issues for dispute, or otherwise cause confusion.

Also, the award may call for establishment of a mechanism through which the parties can work on specific problems in the bargaining relationship or on a substantive issue of interest, particularly if it has been or is likely to be a point of disagreement or contention. This may take the form of a local labor-management committee to meet regularly on the issue, sometimes with the presence of a neutral. In one case an award was issued specifying that within sixty days the parties would negotiate a compromise on a remaining noneconomic issue of substantial emotional impact and had up to that point delayed agreement on the remainder of the contract. Sixty days later, with the other issues settled, with better relationships, and with tempers cooled, the matter was settled. In another case where a city was in fiscal trouble, a labor-management committee was formed with a neutral chairperson to seek cost savings that might be applied to wage increases.

One of the Committee's objectives is to improve the quality of labor relations practices in the public sector where rotating or new leadership makes it difficult to gain expertise and where the typical management representatives have a wide range of daily considerations that keep them from ongoing attention to labor-management matters. While the Committee works to improve bargaining skills on both sides of the table, it particularly encourages improvement on the management side by bringing together, as members and staff, a cadre of experienced and talented representatives of management, by providing them a forum for using their skills, and by encouraging them to communicate with and learn from other management officials.

Education of the Parties

The desire for improving the labor relations skills of municipal management has some educational manifestations outside the Committee's more obvious case-resolution tasks. These efforts have been limited by the difficulty of freeing for Committee involvement municipal managers with sufficient labor-management experience. However, the management members or the management staff—or the labor staff or members—dealing with their counterparts in a particular dispute are able to share their experience with those who have less knowledge. Contacts between the Committee or staff person assigned to a case and the labor or management negotiators, in addition to serving as vehicles for exchanging case information, often provide more general education as "war stories" are swapped or advice or techniques are sought or offered in an effort to deal with the problem at hand. Often the conversation may turn to another labor-management problem or relationship for which the Committee representative can provide some helpful background, advice, or contacts.

Committee members and staff, both labor and management, also seek to be active in their respective professional associations. They give talks and seminars, provide technical assistance, and in other ways informally work to improve labor-management relations in the state. Several members and the chairperson have written articles in professional journals or newsletters about the Committee and dispute settlement. Others have invited peers to Committee case meetings or visited management in their home jurisdictions to discuss general problems and the types of Committee assistance available. Not incidentally, these activities expose labor people to management and management to labor leaders. In the early years some of this activity was intended to inform potential "customers" of the Committee's existence and practices. As the Committee's case handling activities have become institutionalized, more of these outreach activities have become possible. In general the Committee serves as an informal resource to parties statewide—occasionally outside of public safety—in handling labor-management relations. In particular, local management leadership previously had no central source of assistance, in contrast to local union leaders, who in most cases could go to a state or international labor organization for assistance or advice.

Peer Communications

In another form of long-term intervention on specific disputes, the Committee staff, members, or chairperson may communicate to the parties some concern or compliment pertinent to their behavior during a dispute or to the general tenor of a collective bargaining relationship. In one instance in which a settlement was negotiated and accepted by the executive branch but rejected by the town council, the Committee formally and through the peer network took the town to task for the poor manner in which the legislative and executive branch of the town government interacted on labor-management matters. The Committee then offered assistance in improving the structure of the executive-legislative relationship. In the opinion of the Committee, a more professional relationship between the two municipal bodies would aid labor relations: It was not a surprise to find that the union mistrusted management (the executive branch) in negotiations when management could not deliver on negotiated agreements.

While the need for ratification by either union membership or municipal legislative bodies is common and often exercises an important discipline on the negotiators, unnecessary disagreement or disorderliness is best avoided if bargaining is to be fruitful. In this specific case, the Committee had a strong judgment and expressed its concern and willingness to assist based on its experience in other towns where this sort of legislative-executive problem had been successfully handled. The letter sent to the town officials was signed by a town administrator and a finance committee member on the JLMC—two people who had some experience in legislative-executive relationships. The results of this intervention, of course, await the next contract negotiation.

In another sort of intervention, the membership structure of the Committee, once again, figures prominently. A Committee member or staff person may call on a principal in a dispute to explain the Committee's existence and processes or its view of a dispute in an effort to win that person's support, or neutrality, on a proposed settlement. In one instance, a mayor coming up for reelection was hostile to a settlement that the union and the mayor's negotiator had worked out, and a management member of the Committee went out to see the mayor. The member, known to the mayor, explained the Committee's purposes and procedures and the rationale behind the proposed settlement, including this person's view of the political advantages and disadvantages. The previously recalcitrant mayor then agreed to the proposed settlement with only a minor face-saving alteration.

Even more intimate involvement may take place where personal or sensitive matters must be taken into account before a settlement can come about. For example, in one difficult case, it was discovered through a Committee member's personal contacts that a highly personal grudge related to a promotion issue was stalling negotiations and had obstructed productive labor relations for years. An election was soon to be held, and the union leader whose grudge seemed to be in the way was expected to lose. Rather than go to arbitration immediately, the Committee awaited the election outcome; a new president was chosen and the dispute resolved by agreement between the parties.

In a similar vein, the Committee may discover through its contacts or experience in other cases that a particular negotiator or attorney representing a party has a separate agenda, is obstreperous, or, in the words of one staff member, is "running the meter." It is possible to work around such obstacles by dealing through the informal channels provided by the Committee's membership or occasionally by urging a change in relationship between one of the parties and its representatives. Occasionally, attorneys or bargaining agents who presented an obstacle to settlement have been discharged and the matter resolved. The informal aspects of the Committee's operations and the range of personal contacts afforded by its structure allow these sorts of problems to be addressed professionally and discretely by the neutral body, but it is not a simple matter.

Informal interventions, peer influence, and information exchange can take place at any time in a dispute resolution process and are techniques used liberally by the Committee to aid in resolving disputes.

Operating the Committee: Meetings on Cases and with the Parties

The JLMC maintains the flow of its operations through weekly meetings that are attended by the entire Committee and staff and at which both general policy and specific case matters are discussed. In addition, "chairmen's meetings" are held at which the chief delegates of the management groups and each labor groups (police and fire) meet with the chair and the vice-chair to plan future activities or to anticipate sensitive policy questions. As described briefly, the Committee also holds informal and formal hearings—usually in a subcommittee—on specific cases, with both parties to the dispute present. Informal hearings are designed to gather information or to decide on a process by which a given matter might be settled; the formal hearings are held to gather information and hear arguments preparatory to a possible arbitration award. Most of these meetings take place at Committee headquarters.

Additionally, the Committee or staff may meet in formal or informal subgroups to deal with specific cases or policy questions. Individual staff or Committee members, in an "assessing" or information-gathering role, will generally meet with the parties to a dispute either before or after the Committee takes jurisdiction. Such meetings may be held with both sides present, or they may be held with only one side at a time. The purposes of such meetings range from very basic information gathering—on issues in dispute or contract provisions, for example—to mediation, or education, or even to taking steps that would lead to an arbitration proceeding.

Case and Policy Meetings

The case and policy meetings are open public meetings, as are the hearings. According to the Committee's procedural rules, sessions in which negotiating or mediation takes place may be, and generally are, closed to the public.[6]

In anticipation of the weekly case meetings, the staff prepared an agenda of cases currently of concern to the Committee; these cases may or may not be under the Committee's official jurisdiction. The agenda and primary internal management information system of the Committee is represented by a simple set of documents. At each case meeting, each member and staff person receives a packet containing a list of cases pending before the Committee, with information on the age of each dispute, whether it is police- or fire-related, and who is assigned to the case (staff, Committee member, and/or outside mediator). Enclosed with the agenda is a list of impasse situations pending before the Board of Conciliation and Arbitration. Frequently, cases from this list are pointed out as cases the Committee should look into and may be added to the agenda for the following meeting. In addition, minutes from the last meeting are attached for review and approval. Generally an informal report is given by the staff member or Committee member most familiar with or assigned to each case, following which a discussion on each case takes place, leading to a collective judgment regarding next steps.

Generally the discussion begins with a status report on the matter by the lead person, and other members or staff with knowledge of the case contribute to the assessment. The person making the original report often will make a recommendation regarding further action. The discussion of the case generally involves both sides—management and police or fire fighter representatives. Each side may present the view of its constituents, which may offer new insight to those on the other side. Because of the composition of the group and the open examination of the case, this discussion method lends itself, the Committee believes, to settlements and settlement processes that are more in the interest of the parties and more relevant to the dispute at hand. The discussion, moreover, educates all members by expanding their knowledge of settlement techniques, substantive issues, and terms of settlement. They believe that the common distribution of this information adds to continuity in Committee activities and judgments in case handling. Periodically, the Committee chairperson and the chairperson of each of the groups represented (police, fire fighters, and management) will meet privately to anticipate or review matters of policy or procedure.

Policies Arising from Experience

Periodically, at case meetings, discussion of individual cases raises discussions of the Committee's philosophy and operational policies. Such general discussion is permitted to flow within the time constraints; thus, experience with real issues breeds policy making. As a general matter, the discussions are frank and disagreements open. This openness has evolved as working relationships, trust, and accommodation have been built and suspicion has been reduced. These relationships are critical to the resolution of individual disputes that reach the Committee level and are not resolved through direct bargaining.

Summary

The Joint Labor-Management Committee and its structures and procedures have evolved out of a history of contention and dissatisfaction with the last-best-offer mechanism, which, in the view of leaders of both the labor and management sides, did not settle police or fire fighter disputes in a manner that promoted equitable or practical settlements. A procedural substitute was sought with the object of increasing the amount of direct bargaining that would take place in the hope that more satisfactory settlements would result.

Through the joint influence of labor and management on its statute and procedures, the Joint Committee has structured and operated itself in a manner that would promote collective bargaining and avoid resolution of disputes by third parties. Its procedures and methods of operation were developed by the principals—senior union and management officials—in line with this philosophy as they gained experience with the sorts of problems posed throughout the state.

The Committee's activities run the gamut from traditional mediation to joint or tandem mediation and mediation/arbitration in several forms—including a peer form of bargaining by proxies—and include more complex and *ad hoc* interactions of Committee members or staff with the parties. These techniques are employed by first allowing for the maximum amount of free collective bargaining, and only as successive impasses are reached are the Committee's activities likely to result in direct influence or to more closely resemble arbitration. There is no one procedure or series of steps that all disputes go through, but rather a number of possibilities and opportunities for techniques to be applied as necessary and appropriate. The sequence, form, and application of these steps often are designed to fit the issues at hand or to address the processes, traditions, or personalities that seem to be preventing settlement of a particular dispute.

Rather than attempt to simply fix a symptom (the dispute) where it can, the Committee seeks to attack the cause of the problem by improving the basic structure or fabric of the relationship. Chapters 4 and 5 provide examples of Committee involvement in two different types of disputes to which different sets of tools were applied to match each problem, then Chapter 6 analyzes the use, utility, and basis of these tools.

Endnotes

1. For example, see William Simkin, *Mediation and the Dynamics of Collective Bargaining* (Washington, D.C.: The Bureau of National Affairs, 1971), pp. 31–33.
2. Massachusetts General Laws, Chapter 154, Acts of 1979, amending Chapter 1078 of the Acts of 1977.
3. *Ibid.*, Chapter 154.
4. *Ibid.*, Chapter 154; and "Rules: Joint Labor-Management Committee," Joint Labor-Management Committee for Municipal Police and Fire Fighters, Commonwealth of Massachusetts, July 2, 1979.
5. *Ibid.*, Chapter 154.
6. "Rules: Joint Labor-Management Committee."

Chapter 4

ADAPTATIONS OF CONVENTIONAL TECHNIQUES IN A JOINT COMMITTEE APPROACH

Case Example: Police Negotiations in Barkfield, Massachusetts

The following case study describes the involvement of the Joint Labor-Management Committee in a dispute between a small local police union and a town in central Massachusetts, which has been given the fictitious name of Barkfield. The case describes the attempts at settlement through the use of joint mediation.

The Barkfield case and a second case study in Chapter 5 illustrate a number of the dispute resolution tools available to a joint committee which are described in the previous chapter and with which the JLMC and staff began to experiment in the first year of its operation. The Barkfield dispute, for example, was one of the first instances in which the Committee used joint mediation and a truncated form of peer bargaining. In general, the tools used by the senior staff representatives and the Committee members in Barkfield represent conventional dispute resolution techniques adapted to the context of a joint labor-management committee structure and mandate. In the years since the Barkfield case, other techniques have been developed and the use of the more conventional tools has evolved further. Analysis in Chapter 6 of the Barkfield episode addresses the dynamics and utility of the tools and approaches used in this case as well as some limits to their specific application.

POLICE NEGOTIATIONS IN BARKFIELD, MASSACHUSETTS

Introduction

The Joint Labor-Management Committee JLMC had begun operations in January 1978 as a legislatively established mechanism to handle labor-management contract disputes between police and fire fighters and their respective municipalities. Municipal management—their views represented by the Massachusetts League of Cities and Towns—had been dissatisfied with the results of the last-best-offer compulsory binding arbitration statute that had been in existence since 1973. Management disliked the fact that a third party with no responsibility to the electorate and without intimate knowledge of other municipal priorities could force a municipality to fund a decision by the arbitrator. Further, management had lost by a 2:1 margin in the decisions rendered since the statute began operation. The public safety labor movement in the state favored compulsory and binding arbitration and, led by the powerful Professional Fire Fighters of Massachusetts, had lobbied strongly for it. The union position was that, in the absence of any other mechanism to do so, compulsory and binding arbitration forced the settlement of contract disputes, a matter of significant importance to organized police and fire fighters; without the right to strike, these two groups of public safety employees were anxious to have a way to ensure that contract disputes would not simply drag on. A bitter political battle between these labor and management groups took place when legislation governing the arbitration process came up for renewal in 1977. A political compromise between the municipal leaders and the union was passed by the legislature. The result was a Joint Labor-Management Committee, with six representatives from cities and towns and three representatives each from the police and fire fighter unions. This committee was empowered to intervene or provide assistance in resolving any contract dispute that arose between public safety officials and muncipalities.

In December of 1978, the chairman of the Joint Labor-Management Committee for Municipal Police and Fire Fighters was discussing a forthcoming arbitration settlement with two members of his staff and two of his Committee colleagues. They had just heard the case, a contract dispute

---

This case was prepared by Jon Brock, Lecturer at the John F. Kennedy School of Government, Harvard University. This case is based on field research, although most names and locations are disguised to protect confidences. It was prepared as a basis for classroom discussion and is not intended to illustrate either effective or ineffective handling of the situation depicted.

between the Police Alliance and the Board of Selectmen of Barkfield, Massachusetts, and were reviewing the history of the case before issuing the award.

In addition to the specifics of the Barkfield case, the Committee members and staff were musing about the evolution of the Committee and its practices. They wondered whether or not it was a mechanism that was useful in the Commonwealth of Massachusetts and further, whether or not it might be useful for other state or occupational groups to study the mechanism for possible adaptation.

Barkfield, Massachusetts

Barkfield, Massachusetts is a town of about 10,000 people resting just to the southeast of Worcester, Massachusetts. Worcester is the largest city in the state other than Boston. Barkfield had recently settled a contract with its highway workers and was trying to wind up contract discussions with the police local. The police contract was more elusive, and six months had elapsed since the old contract expired. The Joint Labor-Management Committee was trying to help settle the dispute and expected soon to issue an arbitration award on the remaining issues.

The town government is a "selectman" form of government, in which a five-member board of selectmen, elected every two years, carries out the town's business. Annual town meetings are held at which the budget and major organizational items are discussed and voted upon.

The police department, although small at ten full-time officers, was regarded in the commonwealth as well-trained in all aspects of police work, including emergency medical training, fingerprinting, crime prevention, photography, and firearms. One difficulty, however, with this highly trained work force was that turnover among Barkfield police was high; surrounding communities hired Barkfield officers away.

The five-person board of selectmen had been negotiating with the two representatives of the Barkfield Police Alliance since late November 1977. Although the contract would not expire until July 1978, the negotiations began early since the contract then in effect specified that the parties would begin negotiations at least sixty days before the budget was slated to be approved. This would be voted upon at the March town meeting.

By June 1978 both sides were frustrated with the course of negotiations. Union leaders, selectmen, and the chief all reported that the negotiations were leading nowhere and virtually no agreement could be reached. They reported that relationships between the board and the police force were strained, and the chief claimed that his relationship with his department was deteriorating. A member of the board later recalled: "Negotiations became very complex, all the issues intertwined. We were really swinging at one another."

The Issues in Dispute

The lack of agreement centered around three major issues and one minor one: (1) wages, (2) work schedule, (3) provision of ambulance service, and (4) Blue Cross/Blue Shield benefits. The first three had been certified for arbitration.

Wages: All parties acknowledged that the Barkfield Police Department was underpaid relative to comparable departments, and Police Chief Richard Dives reported losing six officers in the previous three years to nearby towns that paid higher salaries. According to figures on patrolman's pay obtained from the Massachusetts League of Cities and Towns by the Board of Selectmen, Barkfield was fourteenth out of twenty-four towns of comparable size located primarily in the rural Berkshire Mountain area. The police union disputed these data and, noting that they were also a year behind, suggested that a more appropriate comparison would be to the towns with which Barkfield was in "competition" for officers and whose police work and cost of living were more like Barkfield; that is to say, those towns surrounding Worcester.

The Police Alliance made their own survey seeking up-to-date data from nine towns to which they believed Barkfield was comparable. This survey found that in only two were the police paid less than in Barkfield. By the police chief's estimate, Barkfield patrolmen's salaries were about 40 percent lower than those of comparable police forces in the area, and yet the Barkfield patrolmen were, in his view, "better trained, offering more services."

In their initial proposals the Police Alliance sought $265 per week plus cost-of-living adjustments each year for the remaining two years of the contract. The town offered $240 per week and 4 percent increases each of the next two years.

The union president said: "The selectmen initially agreed with us on the appropriateness of the comparison; they know we're doing the same job as the cops in those communities. Our brawls are just as big."

Generally, the board members favored granting additional wages and other benefits to their police force, but as one of them noted: "I'm for it, but not all at once. They'd been so underpaid and overworked, that lots of improvements were in order." Another selectman recalled: "The police deserve a healthy raise, but that was an awfully large percentage increase they sought in the first year. It doesn't look good to the townspeople. The police wanted an increase on wages alone that would have been better than 20 percent, never mind the extra holidays and everything else we gave them."

"We only wanted average pay, not the top," one union leader said, "so we just averaged everything out. At the end of the old contract our base patrolman's pay was $221 a week. We have to pay for the same loaf of bread as the other towns in the area, who were making about $260, and by the time our contract went into effect, even more than that. After the selectmen agreed that these nine towns made the right comparison, we made thirty-five phone calls to police chiefs and union leaders and compiled a lot of information on the full range of pay and benefits. We put it into a booklet and later presented it to the Joint Labor-Management Committee when we went to Boston for a hearing on the issues."

Barkfield, in June 1977, had settled with Local 495 of the Service Employee's International Union who represented the employees of the Barkfield Highway Department. The town had agreed to a full cost-of-living adjustment. One observer reported: "The town had just been run through by Local 495 and their professional negotiator, and had given away this uncapped cost-of-living adjustment. It was a little difficult to cry poverty to the police."

Work Schedule: The police officers in Barkfield worked a "5-and-2" schedule—five days working and two days off in a seven-day period. Usually, an officer worked the same shift, all seven days, either 8:00 a.m. to 4:00 p.m., 4:00 p.m. to midnight or midnight to 8:00 a.m. This was unsatisfactory to the officers. They preferred a 4-and-2 schedule. As the union president explained: "Compared to most of the towns in our survey—all of which had either a 4-and-2 schedule, received educational benefits, or received longevity pay—we were in a lousy position. Most of the other towns had both 4-and-2 plus either education or longevity. We couldn't get all three so we decided to go for one this time. We had a lousy schedule and schedule improvement would benefit all of our members, not just the old, not just the young: Educational incentive would help the younger guys get a few extra dollars; longevity pay would help the older guys, who were less likely to go to school. As it was, only one guy had a bachelor's degree, so educational pay wasn't going to help much. Under the operation of our 5-and-2 schedule some of us ended up working seven, eight, or nine days in a row without overtime—since the time was worked without working over forty hours in any one week and officers without seniority always ended up working nights and weekends."

Bob Batley described the scheduling problem. He was a police officer in another town, who, as an alternate member of the Joint Labor-Management Committee, served as one of the mediators later sent by the Committee. "There was no fixed schedule. It was at the whim of the chief, who put up a new schedule every week or so. The shifts seemed to be built around the convenience of part-time officers. The overtime was offered first to part-time people rather than full-time officers. The part timers seemed to be the protected species rather than the full-time officers. Part of the problem was the contract; it was poorly written and didn't specify the operating schedule, seniority for overtime, and related things. The chief could do it any way he wished. It seemed as if he was trying to save money without regard for the welfare of the men."

The union contended that the change to a 4-and-2 schedule would not require more full-time patrolmen and would not itself cost the town additional money. However, the head of the union noted that under the contract they were seeking to negotiate, there would, in fact, be increased costs related to manning the new schedule: Currently, overshift hours were worked largely by part timers who were paid straight time. By the requirement in other parts of the union proposal that full-time officers get preference for overtime assignments and be paid time and a half, costs of manning a shift would increase by virtue of the higher hourly cost of full timers. The union contended that no additional full-time officers would be needed if the existing complement of full-time officers were used first, based on seniority, and part timers used as necessary to fill in.

Another feature of the 4-and-2 schedule that appealed to the union was the fact that it would rotate the days of the week that an officer would have off. Under the 5-and-2 schedule, days off tended to fall always on the same day of the week; if an officer began his or her workweek on Wednesday, they would work through Sunday and have each Monday and Tuesday off, week after week. Although officers would work their shift based on seniority, under a 4-and-2 schedule, days off would rotate automatically such that junior officers would not always work on weekends as they currently did. Finally, the officers contended that the practice of working an officer seven or eight days in a row would cease to provide a cost advantage if the 4-and-2 schedule were adopted with overtime and other language designed to prevent the practice. Overall, the union felt that the 4-and-2 would be less demanding and would disrupt family life less than the current 5-and-2 schedule. The union made this one of their key demands.

The chief had a somewhat different view of the costs of the 4-and-2 work schedule. "It cuts the work week by 3.5 hours per man. With ten men, that's two and a half man days for which we would have to pay time and a half. That's about $24,000 a year. Hire another man for less? Sure, but that would put the department over the limit for the 'ratio law.' That law specifies that when the force is up to twelve men, they have to pay me 1.8 times the salary of the highest paid officer rather than 1.5 if it's under twelve."

State law also defines the powers of the chief relative to the other town authorities. Under one application of this law, the Barkfield police chief was, formally, a "strong chief," which gave him rather more latitude and independence with respect to controlling the department. If he were not a "strong chief," he would have to share more managerial authority with the board.

"I run a pretty tight ship, have for fifteen years as chief. There's been a lot of bitching about the shifts and the overtime. I was guilty and my sergeant was guilty about making those assignments. On the other hand, we rarely have enough overtime in the budget and often go back for supplemental money. The old contract was too vague and didn't specify the way overtime was to be handled so we did it in expedient ways."

Joe DeCata, who acted as one of the two Committee mediators, recalled that during mediation, he had noted among the police a lot of bitterness concerning scheduling. He and Batley urged the selectmen to influence the chief to be more orderly and fair about it. Although the selectmen promised to speak to the chief about the practice, there was no change during the negotiation period.

Ambulance Service: The Town of Barkfield had provided an ambulance service to the local community for the past thirty years. The service always had been operated by the police department. Emergency medical training had been a part of a patrolman's job description as long as anyone could remember (see Exhibit I) and most members of the force had been certified as emergency medical technicians (EMTs).

Robert Tucker, president of the Police Alliance, was a qualified instructor of EMT and carried on most of Barkfield's training. He recalled: "We were getting a lot of complaints for being on the ambulance. We only run three men on a shift. One is at the desk in the station house and the other two are out in cruisers. When an ambulance call comes in, one of the cruisers goes to the scene and the other goes to get the ambulance. One of us drives the ambulance to the hospital and the other administers emergency care in the back. The town is left with no police protection on the streets while we're on ambulance duty.

"Someone else should take the time to go to the hospital and otherwise administer aid. We are police officers first, although we are first responders on anything and everything. The selectmen wanted us to stay in the ambulance business but weren't willing to pay us for the training and skills. We're all qualified technicians and periodically have to retrain to stay certified. We wanted the town to pay us for our efforts to keep our skills and for performing this service. Initially we asked for $2,000 per certified officer. It would have cost them a grand total of $20,000."

The chief described the ambulance service: "The ambulance service has been offered free of charge for over thirty years and the cops here have always been qualified EMTs. It's the only thing the department does that every citizen appreciates. Everything else you do, you make at least one enemy and maybe one friend. If you help an accident victim, bandage him, save him, everyone remembers the good police officer, remembers that the police is your friend, like they used to tell you in grade school. The ambulance service has built a lot of good will for us. For example, when we wanted civil service protection and the issue was coming up for a town vote, we took out the old ambulance lists and wrote letters explaining our position. Those people felt good about us and supported us.

"It's certainly true that the ambulance service left us without police protection periodically. While continuing to be untenable in the short term, the goodwill and support it bought for the department would, it seems to me, have paid off in a few years. My guess is that the way the town is changing, we would double the size of the department in two years, leaving us plenty of coverage. Without the service and with some of the bitterness that this contract negotiation caused, I don't know . . .

"Some of the men were against the ambulance service for personal reasons. It's difficult for some people to deal with a dying person; they often feel they could have done more to save him."

In January of 1975 the Massachusetts Police Institute had submitted a manpower study to Chief Dives, which analyzed the services and operations of the department. It noted the heavy manpower demands and the consequent lack of police protection caused by the ambulance service and suggested that a citizen's committee collaborate with the police department in seeking a solution. (See Exhibit II for an excerpt from this study.)

The ambulance service/EMT issue had been a dominant subject of discussion throughout the negotiations in late 1977 and during 1978. Just before negotiations began, when the board refused to provide overtime funds, the chief suspended all EMT training. Later, in the spring, the head of the union was removed from his EMT training duties and the officers formally served notice that they would not serve as EMTs after the end of 1978.

"At that point," Tucker recalled, "they threatened to fire us and we said, 'go ahead.' If you believe in something like that, you get ready to take the consequences." The EMT work, however, was in the patrolman's job description. It was the chief's view that a patrolman who refused to carry out those duties could and would be dismissed, and he intimated that in a subsequent letter to the board.

Blue Cross/Blue Shield: An important side issue concerned disagreement over the percentage of Blue Cross coverage that the town would pay. Several years before, the highway department's employees failed to negotiate an increase in the town's contribution to health insurance. The town had been paying 50 percent, and the highway department workers wanted 90 percent. Failing to win it through negotiations, the local representative of the highway workers circulated a petition to put the matter to a town meeting vote. After some questioning of the petitioning procedure, the town meeting voted to increase the proportion to 90 percent effective for all town employees in February of 1977. The Board of Selectmen filed a prohibited practice complaint over technicalities regarding the petitioning procedure. The Massachusetts Labor Relations Commission found for the union. The issue was still a source of friction as the town sought in their various 1978 contract negotiations to negotiate back down to 50 percent. The police were willing to settle for 75 percent as had the other unions but insisted that the town live up to its voted upon commitment to pay 90 percent for the period from February 1977 until a new police agreement was signed. An appeal by the town to the Labor Relations Commission ruling was pending.

The Board of Selectmen

This was the second labor negotiation for most of the members of the board. The first had been the negotiations with the highway department workers, part of which had overlapped the beginning of the police negotiations. The highway department settled in June 1978. In that instance, the board negotiated as a committee with Selectman John Borghese as their chairman. Ordinarily, Robert Castman was chairman of the Board of Selectmen. However, in his regular, full-time job it turned out that he was a member of the same union that represented the highway department in Barkfield. He, therefore, would have been in a conflict-of-interest situation had he chaired the board during those negotiations.

At first, the board negotiated as a "headless" committee, but a chairman was chosen after the board had several times confused the facts of the two negotiations that were being conducted concurrently. Borghese noted later that as the person in the chair, he "prepared for two weeks at a time prior to negotiation meetings."

One of the Committee mediators recalled: "There was a lack of unity and communication among the selectmen. I could see problems on the board. Borghese was a strong, articulate guy, who wanted to be chairman. Castman is the chairman and seems to be seeking a higher office. He recently ran for a county-wide position. The lack of communication between them made it very difficult to settle the dispute since agreements among the selectmen were even more difficult to achieve than between the parties. They didn't spend a lot of time together and had different views of the politics and propriety of small items. There was little disagreement, however, that the cops deserved more money."

Negotiations were time consuming. One board member pointed out: "We're only part timers. Besides, we have other town business to perform. These negotiations had gotten so complex and time consuming that we began to schedule bargaining sessions for evenings that were not regular board meeting nights. We had to do other business and it seemed important that the police negotiations get more continuous attention and be held in private. Board meetings are open meetings, although the state's collective bargaining laws permit closed meetings during negotiations. The union requested closed meetings, although such a practice was rare for us in Barkfield."

The board's meetings take place in the basement of the Town Hall every Tuesday at 7:30, where candid and open discussions are held on issues ranging from rules of conduct for teenagers in a town park, to expenditures and construction specifications on a dam, or sewage system, or a high school track.

There was a lack of expertise regarding police work and collective bargaining, one selectman admitted, and he attributed this to the turnover that inevitably occurs when the board's seats are filled every two years.

The police chief, Richard Dives, noted that "the police officers had done their homework and had all the facts and figures. The selectmen were less prepared." Two members of the Board of Selectmen composed a police subcommittee of the board who met with the chief once per month. According to Dives, they "rarely got into great detail" and were especially wary of getting involved with the financial statistics, which were divided up into some forty-two line items. "No one comes down to see how things work," the chief said.

One observer reported: "It's not the ideal board for conducting police labor negotiations. There were two brand new members and the others didn't have much experience with these sorts of things. Only one member has a college education, some don't have a high school education, and only one owns a business where he has to meet a payroll and calculate true operating expenses. The average board member makes less than a cop. One of them is our mail carrier. One is a member of another union, and all of them do this on a volunteer basis. The town has just established a personnel board to handle a variety of employee-related issues, so perhaps that body will begin to be involved with labor negotiations."

Since the selectmen had their own jobs and businesses to attend to, a full-time "administrative assistant" acted as a staff to the board and carried on communications and monitoring functions on its behalf. He was well regarded by all of the parties and townfolk, although by the nature of his position his policy influence was minimal. An astute observer, he viewed himself as an honest broker and rarely was identified with a particular faction on any issue or in any controversy.

The Police Alliance

The Barkfield Police Alliance was represented by two officers, Robert Tucker and Bruce Angelli. The Alliance represented only those officers who were full-time, and, in fact, the Alliance had only registered as a bargaining agent some three years before; previously, it had been a loose gathering of police workers, including the chief and part-timers. It dealt with community activities, improvement of law enforcement, and the like. In previous negotiations the Alliance had been represented by another officer, but recent elections were won by Tucker and Angelli as the tenor of the organization changed toward that of a labor union, responding to the economic position of the Barkfield officers.

It was their first negotiation. In preparation, they consulted with their members and began to gather facts and information that would guide them in their negotiations. Examples of their preparation include the survey of nine nearby communities that they carried out to determine key features of other police contracts. Early in the negotiations the union leaders often asked the police chief for facts and figures as they analyzed, developed and advocated their bargaining position. Similarly, the chief provided figures to the selectmen. The chief, of course, was not in the bargaining unit and technically was part of management.

In the 1977–78 negotiations the union president reported, "we never argued about the number of men or any of the things that were up to management, we only wanted to be paid and treated fairly for our efforts." On several occasions, these union representatives went to Boston to represent their interests in formal and informal hearings before the Joint Labor-Management Committee.

The Chief

Richard Dives had been an officer in Barkfield since 1946 and chief since 1963. An observer from the Joint Labor-Management Committee remembers his impressions of the chief's role: "The chief—we never met him. He seemed to be trying to save money by avoiding overtime, running that brutal schedule, and using part-timers. He showed no regard for full-time officers. He wanted the ambulance service kept intact. He liked it so much that he's spent thousands on the ambulance and EMT equipment, but wouldn't seek equivalent funds for regular departmental vehicles. There was some sort of antagonism between him and the board. Why, for example, were the selectmen so bent on keeping the department below twelve men? It was just to keep the chief from getting paid more. So what? They'll pay out the money in overtime. Still, Dives is a pretty expert politician. The selectmen were buffaloed by him. They're very deferential to him in his presence, but recently they overruled him on selection of an officer."

The chief of police recalled that in negotiations neither party seemed to know what they were doing, that there was lots of posturing among the board members, and often a difference between what they said in public meetings and what they said in caucuses or with only the two parties present. "For a time I was regularly present and a part of management's caucuses. I was also the source of statistics for both sides. I finally walked out; I was the fall guy. After that I'd get a letter every now and then on some question or another."

In his own view: "I'm a strong chief as far as the law goes, but I'm not hard to get along with. Every now and again the selectmen will get some political heat to put on a special detail or cover some shift, without regard for cost or anything. I just smile. Often I just ignore it and generally they don't care. Just the same, I think that they'd like to get the department out from under the provisions of '97a' [the strong-chief law] so they'd have more control. On the other hand, these negotiations educated them a bit about what it takes to run a department, and maybe they'd just as soon leave it to me. I'm not sure why they're so concerned about the ratio law. I had already been technically over the manpower limit for a year and a half and didn't put in for the money due me. As a matter of fact, I've waived my right to it. I guess as part timers, they don't know the law well."

Some selectmen observed: "The chief is a tough nut," and, "He was pretty arbitrary."

Negotiations

In September the decision from the Massachusetts Labor Relations Commission had mandated that the town pay 90 percent of the cost of Blue Cross/Blue Shield benefits. In November the chief went to the board with his supplemental request for overtime money. The overtime allocation in the town budget passed just six months before was exhausted. "I told them it wasn't enough," the chief said. "We needed about $24,000 and they voted $9,900." Subsequently, when the money ran out, the selectmen voted against the increment requested by the chief. He responded by suspending all EMT training (see Exhibit III). Since the regular recertification of all ten officers took place in off-duty hours, which were compensable at time and a half, EMT training was a large consumer of overtime dollars. The officers responded with a grievance.

In late November, the Police Alliance wrote to the Board of Selectmen, seeking to open contract talks. Opening proposals were requested by the board and submitted on December 7, 1977, in advance of a scheduled December 12 meeting of the board. In that communication, the Alliance requested a closed meeting and laid out some nineteen items: the Blue Cross issue, clothing allowances, and pay for court time, to vacations, wages, education, and longevity pay as well as EMT pay of $2,000 per year. Particular attention was paid to the work schedule and to overtime. A few negotiating sessions took place after the Christmas holidays and the board made some counteroffers.

By February some agreement and change in position had occurred. The Police Alliance had backed off a bit on their wage demands and insurance proposals. However, the wage question was far from settled, the scheduling demands had barely been discussed, and the EMT pay, training time, and other issues had yet to be agreed to. Bargaining took place on February 1 and February 10, and then paused as the board began to prepare the town budget for submission to the March town meeting. No provisions for altered police costs were included.

Negotiations continued following the budget "season" and in mid-April some additional progress was made. The selectmen had offered $240, based on a calculated average of $236 for comparably sized towns in the state. The union, whose representatives had started their demands at $275 per week, effective July 1, 1978, were now willing to accept the town's offer of $240, with the proviso that on January 1, 1979, a survey of police wages in the Worcester area would be taken and the average paid to the Barkfield officers. The Alliance noted that the current average for the relevant surrounding towns was already above $260, but they reasoned that with a January 1 adjustment, they would come out in an acceptable position. For the next two years of the contract, the officers sought a cost-of-living adjustment based on the Consumer Price Index for Boston, the same adjustment won by the highway workers. If this wage adjustment package was accepted, the union would drop demands for longevity and educational pay. They had backed off on part of their demand for an increased clothing allowance and were willing to accept the 4-and-2 schedule in the second year of the contract rather than immediately, as originally proposed.

On April 27, Officer Tucker was removed from his duties as a training officer for EMT certification. The chief noted in his letter (Exhibit IV) to the Board of Selectmen that this was done so that certification training could begin outside of the normal channels. The ambulance service soon would be jeopardized since certification of a number of officers was about to expire. The EMT controversy raged during the month of May with the board seeking to reestablish certification without increasing costs. Through Anslow, the administrative assistant, the board wrote to the Alliance asking if they would train for EMT during working hours. The union responded with a grievance and a succinct statement of their position:

"We are willing to take EMT training as part of our regular forty-hour tour of duty or take compensatory time off on the basis of one and a half hours for every hour of EMT training done on our own time. . . . Our willingness to cooperate in this respect, however, shall not constitute a change of our job description so as to include the requirement for EMT training and ambulance service. We shall continue to perform first-responder duties and CPR duties. We are agreeable to continue EMT duties through December 31, 1978, or until other arrangements are made. . . . If it becomes necessary to perform EMT duties beyond [that date] we would expect that we would receive compensation as outlined in our collective bargaining discussions."

The chief reviewed the letter and responded angrily to the board when they asked him to work up the cost implications of the officers' statement. He referred to the officers' "ultimatum" and suggested strongly that the board not be led around by the officers.

The Joint Labor-Management Committee Gets Involved

In late May 1978, Bob Batley, an alternate labor member of the Joint Labor-Management Committee and a police union president himself, heard through the police grapevine that Barkfield's negotiations had run into difficulty. At around the same time, a management Committee member who hailed from that part of the state communicated to Batley what he had learned of the Barkfield situation. Since the JLMC was a new and not a well-known institution, Batley had made it a practice to "prospect" for situations where the JLMC might lend a hand in bargaining. To maintain a neutral posture in accordance with the JLMC's normal practice, Batley kept the senior management staff member informed of such contacts. When out near Barkfield working on another case, Batley called Robert Tucker to introduce himself and talk about the bargaining situation. On June 20, he stopped by Tucker's home for a cup of coffee and a description of the bargaining situation. On the same trip he "touched base" with half a dozen or so other police departments in the state.

The Barkfield contract expired on July 1, 1978, and Batley and Tucker had kept in touch until then. Later, in July, Batley, accompanied by Joe DeCata, the senior management staff member of the JLMC, spent a day in Worcester seeking to resolve some collective bargaining problems in that part of the state and to acquaint jointly some union people with the mediation and other services offered by the Committee. A handful of police union people stopped in and talked informally about their situations, received some information on the Committee, and generally received guidance on collective bargaining matters.

Several members of the Barkfield Police Alliance stopped in and told their "tales of woe," as Batley put it, this time to Batley, of union background and DeCata, with a management background. Since Batley and Tucker had last talked, the Barkfield Police Alliance on July 11 had written a letter outlining their position. They sent the letter to their attorney for transmittal to the board. There had been no bargaining since April, and their letter was intended to restate their position in a hopeful attempt to restart negotiations, presumably at the July 18 meeting of the board. They had received no reply to the letter and as the July 18 meeting of the board went past, the Police Alliance wrote to the Joint Labor-Management Committee asking that it take jurisdiction of the case.

The Committee considered the petition, but, as was their practice, asked Joe DeCata, the management senior staff representative, to get some input from the management side (the selectmen) before any official Committee involvement would take place. DeCata called Larry Anslow, the administrative assistant, to learn about the situation from management's point of view. Anslow confirmed the issues and communications problems that Batley had gleaned from his contacts with the police. He agreed to check with the board to see how they would react to JLMC involvement. Although the Committee could simply exercise jurisdiction, they sought the agreement of the parties to their involvement. The board didn't demonstrate much knowledge of the Committee, but agreed to the Committee's staff coming out if it could serve as a "lubricant" to negotiation.

Mediation at the Staff Level

Arrangements were subsequently made for DeCata and Batley to meet on August 15, first with the police union and then with the board. After a "productive" meeting with the police, DeCata and Batley walked across the street to the Board's meeting and began to explain their presence and function as mediators and problem solvers. Batley reported, "We got a bad reception. They didn't trust who Joe was and they didn't even want me in the room." (Batley was president of a local police officers' union elsewhere in the state and therefore suspect to them. DeCata, a knowledgeable labor relations specialist, with years of municipal experience, was often mistaken for a union leader because of his physical appearance.)

At the next selectmen's meeting Batley and DeCata returned and brought along Dick Horne, an appointed member of the Joint Labor-Management Committee and recent past president of the Massachusetts Selectmen's Association. Most of the Barkfield selectmen knew Horne or knew of him. He explained the Committee's role and functions, to save time and money and promote settlements that the parties could live with. The Committee provided mediative and other assistance and was composed jointly of individuals with management experience and people with labor backgrounds. Their assistance was free and expert, and he urged them to accept the help. Help would come first in the form of mediation. If the parties could not agree, other types of assistance were possible and binding arbitration under Committee auspices could still take place, and at less cost, with less time elapsed than under the normal state procedures. Horne suggested that through mediation, a significant degree of agreement probably could be reached before arbitration might be invoked on any outstanding issues. Much of the time that evening was spent "selling" the Committee, as one observer put it.

Horne began his remarks by referring to Batley in his folksy and casual brogue, "By the way, gents, do you mind if Mr. Batley here remains with us in this little management session? We consider him one of us . . ." The selectmen agreed to Batley's presence. The police, based on Batley's introduction and the meeting in Worcester, had already agreed to DeCata's presence in their caucuses. Batley, however, later passed a remark on the way the ambulance service in his own town was run. John Borghese, sitting as chairman of the board that evening, attacked Batley for his "biased, police views," although their relationship improved as time went on.

Mediation under committee auspices began at that meeting. To get a sense of the status of each side's position, Batley met with the police separately and DeCata and Horne met with the board. After DeCata, Batley, and Horne caucused and compared notes, confidentially, they decided to bring the parties together into the same room, an event that hadn't occurred in the past four months.

The police, among other things, outlined their problems with the work schedule; they were working more than a forty-hour week, receiving no overtime pay and receiving their assignments on short notice, which disrupted their family lives. The selectmen listened sympathetically and promised to try to get the situation changed. That evening the union also noted that they had sent a letter via their attorney outlining their latest position and seeking to meet with the board during the regularly scheduled July 18 meeting. Why hadn't the board responded? Apparently, they had never seen the letter and had not learned of the union's renewed interest in negotiating. It seemed that the union's attorney and the board's attorney had communicated, but the letter or its contents had not yet been forwarded. Somehow, the attorneys representing the parties had not completed the communication. This realization broke some of the tension and distrust, and the two mediators began, with the parties now sitting across the table from one another, to list on paper all of the contract issues under discussion, separating them into agreed upon and open issues.

Mediation Techniques

DeCata recalled the mediation process: "Bob and I had worked together in the Framingham case, where we also got to know Al Erskine, a management member of the Committee from that area. The Framingham case came early in the Committee's existence and our tools and procedures weren't fully developed. We somehow fell upon the tandem, or joint, mediation technique and it worked very well. We had a lot of trust between us, so we decided to try joint mediation in Barkfield, where the mistrust between the parties was rampant and the parties' bargaining experience limited. Sometimes we met together with one or both parties, sometimes separately with our respective sides, but we were in constant communication. By reducing the issues to a written list, going over the list at each session and by going back and forth, probing for give-and-take, the neutrals can keep control over the process so that old enmities and side issues don't flare up. The two sides are kept honest and their feet held to the fire, or to the issues, if you will."

"The list of items," Batley observed, "forced them to focus on the substance, leave out extraneous stuff and personalities. By going over it each time, we narrowed the differences step by step. We would listen and then try to capture the issues and then see if the parties would agree that those were indeed the issues. Otherwise, we'd redefine them so there was agreement on the formulation of the issues. You need to know what the issue is if you're ever to resolve a dispute on it."

In a few sessions after the August 15 meeting, the police came back with new proposals in time for a meeting on August 22. The mediators were able to clear away such issues as death benefits and funeral expenses because of the mediators' familiarity with practices in other communities and applicable state laws. Vacations and pay for court time were susceptible to similar handling. The overtime issue was a bit more difficult. While there was a law requiring overtime pay over forty hours of work in a week, the chief ran the schedule so that rarely did an officer work more than forty hours in a calendar week but worked six to eight days in a row, over two separate weeks. The change had to come in management practice, but this change was related in the officers' minds to the 5-and-2, 4-and-2 controversy. Batley gave DeCata a quick tutorial on 4-and-2 and 5-and-2 in the Barkfield context.

In the course of mediation, the Committee mediators learned about the substance of the issues that separated the parties and became aware of the emotions on both sides. They also discovered the strong resistance of the selectmen to a larger force level, and their sensitivity to the public's reaction to cost increases.

By late August, the sides had agreed on all but five issues: wages, including educational incentive and longevity pay; clothing allowance; retroactivity in Blue Cross/Blue Shield; the work schedule; and the ambulance service. At the end of a mediation session on August 30 that lasted until 2:30 in the morning, DeCata and Batley left the two sides in a room together. They were closer together on the remaining issues, and the mediators, exhausted, but hopeful left them there to resolve the rest of the issues. "Do your best, call us tomorrow." As they walked out the door they said to each other, "If this doesn't settle it, there's nothing else we can do." They began the three-hour drive home.

The second and third year wages had yet to be worked out and there was $25 difference between the union and the town in the second-year clothing allowances. There was also disagreement on the number of credits that would have to be earned to qualify for educational incentive pay. The Blue Cross issue was a matter of getting the town to drop its appeal to the Labor Relations Commission and ironing out the dates for retroactivity, which DeCata essentially had worked out with the board a few days before. The town had agreed to try a 4-and-2 schedule in the third year of the contract, assuming that a citizen's committee found it feasible, but sought a proviso that the number of full-time officers required would remain constant and that overtime costs wouldn't be excessive. Finally, there was the ambulance issue.

To the mediators and the parties it all looked close, but old animosities emerged, the discussion reverted to name calling, recrimination, "Look what I've already given up," and the discussion ended. The mediators returned on September 20 to try and resolve these questions (see list of items, Exhibit V), but couldn't bring the parties any closer.

A Hearing on the Issues

DeCata and Batley reported at one of the JLMC's weekly meetings in early October that mediation efforts could bring the parties no closer. Another of the Committee's tools would be required. It was decided to invite the two sides for a hearing, hoping that something would shake loose, or that in a different forum a new mediative approach might prove fruitful. "It lent the process some additional legitimacy," DeCata suggested, "at a point where things had stalled."

A hearing on the issues was scheduled for October 6 in Boston, but was canceled because the selectmen were unable to attend. The next date was October 18, and John Borghese and Thomas Mullen of the Board showed up along with Larry Anslow, the administrative assistant. DeCata and Batley sat as "assessors," advising the Joint Committee's chairman, Professor John T. Dunlop, a labor economist and mediator from Harvard University and former Secretary of Labor. The chairman opened the hearing by discussing possibilities for future mediation or other ways to resolve the dispute. They hoped to find agreement on a process that might lead to resolution of the issues in dispute. Barkfield's Board of Selectmen had not authorized Borghese and Mullen to negotiate, so no additional progress was made that day and no subsequent negotiations took place back in Barkfield. It was simply agreed that another date would be set.

It was hoped that at the next hearing appropriate representation from the board would permit some further negotiations under the chairman's auspices. Ordinarily, some additional negotiations took place at these hearings or subsequent to them. At a minimum, a new approach to negotiations was usually fashioned.

The Committee held another hearing on November 10, hoping to carry on some further mediation, but only one selectman showed up, again with orders not to negotiate. Chairman Castman and Selectman Borghese, who had been active in the negotiations, at the last minute were not able to attend. In the time between the October 18 hearing and the November 10 hearing the parties had no formal or informal communication.

The assessors at the hearing—who had served as mediators in the case—recommended to Dunlop in a caucus that the case be handled by arbitration of the outstanding issues. They discussed this with their respective sides and then with both parties together. The union and management, weary of the dispute, agreed to conventional arbitration by the Committee as the preferred method of resolution. According to its procedural rules, before the Committee could actually take the case for arbitration the full committee had to vote on a motion to do so. At the next Committee meeting, DeCata raised the issue and Al Erskine moved that the Committee take the staff recommendation to arbitrate. The Committee voted unanimously to take the case for arbitration in the Committee's own form of that practice.

Arbitration

DeCata and Batley were disappointed that they couldn't resolve the dispute through mediation, but later expressed the view that their mediation had narrowed the gap on the outstanding issues and had resolved many of the others. Indeed, when, on December 5, the case was certified for arbitration, three issues remained and all others were found to be in agreement as a result of the summer and fall mediation. The arbitration panel would have to decide on wages, the work schedule, and the EMT ambulance problems. DeCata had in the meantime persuaded the town to agree to the union's Blue Cross proposal, and Batley had convinced the sides to agree on the clothing allowance.

On December 19 an arbitration hearing was held where Chairman Dunlop presided and the Committee members, Al Erskine, a leading town finance committee officer, and Dave Morley, a police officer and labor member of the Committee, sat as members of the panel. Prior to the hearing, DeCata and Batley had briefly explained the issues to the panel members and the chairman and had outlined the current and candid positions of the parties. The police union made a presentation that included the wage and benefit comparisons they had surveyed and listed their positions on the issues. The town's administrative assistant, representing the town, had brought with him the town's "last" offer (see Exhibit VI). The parties' real positions had changed little since the September 20 meeting, (see list of issues in Exhibit V) but, in fact, some hardening in their stated positions was evident in their positions as they outlined them to the arbitration panel that day.

Immediately after the final hearing, DeCata and Batley discussed their views with the arbitration panel members (Dunlop as neutral chairman, Dave Morley on the police union side, and Al Erskine for management). DeCata and Batley gave the labor (Morley) and management (Erskine) panelists further background and history on the situation and their views of the parties' most important priorities and concerns.

Exhibit I.   Barkfield Police Patrolman Job Description

Richard Dives, Chief

DUTIES OF A PATROLMAN: September 27, 1977

Immediately after reporting for duty, each officer going out on duty relieves the officer, as assigned, whose tour of duty has expired. He confines his Patrol within the limits of his route, except in the case of Fire, Arrest of a prisoner, or other cause of necessary absence until he is regularly relieved, unless sooner ordered elsewhere by a superior.

Because he serves his entire Town, and not merely a particular place or route, it is his duty to give proper attention to violations of law committed in his sight anywhere within his Town, especially such as involve injury, or the risk of injury to person or property.

When a Patrolman becomes sick during his tour of duty, he reports at once to his Station House or to his Sergeant.

He especially avoids giving cause for gossip, or scandal by conversing with women in the streets at night when he is in uniform, whether on his route or not. He constantly patrols his route except for his halts necessary to the proper performance of his duties. He does not sit down, lean against walls, posts or trees, or conduct himself in any respect other than as a responsible official exposed to public observation and criticism, with important work to do.

When assigned to crossings, he will give his entire attention to such duties, avoiding all unnecessary conversation.

He renders such aid as may be consistent with his duties to persons requesting it. He keeps his number in sight, and gives his name and number to all who request it.

He directs strangers and others, when requested, by the nearest and the safest way to their destination. If he hears a call for assistance, he proceeds to render aid with all dispatch, taking every practicable precaution for his protection of his route when he leaves it for this or for other purpose.

When any Way becomes blocked by vehicles, he, using his best judgement, aids in disentangling the same. When the stream of travel is continuous, he opens a way for foot travelers, attending especially to women, children and the aged wishing to cross.

When a disturbance occurs, he instantly proceeds to the spot and uses his best efforts to restore quiet.

He also notes during the night all vehicles which in any manner excites suspicion.

So far as possible, he attends at School Buildings on his route before and after sessions for the purpose of preserving order and protecting the children from injury.

Insofar as he can, without intruding on the privacy of individuals, the Patrolman notes all movements into and removing from the limits of his route. He acquires sufficient knowledge of the residents as will enable him to recognize them. He makes himself thoroughly acquainted with all parts of his route, and with the streets, private ways, houses, buildings, stores, and business concerns included in it.

He constantly observes the conduct of all persons of known bad character. He notes their movements and the premises they enter, learns their names, residences, and occupations. He reports to his commanding Officer any useful information he may obtain concerning them. He fixes in his mind all characteristics necessary to identify them.

He takes particular note of all places where intoxicating liquors are sold. He reports all unlicensed plates, and all places where the terms of the License under which the liquors are sold are not fully met.

He notes all street lamps out of repair, not lighted at proper times, or extinguished too late or too early. He notes all buildings erected, or in the process of being erected contrary to Law, or defectively built or which have become unsafe, or in which any noisy, dangerous, or unwholesome trade is carried on. He reports all this to his commanding officer without delay.

At night and during the time that business buildings are closed he exercises the greatest vigilance, giving particular attention to vacant or unoccupied buildings and dwellings. Once each night shift he examines and tries accessible doors, windows, gratings of such places and investigates all suspicious and unusual circumstances, such as open doors. lights out over safes, and open safes. In the daytime he examines in a manner all vacant or unoccupied buildings and dwellings in his patrol area. When a door or window is found open under suspicious or unusual circumstances on any tour of duty, he makes a thorough investigation and determines, if possible, whether burglary, or any other crime has been committed, and whether the door or window can be secured. He notifies the dispatcher to inform, if possible, the owner or person having control of the premises. He gives special attention to all vacant dwellings to prevent depredations. He is vigilant to prevent fires, waste of water, and to see that fire escapes are not obstructed. He calls to the attention of the abutters the state of the sidewalk and roofs, where, by snow, ice or other cause, they are rendered dangerous, or when obstructed with goods, or where ashes, or garbage, dead animals, or other offensive matter are thrown in the streets. If the law, ordinances, by-laws, orders, rules, or regulations that govern such cases, upon notice given, are not forthwith obeyed, he ascertains the names of the offending parties and reports same for complaint and prosecution.

He takes care that the sidewalks are not obstructed by persons loitering thereon to the inconvenience of other pedestrians.

He carefully preserves any property which comes into his possession in his official capacity, and marks and delivers it to his commanding officer.

He strictly complies with the requirements that he should not have in his possession a key to any premises, not his own, on or near his route, except with the knowledge and consent of his commanding officer.

He will not leave the boundaries of the Town of Barkfield except in compliance with standing general orders.

He will keep abreast of all changes in Mass. General Laws as well as Town by-laws within his jurisdiction and enforce them to the best of his ability.

He shall hold a current E.M.T. card certified by the national registry and also a CPR certification.

He shall attend all schools, courses, classes as required to keep both certifications current.

He shall also be required to attend all courses, classes, seminars as is required to keep abreast of laws and by-laws.

He shall be required to perform any and all duties related to his work as a Police Officer. (The word "He" as stated shall be interpreted to signify either "He" or "She.")

**Exhibit II.   Excerpt from Massachusetts Police Institute
Manpower Survey**

Ambulance Service

Another major factor concerning the utilization of police personnel in Barkfield
involves the police ambulance service. The extent to which the Barkfield Police
Department is a virtual prisoner of its ambulance service tradition is seen when one
considers the extent to which personnel are committed to provide this service. The
following chart indicates the ambulance run activity for 1972 and 1974. Due to
nonavailability of accurate figures for 1973, that year was not computed.

It should be pointed out that for every man-hour spent providing the community
with ambulance service, there is an equal amount of time where police protection
within the community has decreased by one half and often times, totally.

Chart #8 shows that for the year 1972, there were a total of 315 ambulance
service runs, and from January to October 1974 there were 338 runs. From 1972 to
1974 the actual number of runs has increased as well as the total man hours required
to provide this *free* service.

The average cost computed by the survey team for each ambulance run, irrespec-
tive of equipment costs, came to ($20.00) twenty dollars. Applying this figure to the
total number of ambulance runs up to October 1974 yields a total cost of $6,760.00.

The ambulance function on an ad hoc basis is certainly an important part of the
total police service provided in some communities. On the basis of the reaction
created by such a service in Barkfield, ambulance service is an important ingredient
in terms of the positive rapport of the Police Department with Barkfield residents.
Yet the routinized provision of such a service as provided by the Barkfield Police
Department detracts from the ability of the department to fulfill its main mission.

Under the recently proposed "Ambulance Regulations," the Department of Men-
tal Health has outlined some provisions which should be of particular interest to the
town of Barkfield. The provisions are as follows:

1. Written policies and procedures on the operation and maintenance of ambulances must be prepared by each department.
2. Each department must have a heated garage large enough to house all ambulances (including all cruiser ambulances).
3. Twenty-four-hour-a-day phone coverage and ambulance service is required.
4. Ambulances must be cleaned, washed, and disinfected inside after each use.
5. Station wagon ambulances can be used to transport sick or injured persons
   until July 1, 1977. After that date, only communities that have a fully-
   equipped Class I vehicle as a primary transport vehicle may use station
   wagon ambulances, and then only as a backup.
6. Even communities which have traditional full-sized ambulances will be required to use these only as a backup to Class I vehicles.
7. The amount of medical supplies required for dual-purpose vehicles, although
   less than that required for other vehicles, may well exceed the space available
   in a station wagon ambulance.
8. One third of all employees who may be called upon to be ambulance drivers
   or attendants must be EMT-A trained (81-hour course) by July 1, 1975,
   another third by July 1, 1976, and all trained by July 1, 1977.
9. All ambulance operators (drivers) and attendants must attend refresher
   courses each year.

Chart #8   Ambulance Calls

	# for 1972	# Police Personnel Involved	# for 1974	# Police Personnel Involved
January	26	47	30	45
February	28	49	33	51
March	23	40	33	44
April	31	36	28	44
May	28	39	51	77
June	29	47	36	52
July	20	34	33	52
August	29	44	38	55
September	27	44	26	42
October	23	43	30	44
November	21	25	—	—
December	30	53	—	—
Totals	315	461	338	456

10. All operators and attendants, while waiting to comply with July 1, 1977, EMT-A requirements, must have Red Cross standard or advanced first aid certificates. In the interim, the person with the higher level of training shall be the attendant, riding in the patient compartment.

Based upon the above possible provisions, it is recommended that the Town of Barkfield establish a Task Force of local citizens for the expressed purpose of investigating the current ambulance service rendered by the Town in relation to the proposed new ambulance regulations and also in relation to the present nonavailability of sufficient police manpower to provide this service.

Police Vehicles

The Town of Barkfield established a policy whereby the Chief of Police was authorized to request purchase of a replacement cruiser every nine months. Currently the department operates a fleet of three cruisers which are identified as follows:

1973 Chevrolet (Wagon)	80,000 miles
1974 Chevrolet (Wagon)	70,000 miles
1974 Chevrolet (Wagon)	50,000 miles

The two 1974 cruisers are presently used on a daily basis to provide for two mobile patrol sectors in the Town. The 1973 cruiser, with 80,000 miles, is held in reserve for spot use. Clearly, from the mileage figures on two of the three cruisers, now is the time to buy a new one. However, the chief indicated that the 1975 budget does not provide for a replacement cruiser.

During the course of the survey, the MPI Technical Specialists were given a complete ride-along tour of the town that covered virtually ninety miles of roads and took four hours. This ride-along revealed that much of the present roadways patrolled by the Barkfield Police are dirt roads or extremely limited access. Patrolling these roads results in detrimental physical abuse of the patrol vehicles. Consequently, the excessive wear and tear caused by poor road conditions, along with the fact that two of the vehicles already have over 70,000 miles, necessitates immediate replacement of these two vehicles. In addition, it is recommended that the previously established policy of vehicle replacement be adhered to in the future.

Exhibit III. Police Chief's Suspension of E.M.T. Training

To: All Fulltime Police Personnel   25 NOV 77
From: Chief of Police Richard Dives
Subject: E.M.T. Training and Personnel Shortage

As of this date 11/25/77 there will be no further E.M.T. Training, unless approved by the Chief of Police for the following reasons:

1. The Board of Selectmen have voted not to pay any overtime (time and one half) for E.M.T. Training, and that officers involved in this training be given time off during the week the E.M.T. training is to take place. That the fulltime personnel involved in E.M.T. Training hours be no more than 40 (forty) hours, E.M.T. Training time included in one week.
2. The fulltime officers have filed a grievance with the Chief of Police on this matter, as set forth in the present contract between the Town of Barkfield and the Police Association of Barkfield. Step 1 and Step 2 have been completed and Step 3 is pending.
3. The Board of Selectmen by a vote of 3 to 2 have refused to request a list to fill the position now held by Dick Harries. On a permanent basis this will cause Dick Harries to revert back to Permanent Intermittent as of 1/3/78. This was done even after the Chief of Police signed a waiver of increase in compensation that the addition of another fulltime officer may entitle the Chief of Police to. This waiver involved only officers Moruzzolini and Harries.
4. At the time the waiver was signed the Chief of Police was already entitled to an increase in the amount of $3,447.60 annually; he has not pursued or intend to pursue the matter any further, and orally stated this to the Board of Selectmen. The Board of Selectmen had been informed officially by the Town Counsel, Darren L. Byne, that the Chief of Police was entitled to the additional salary increase.
5. It would seem that certain members of the Board of Selectmen are not at this time willing to provide adequate personnel on a fulltime basis, for reasons that they have not stated. They have officially voted to reduce the fulltime force even further. The manpower of the police department will be at a critical point. Therefore I as Chief of Police must control the working force with a careful displacement of officers and the hours worked. I do this at this time of the year with regrets; it is a situation over which I have no control, and have tried to the best of my ability to correct. Should this matter change, I will advise you. As I am sure you can see this will have an adverse effect on planned vacations, but it is a matter that I have talked over with the Selectmen and they have moved not to help with this situation. Again I will state this is not the Board as a whole, but only certain members. The records are open to the public, you may want to read them, as all of this is a matter of record.

Richard Dives
Chief of Police

Exhibit IV.   Letter from Police Chief Removing E.M.T. Officer

Board of Selectmen   1 May 78
Town Hall
Barkfield, Massachusetts

Gentlemen:

This is to advise you that on April 27, 1978, after having a conversation with Patrolman Robert Tucker, in my office at the Barkfield Police Station, I have removed him as training officer for E.M.T.

The reason for this was not in anyway related to his ability to perform this assigned duty, or in anyway a disciplinary action.

As I am sure you are aware this matter is very much involved in the present contract negotiations between the Barkfield Police Alliance and the Town of Barkfield (i.e., your Board).

As there has been no training conducted of any type since collective bargaining commenced, I am of the opinion that the total ambulance service of the Town of Barkfield would indeed suffer if immediate action is not taken to start a recertification training program. With this in mind and a deep concern for the future status of the ambulance service of the Town, I intend to meet with several qualified persons in the area who carry on continuing recertification programs. After this is done, I will meet with your Board so that we can resolve the current problem of recertification to the satisfaction of your Board.

I feel that your Board should be aware of the following: Of the eight fulltime officers and one temporary fulltime officer, there may be a question of E.M.T. status requirement of six officers, they are:

Sgt. Derek Frost
Sgt. William Donovan
Ptlmn Fevyer*
Ptlmn Cardillo*
Ptlmn Stevens*
Ptlmn Bornot*
Ptlmn Tucker

As I have stated, as has our previous Town Counsel, that ambulance work and duties have been a part of the duties and responsibilities of a Sergeant or Patrolman of the Barkfield Police Department for about the past thirty years. This was of course prior to the department becoming fulltime in 1955. There are many more facts to be brought forward in this matter but they are best to be held until they may be needed.

---

* One of these officers will be appointed Sergeant; more than likely he will to be an E.M.T. as it is in his job description. This will leave six officers, of the six remaining the final answer to their being required to be E.M.T.'s will be settled in the Courts. As I am sure you are aware that I will take immediate action, should an officer refuse to continue his training or duties as an E.M.T. I will suspend him and request that he be dismissed permanently at a hearing held by your Board.

All of the part-time officers that are active must be E.M.T. with the exception of James William, and he has kept his E.M.T. status current on his own through various courses available.

The following is for your information on the E.M.T. status of the Town of Barkfield.

+ Must maintain E.M.T. status
* They may question if they are required to be E.M.T.s
− E.M.T. status at present

		"Fulltime"
1.	Sgt. Derek Frost	* −
2.	Sgt. William Donovan	* −
3.	Ptlmn John Fevyer	* −
4.	Ptlmn Jack Cardillo	* −
5.	Ptlmn Reginald Stevens	* −
6.	Ptlmn Robert Tucker	* −
7.	Ptlmn Paul Borot	* −
8.	Ptlmn Dick Harries	* −
9.	Ptlmn Harry Pady	* −

		"Part-time"
10.	Ptlmn George Mabon	+ −
11.	Ptlmn Kevin Hale	+ −
12.	Ptlmn Rachel Gordon	+ in training
13.	Ptlmn Gwyn Davies	+ will train soon
14.	Ptlmn Thomas Mullen	+ −
15.	Ptlmn David Muir	+ will train soon
16.	Ptlmn Kevin Lucas	+ will train soon
17.	Ptlmn Marcus Kent	+ will train soon

		"Special Police"
18.	Ptlmn Pamela Miller	+ −
19.	Ptlmn Victor Hills	+ −
20.	Ptlmn Bernie McPhee	+ −

		"Other E.M.T.s"
21.	C.D. Director Graham Brown	−
22.	F.M. Matthew Carse	−
23.	Nurse Graham Nelson	−

Very truly yours,

Richard Dives
Chief of Police
Barkfield, Massachusetts

Exhibit V. Town of Barkfield Selectmen-Police: Status of Negotiations

ITEMS IN AGREEMENT

Article 6. Court Time
Agreed to a four (4)-hour straight time minimum. Beyond four (4) hours is computed under OT formula.

Article 8. Vacations
1 year - 1 week; 2 years - 2 weeks; 7 years - 3 weeks; 12 years - 4 weeks.

Article 10. Holidays
Same as existing contract with wording that does *not* require the working of day before and after for eligibility.

Article 11. Bereavement Leave
Agreed - A. three (3) days for immediate family defined as mother, father, son, daughter, spouse, brother, sister.
Agreed - B. Add one (1) day for grandparents of either spouse, brothers-in-law, and sisters-in-law.
Agreed - C. Personal Day - One (1) day per year.

Article 12. Work Schedule and Overtime
A. Accept a 5-and-2, forty-hour schedule in concept (2 years) (with trial period).
B. Overtime in accordance with Chapter 147, Section 17E, accepted by the Town on March 13, 1971. More specifically, time and one half after forty (40) hours.

Article 13. Insurance
Agreed - B. Life Insurance - $6,000.
Agreed - C. False Arrest - $100,000/300,000 limits.

Article 13A. Insurance
C. Drop appeal with Labor Board.
D. No payment of legal fees.

Article 14. Sick Time
1¼ days per month accumulative to 90 days.

Article 15. Education
Agreed - A. Same as present.

Article 16. Mileage
Agreed as per Town practice in effect.

Article 24. Funeral Expenses
Selectmen will place article for acceptance of Chapter 41, Section 100 G (Duty-related death funeral payment) on Town Meeting Warrant.

Article 25. No Strike Clause
Agreed in principle.

Article 26. Training
A. Overtime if mandatory training is off duty and beyond 40 hours a week.

ITEMS IN NEGOTIATION

	Issues	Present	Union	Management
1.	Wages	$221.00/wk	$240.00/wk now Avg. pay after 1/1/78 plus C.L.A.** for 2nd and 3rd year per B.C.P.I.**	$240.00/wk 4%—2nd 4%—3rd
2.	Clothing Allowance	$250.00/yr	$250.00—1st yr. $275.00—2nd & 3rd drop holster & gun	$250.00/yr and revolver and holster for new man.
3.	Educational Incentive	Own Plan	$250.00—30 Cr. $500.00—60 Cr. Or Longevity: 1%—5; 2%—10; 3%—15.	$250.00—A.S. $500.00—B.S. And Longevity: 1%—5; 2%—10; 3%—15.
4.	BC/BS	In Litigation	75/25—90% Retro from 2/1/77 to present.	75/25; Split 90/10 2/1/77 to 6/30/77.
5.	Work Schedule	No Fixed Schedule	5-&-2; 4-&-2—3rd yr.	5-&-2 (one-year trial schedule) 4-&-2 possible in third year.*

* Study Committee for 3rd year implementation.
** C.L.A.—Cost of Living Adjustment.   B.C.P.I.—Boston Consumer Price Index.

Exhibit VI.   The Town's Final Offer on December 19

December 19, 1978

Commonwealth of Massachusetts
Department of Labor and Industries
Joint Labor-Management Committee
Attention: Chairman, John T. Dunlop
Room 408 - 130 Bowdoin Street
Boston, Massachusetts 02108

Gentlemen:

Attached is a copy of the last offer of the Barkfield Board of Selectmen to the Barkfield Police Alliance in the matter of contract negotiations for the period beginning July 1, 1978.

It is the feeling of the Selectmen that the offers they have made are reasonable and equitable and they do not propose to make any increase in their offer.

It should be noted that the value of the offer, expressed in terms of the average patrolman per week is 15.26% more than the Fiscal 1978.

Sincerely yours,

Lawrence Anslow
Administrative Assistant
Town of Barkfield

LA/mkd
Enclosure

SELECTMEN'S LAST OFFER - POLICE

Article 6	Court Time: 4 hours straight time; minimum time ½ over 4 hours.
Article 7	Patrolman Base: $240.00 1st year, 4% 2nd year, and 4% 3rd year.
Article 8	Vacations: 1—1, 2—2, 7—3, & 12—4.
Article 9	Clothing: $250.00 per year.
Article 10	Holidays: Same as existing contract but change the wording.
Article 11	Bereavement

A. 3 days for immediate family (mother, father, son, daughter, spouse, brother, and sister).

B. 1 day for grandparents of either spouse, brother or sister-in-law.

C. Personal Day—1 per year.

Article 12   Work Schedule & Overtime

A. 5-+-2, 40-hour schedule.

B. Overtime in accordance with Chapter 147, Section 17E, accepted by the Town March 13, 1971 (time ½ over 40 hours).

C. Willing to discuss 4-+-2 week provided that manpower is not increased and budget does not require more for part time.

Article 13   Blue Cross/Blue Shield

A. 75/25 from July 1, 1977 on through the contract.

B. Life Insurance—$6,000.

C. False Arrest—100,000/300,000 limits.

Article 14   Sick Leave: 1¼ days per month, accumulated to 90 days.

Article 15   Education Incentives; Article 22—Longevity Combined
  A. (Same as old contract) Town pay for materials required for courses.
  B. $250.00 cash bonus for associate's degree payable once a year. $500.00 cash bonus for bachelor's degree payable once a year.
  C. Longevity—1% for 5 years; 2% for 10 years; 3% for 15 years *on base pay*.

Article 16   Mileage—Per Town Vote, 10¢ per mile.

Article 22   Longevity: see Article 15.

Article 24   Funeral Expense: Agreed to place article for acceptance of Chapter 41, Section 100G (Duty-related death, funeral payment) on Town Meeting Warrant.

Article 25   No Strike Clause: Agreed in Principal.

Article 26   Training
  A. Overtime if mandatory training is off duty and beyond 40 hours per week.
  B. Ambulance - willing to discuss variation if Police keep service in Department.

Exhibit VII.   Chronology: Barkfield Police

September 2, 1977		Decision by Massachusetts Labor Relations Commission re: prohibited practice on health insurance. Decision against town.
November 25, 1977		EMT training halted by Chief in response to overtime deficit.
December 7, 1977		Opening collective bargaining proposal presented by Barkfield Police Alliance.
February 1, 1978		Meeting—Board and union
February 10		Meeting—Board and union.
April 22		Unfair labor practice charge.
April 25		Tucker removed as EMT training officer.
April 27		Batley first hears of Barkfield negotiation problem.
June 20		Batley goes west and touches base with several police departments. Meets Tucker, President of Police Alliance.
July 1		Contract expires.
July 11		Letter sent by union to attorneys seeking to restart discussion on July 18.
July 25		DeCata and Batley go to Worcester, meet with various unions, talk about their role, union problems. Barkfield police come in and tell "tales of woe."
August 1		Union requests JLMC jurisdiction.
August 15	7:30 p.m.	Batley, DeCata go to meeting with Alliance.
	8:00 p.m.	Batley, DeCata go to Selectmen's meeting
August 16	5:30 p.m.	Batley and DeCata and Dick Horne go to selectmen's meeting—Horne explains Committee's purposes. Selectmen agree to talk to Chief re: schedule.
August 22	7:00 p.m.	Mediation session.
August 30	7:30 p.m.	Mediation and negotiation
October 2		Grievance withdrawn
October 6		Hearing scheduled, cancelled.
October 18	1:30 p.m.	Hearing on the issues.
October 18 until mid-December		Phone calls with parties re: contract language lawsuits, grievances.
October 19		DeCata discusses case with Horne.
November 10		Hearing—Anslow only appears on town's behalf.
December 5		Case certified for arbitration.
December 19		Batley and DeCata meet with Morley and Erkskine, prior to arbitration hearing.
		Arbitration hearing.

Chapter 5

NEW TOOLS FROM A JOINT COMMITTEE STRUCTURE

Case Example: Fire Fighter Negotiations in Seabury, Massachusetts

This case study is taken from one of the first cases handled by the Joint Labor-Management Committee. Prior to the JLMC involvement the dispute was one of several years duration, characterized by a settlement that was rejected by the town and a subsequent arbitration award that was contested and later overturned. A long history of dissatisfaction and poor relationships with the fire service interfered with productive labor-management dialogue. The new town manager was faced with negotiating an agreement and winning approval under difficult circumstances where historical personality and political clashes had impeded progress.

To resolve the dispute, the Joint Labor-Management Committee chose to use its membership's working knowledge and peer network to encourage movement by the two sides. The interplay between and among the Committee members and their peers in the dispute is illustrative of the possibilities—and some of the dangers—in using the Committee's membership in rather unconventional and unstructured mediating capacities. This case presents an opportunity to examine these novel aspects of a joint labor-management committee. Included in Chapter 6 is an analysis of these tools and their application.

FIRE FIGHTER NEGOTIATIONS IN SEABURY, MASSACHUSETTS

Founded in 1634, the town of Seabury is one of the oldest in the United States. It is located in Suffern County on the southern coast of Massachusetts. Its population is quite diverse. In the 1950s the inhabitants were primarily old Yankee and their descendants, Greek, Polish, and French in origin. Since then it has included others who have moved out from Boston and the inner suburbs as the town has grown. The town supports churches of eleven different denominations. The community's work habits also reflect diversity. Some of the inhabitants commute daily to Boston and other urban communities; some others work at the local Sylvania plant and in the shellfish industry. The largest group of workers, however, is employed by the Town of Seabury as teachers, by the power company (a town-owned enterprise), as municipal workers, police officers, or fire fighters. There is also a thriving downtown business community. Most residents are not wealthy. Data compiled by the Massachusetts Municipal Association for 1979 showed that the average income in Seabury was 5.6 percent below that of Suffern County and one-half percent less than Massachusetts as a whole.

Strong community feeling is not new to the town. As early as 1687, irate Seabury citizens staged a rebellion against a British tax levy. The town green displays a plaque which records the event, and the town seal bears the legend "The Birthplace of American Independence." Like their predecessors, modern voters are politically active (attendance at annual town meetings averages around 800 voters). In the late 70s the Board of Selectmen, made up largely of local merchants, many of whom had high school educations, were described by one resident as having "a different world outlook" from the Finance Committee, which was composed primarily of college educated professionals and who were appointed and who, therefore, did not have political ties.

The Origins of the Fire Fighter Dispute

The beginnings of the dispute may be marked when a special town meeting was called in Seabury for November 25, 1974. The meeting, required by law,[1] was called for the purpose of appropriating money to fund a newly

---

This case was originally prepared by Adele M. Langevin, then a master's candidate at the Graduate School of Education, Harvard University, and the author gratefully acknowledges her willingness to permit its adaptation and use. While the case is based on field research, certain names and facts have been altered in the interest of presentation. The case was prepared as a basis for classroom discussion. It is not intended to illustrate either effective or ineffective handling of the situation depicted.

[1] Massachusetts General Laws, Chapter 150E, Sec. 7: ". . . the employer shall submit to the appropriate legislative body within thirty days after the date on which the agreement is executed by the parties, a request for an appropriation necessary to fund the cost items contained therein."

negotiated fire fighter's contract and to supplement the depleted fire fighter's overtime fund. The fund had become depleted because, in part, the manager had ordered that the economic provisions of the contract be implemented prior to Town Meeting appropriations. Another of the costly economic items was a minimum-manning clause, and the town meeting voted not to fund either item. It marked a political setback for the then town manager, Robert Trent, who in March 1974 had negotiated the contract with Local 209, International Association of Fire Fighters (IAFF). The contract was to be effective retroactively to July 1, 1974. This contract had included a minimum-manning clause (providing for four fire fighters and one officer per shift) and its provisions had been in force since July 1, 1974, pending town meeting approval of the cost items. Because of the minimum-manning clause, however, overtime costs had increased and the overtime fund was completely exhausted by August 14, 1974. By its refusal at the November 25 meeting to provide additional funds, the manning provisions could not be carried out and the town had, in effect, rejected the whole agreement. From that point the town administered its relations with the union under the provisions of the fiscal year 1974 "Jefferson" contract negotiated under Trent's predecessor (surnamed Jefferson) as town manager. Trent, the third town manager in less than ten years, was worried: Because of the recent action by the town meeting his job was on the line in a town which had been called "a town manager's graveyard."

Impasse Procedures Begin

According to Section 7 of Chapter 150E of the General Laws of Massachusetts, "If the appropriate legislative body duly rejects the request for an appropriation necessary to fund the cost items, such cost items shall be returned to the parties for further bargaining." As required, negotiations resumed. Although the town had indicated a willingness to change its position on salary items in exchange for a union concession on minimum manning, union counsel, Thomas Bergen, recommended that the union hold to its position. An impasse petition was filed by the union with the Massachusetts Board of Conciliation and Arbitration, which agency was then exclusively responsible for handling impasses in public safety employee negotiations in Massachusetts. After an impasse investigation and brief attempt at mediation as required by the statute then governing impasse procedures in public safety disputes, a fact-finder would be appointed as the next step in the statutory process. If mediation, fact-finding, and additional negotiation did not result in settlement, an arbitrator would be appointed to hear the parties and choose between the last-best-offers of each party following the conclusion of the hearings.

The fact-finder's report was issued on April 1, 1975, and included reference to the minimum-manning issue. Although *per se* this was not a mandatory subject for bargaining under the state's collective bargaining laws,

Trent and the union allowed its inclusion.[2] (Neither the Board of Selectmen nor the Finance Committee knew it was only a permissive subject and they assumed it was a mandatory item.) Since the parties could not agree on the fact-finder's report the Board of Conciliation and Arbitration appointed a three-member arbitration panel, as the law required.

In submitting its final offer to the arbitration panel, the Seabury fire fighters' last-best-offer was based largely on the terms of the March 1974 agreement that had been rejected by the town meeting. Their final offer included a minimum-manning clause and a special retroactive feature calling for compensation for the overtime that would have been worked had the minimum-manning clause been in effect since then. Much of this was "phantom" overtime, since after the town meeting in November it was neither scheduled nor worked by the fire fighters. It would *only* have been required had the manning clause been in effect. The union was apparently hoping to have enforced as an arbitration award the same contract they had negotiated with Trent. An arbitration award was not subject to a town vote as a negotiated agreement would have been. The arbitration award would require that the town fund the contract so awarded.

The town's last-best-offer did not contain a provision for minimum manning, but it did contain a better salary schedule (an 8 percent increase) than provided for in the fact finder's report (6 percent) as well as increased longevity benefits, uniform allowance, and educational incentive benefits.

"I'll See You in Court"

The arbitration panel chose the union's last-best-offer and issued its award on December 17, 1975.

As the statute permitted, following the award the town filed a motion for summary judgment before the Essex County Superior Court in December challenging the inclusion of minimum manning in the award and seeking to vacate the arbitration award. The union filed a counterclaim seeking enforcement of the award. Various other petitions were filed during 1976 and 1977. While this worked its way through the courts, no bargaining took place due to "lack of interest." In the spring of 1977, the union sought to resume bargaining, but the town declined unless the court actions were a subject of bargaining. The union would not accept this condition. The town, by this time under the leadership of James L. Porter, who became town manager in the fall of 1976, refused to bargain further, claiming that it was awaiting the court's decision. In June the union filed an unfair labor practice complaint with the Massachusetts Labor Relations Commission, charging that the town was refusing to bargain in good faith.

---

[2] Outside Section 4 of Chapter 150E specifically states that "no municipal employer shall be required to negotiate over subjects of minimum manning of shift coverage with an employee organization representing municipal police officers and fire fighters."

During August of 1977, Edward Best had replaced Porter as town manager. Shortly thereafter, several of the pending actions came to closure. In December of 1977, the MLRC issued a ruling in favor of the union and ordered the town to "cease and desist," and to take ". . . such affirmative action as will comply with the provisions of Section 10," ordering the town to bargain in good faith.

Also, on December 14, 1977, Superior Court Justice Albert Murphy vacated the entire 1975 arbitration award, ruling that although ". . . a shift manning clause is a permissive subject of bargaining . . . the arbitration panel's selection of the union's last-best-offer containing the minimum-manning clause and retroactive overtime pay was in excess of its authority and the decision cannot be enforced." He also ruled that "bargaining and agreeing on a permissive subject do not make it a mandatory subject of future bargaining." Further, he took the arbitration panel to task for choosing portions of each party's last offer, contrary to the provisions of the statute.

The court provided no further remedy or direction beyond those rulings. The fire fighters had been without a contract or a raise for over three years. They appealed the case to the Supreme Judicial Court. In the meantime, under the MLRC ruling to bargain, negotiations resumed.

Negotiations Begin Again: 1978

Edward Best, in his job for five months, was determined to be a successful town manager and complete his three-year contract, even though this included resolving the impasse with the fire fighters.

Best, at 34, was an energetic young man who had a reputation for hard work and total commitment to a task. He was new to Seabury and in his first job as a town manager. His academic background included undergraduate and graduate degrees in government, and he had served as an assistant to the city manager and with the Municipal Association in the state of Connecticut. His last job before coming to Seabury was a position as Assistant to the Board of Selectmen in West Harbor, Connecticut.

On Edward Best's first day on the job he assumed principal responsibility for negotiations with the town's Local 362 of the American Federations of State County and Municipal Employees (AFSCME). He had never negotiated a labor-management contract before, and found in place an inexperienced and untried negotiating team. That group had been assembled by Best's predecessor just before Best took over the town manager's job. James L. Porter had seen in the controversial fire fighter negotiations the need for a "buffer" between the manager and the town meeting. Best kept the team. The team included Ellen Harding, a Finance Committee member, Susan Simmons, a member of the Board of Selectmen, and George Hannen, the Town Accountant.

Best had been appointed by a split vote of the board. He had inherited a situation where feelings against the fire fighters ran high: The many court actions were important matters of cost and principle to the selectmen and Finance Committee, who would have to approve the agreement. The town, it seemed, was very much behind their elected representatives on the issues. People in the town thought the fire fighters were "wrong" in their pursuit of minimum manning and phantom overtime.

Best prepared to enter negotiations with the fire fighters following the MLRC ruling and the Court decision. He was able to secure from the Board of Selectmen funds to retain counsel, and hired John Carmichael, of Lewis, Stearns, and Carmichael, a prestigious Boston law firm that specialized in labor relations, and whose uncle had done work for the town years earlier. Best wanted a legal opinion of Judge Murphy's ruling and needed to know "Where do we go from here? Do we start from ground zero; if not, then what?"

Best and Carmichael felt that the Trend contract had "given away the store," and noted that some of its major provisions had been vacated by Judge Murphy's ruling. Since the town had been operating under the last effective contract—the expired Jefferson contract—Best and Carmichael agreed that the basis for negotiations should include not only a retroactive contract for three years, but a new agreement for fiscal years '78 and '79. Thus they would be dealing with a five-year period, despite the fact that state law limited the length of an individual contract to a maximum of three years.

On January 9, 1978, Best met with the fire fighters' counsel, Thomas Bergen, to discuss the basis for negotiations. Although he thought using the Jefferson contract was an "interesting concept," Bergen counterproposed that new salaries be superimposed on the Trent contract. Best maintained that, as a new town manager, he wanted to deal with the situation comprehensively; therefore, he wanted to go back to the FY 1974 contract as a point of departure.

During a series of January meetings, negotiators for the two sides continued their efforts to decide which contract should be the basis of the actual negotiations. At a January 31 meeting, Best stated that since the past years were just water over the dam, only wages needed to be dealt with in the retroactive part of the contract. He felt any other benefits would, in effect, be meaningless. He proposed to add more money to the Jefferson contract, making the amounts retroactive to 1974 and to submit this retroactive contract, plus a new one for two years, to the approaching Town Meeting for funding, provided, however, that the union drop its appeal on the Murphy decision, which vacated the arbitration award. The union was agreeable, but wanted new issues introduced for the prospective portion of the proposed contract; in addition to wages they introduced clothing allowance, additional holidays, education incentives, longevity pay, and expanded vacation benefits as issues in the prospective portion of the contract. A major issue was their desire to go to a forty-two-hour workweek from forty-eight. The police had gone from forty-two to thirty-seven hours and the fire fighters sought a kind of parity there as well.

The Joint Labor-Management Committee

Present at the January 31 negotiations was an observer from the newly formed Joint Labor-Management Committee for Municipal Police and Fire Fighters (JLMC). The Committee was a new state agency with broad powers to intervene and take jurisdiction in any and all labor-management contract disputes involving municipal police or fire fighting negotiations. Committee members served on a voluntary basis while retaining their fulltime jobs. Typically, they were active members in their respective union or management communities. The intention of the JLMC was to intervene informally whenever possible, seeking agreement between parties rather than using the formal arbitration powers available to it. In fact, the Committee's philosophy and policy were to try to encourage an agreement between the parties themselves rather than to arbitrate.

The fire fighters' situation in Seabury had been brought to the JLMC's attention by T. Dustin Alward, President of the Professional Fire Fighters of Massachusetts and the chairman of those members of the JLMC who represented the fire fighters. (The police and the management representatives each had a chairman, and the Committee had an overall neutral chairman.) As an elected union leader he was sensitive to the needs and mandates of his electorate and at the same time was widely regarded inside and outside the union as a strong union leader.

"Dusty" Alward was concerned about the status of negotiations in Seabury for many reasons. As a fire captain who still worked in the firehouse he knew that the fire fighters in Seabury were getting frustrated over the uncertainty and years without a raise or other changes in working conditions. In addition, having watched hundreds of negotiations from his vantage point as a union officer, it seemed to him that the two sides had taken a "litigate rather than negotiate posture," a posture unlikely to yield satisfactory or quick results.

Part of his view also came from the fact that the Seabury local had a pending appeal in State Supreme Court. Alward estimated that the appeal could cost his state organization—which sometimes financed such actions by locals—$30,000. Alward had to decide whether or not to proceed with the case. Based on legal precedent, it did not seem that minimum manning was a strong issue for the local since the MLRC had already ruled in management's favor in a precedent-setting decision involving the Danvers fire fighters, Local 2038, IAFF. The ruling, issued on April 6, 1977, stated "the decision regarding the overall number of employees to be hired by a municipality to deliver a given service falls squarely within the managerial control of the governmental enterprise, and should be negotiable only at the will of the public employer." In any event, Alward was anxious for the parties in Seabury to reach agreement and avoid further contention, litigation, and uncertainty.

With the advent of the JLMC, he brought to the Committee's attention the Seabury case at one of the JLMC's first regular case meetings, hoping that with its flexibility to assist in disputes, the Committee might be helpful. After some discussion and, reportedly, some hesitation, the labor and management members of the Committee agreed to send one of its fulltime staff representatives to Seabury as an "observer," expecting to get an objective analysis of the situation. Once they had some information, perhaps some constructive course of action might be chosen. Also, it was possible that the presence of neutral observers might have a salutary effect on negotiations. Following its philosophy of minimal intervention, observer status would be less intrusive to the parties and would not obligate the Committee to any particular involvement or action.

Gaining Acceptance

The chairman of the management side, Demetrios Moschos, Assistant City Manager of Worcester, Massachusetts, called Edward Best to offer the services of the JLMC in the Seabury dispute. Best recalled the conversation: "He came on like gangbusters. They were going to take jurisdiction, he said. 'I won't put up with it,' I told him. They weren't going to nose in on our affairs. 'We'll handle it ourselves.' And I hung up."

Later that day Best was called by Dick Brown, a management member of the Joint Labor-Management Committee and himself a town manager. Brown recalled: "I took this one. I should have been able to do something. Although we didn't know each other well I know him from some meetings of the town managers' association. He'd have to listen to me. I was pretty high on the informal management hierarchy in the state. He's a pro, a strong guy and would listen to reason." When Brown called Best, Best told him to "go to hell. It's a local problem; we'll handle it. Who needs you?"

Brown: Don't give me that shit—I'm a very busy town manager.

Best: So am I!

Brown: Not for long, you're not. You're trying to be a hero on the wrong issue. Realistically, you have three options:

You can go to last-best-offer arbitration where you're likely to spend a lot of money, take a lot of time and maybe lose your pants.

You can do nothing, and we'll take over without your permission and do it our way; we have the authority, or

You can let us come in and work informally; after all, we don't cost anything. If we can't help, then take one of the other alternatives.

Softening his approach, Brown continued: "Hey, there's nothing in this for me. We're trying to do this on a peer basis and help avoid arbitration. I'm a manager and see it from your point of view. I'm familiar with this sort of situation. It's a problem that I've got, every town manager has. If you won't take help from your peers you're out there by yourself. The other side is taking all the help they can get."

Best finally agreed to some informal involvement and Alward secured the union's approval for similar involvement on his part.

Observation

Following the Committee's consensus to send an observer and agreement of the parties, Paul Quirk, the senior labor staff representative of the Committee, was asked by the Committee to go to Seabury and sit in on negotiations. He arranged to attend the negotiating session on January 31, 1978, which was to be held at the Seabury Power Company.

Paul Quirk had been a leader in the state labor movement and was selected by the union side of the Committee to be the senior staff representative for labor. In addition, he had the respect of people from across the negotiating table; he was known to have breakfasted frequently at the home of a chief management negotiator before and after hard negotiating sessions, at which negotiations each would have done their damndest to "stick it" to the other. Yet they maintained each other's respect. Unlike many of his labor colleagues, Quirk was a college graduate, a former Peace Corps volunteer, and a recent graduate of the 13-week Trade Union Program of the Harvard Business School.

To be sure, he had his detractors. Quirk had gained some publicity in Massachusetts for organizing an 8,000-member state employee local, and then in 1976 leading the first state employees' strike. His goals in working with the JLMC "were not just to effect local settlements," but rather to improve public sector labor relations more broadly. He "wanted to make the world safe for collective bargaining," through the development of professional skills and understanding in the parties to collective bargaining disputes. He was eager to see the Committee succeed "by finding and fixing problems in a way that would allow for good bargaining."

When Quirk arrived in Seabury, he was questioned by John Carmichael, the management counsel. Carmichael had seen Quirk on television news programs during the state workers' strike, and he suspected Quirk's motives for coming to Seabury. Quirk tried to allay his fears during their conversation:

Carmichael:	On what grounds are you here? We haven't asked for any assistance.
Quirk:	As a joint labor-management group we're keeping an eye on the case, but only as observers.
Carmichael:	No dispute exists; we haven't ever dealt with this union and feel we're in the position of initial negotiations.
Quirk:	We realize there's no dispute now, but we're interested because of the long history of dispute.

Quirk was permitted to stay as an observer, but Carmichael still wasn't sure about him, knowing Quirk's background.

At the next meeting in Seabury, Quirk was joined by Robert Curley, the new full-time management representative of the JLMC. A native of Maine, Curley had spent five years as Personnel Director for the city of Portland, Maine, and six years as the Director of Personnel Services and Labor Relations for the Maine Municipal Association. He had also served on the Maine Labor Relations Board. Beside having an outsider's objectivity, Curley was known to be a highly organized individual, methodical in his work behavior. In addition to his negotiating skills and his experience as a neutral, he was familiar with technical and legal aspects of labor relations and labor contracts as well as with traditions and customs of collective bargaining. Curley's manner and appearance caused him frequently to be mistaken as a union representative, a trait which did him no harm in his neutral role as senior staff representative for management; as Quirk had discovered the week before, many in the business would not easily forgive one's past. Curley had the respect of labor people with whom he had dealt for his fairness and professionalism. Curley was an experienced negotiator, mediator, and arbitrator, and the management members of the JLMC and municipal association were extremely pleased at being able to obtain his services.

Quirk and Curley reported back to the JLMC on February 6, 1978, at a meeting at Baker Library on the Harvard Business School campus where the Committee held its meetings pending state appropriation of funds for office space. The full Committee and its chairman, John T. Dunlop, a professor at Harvard University, decided, based on the information that Quirk and Curley had gathered, to monitor the Seabury case more closely.

Meetings in Seabury scheduled for February 5 and 10 were postponed because of the Great Blizzard of 1978, which shut down most of eastern Massachusetts for more than a week.

The members of the town's negotiating team found Curley helpful and were interested in hearing his views as an objective outsider with extensive labor relations experience and a very practical sense of what to do next. One member of the negotiating team recalled: "We had many opportunities to talk during waiting periods. We'd talk about various experience in his labor relations background. We learned to trust him."

He advised them when they should "hang tough" and when they needed to bend, where further resistance would gain nothing or might have costs. Carmichael initially had doubts about Curley's authority to be there, but subsequently found him helpful. He said later that both Quirk and Curley "behaved like federal mediators" (federal mediators are regarded in the field as highly professional and impeccably neutral), and was "pleased with their performance."

Still, it had become evident that several obstacles were preventing further movement by the parties. One problem was a management perception, apparently shared later by the union, that union's counsel almost seemed more interested in prolonging negotiations rather than resolving them. "He was always moving the boundaries," said Ellen Harding. The fire fighters were beginning to agree: Subsequently, "Bud" Chandler, a cigar-chewing veteran fire fighter and president of the local, labeled him "useless." "We were a 15-man local, owed him $15,000, and still didn't have a contract." The fire fighters, in the middle of negotiations, "sidetracked" Mr. Bergen and ultimately fired him.

Other problems began to surface. When negotiations had begun in 1974, longevity pay was a key issue. By 1978, retirements had caused older members in the local to be replaced by seven younger fire fighters who were more interested in educational incentive pay and achieving parity with the town police officers' base wage than they were in additional pay based on years of service. Yet, during this late winter period of negotiations the leadership maintained the need for longevity.

On the other side it became obvious that the fire fighters in town had an unfavorable public image—only partly a result of the protracted dispute. This was an unfortunate situation for both union and management negotiating teams since the citizens in town meetings had to approve the cost items in any contract that was negotiated. One resident stated, "They're a bunch of lazy bums. In every significant fire in town in the last five years, the buildings have burned to the ground." The town relied on call (volunteer) firemen to supplement the full-time fire fighters. It was widely perceived in the town that the more dangerous and important work was performed by the call firemen.

Defending themselves, the fire fighters cited a report by a private consultant on the status of the town's fire protection, which noted that Seabury was one of the largest towns in the state, covering thirty-four square miles. Therefore, it recommended that 15 men be on duty at all times. In fact, the average per shift was four. The report also addressed other fire safety issues such as water pressure, smoke alarms, etc. Office furniture in the single fire station (the desk, typewriter, clock, lamp, and chair) had been donated to the station or purchased privately by the men. Part of the alarm apparatus, itself antiquated, one fire fighter said, had been broken for years. Another fire fighter claimed that "every life lost in a Seabury fire over the last twenty years happened when the shift was shorthanded and the town had refused to fill the vacant spot."

Attitudes and Obstacles

On February 17, a "nuts and bolts" negotiating session took place. At this point after a request by the JLMC, it was agreed by both parties to allow Quirk and Curley to monitor the negotiating sessions and to attend caucuses of their respective side. It was unusual if not unique to permit outsiders into private caucuses of the parties. Negotiations continued, and by

March 14 the issues in dispute were narrowed down to wages, where the
fire fighters sought parity with the police, and longevity pay. The union
wanted parity with police wages, but the town's position was that parity
hadn't existed in fifteen years and shouldn't now. Unlike the fire fighters,
the police were well regarded in the town and parity seemed unreasonable
in light of that.

Quirk, Curley, and Brown communicated with the full Joint Labor-
Management Committee as events progressed. It seemed that in addition
to the problems on the union side related to the membership mix and the
longevity issue, the desire for parity with the police and their lawyer's
behavior, there were also problems on the management side that were
blocking progress. Among other things, the town negotiating Committee
held the same view as that of the bulk of the town regarding the fire fighters
and were unwilling to make much of an investment in the fire fighters or
fire protection. The town wanted improvement, "but we wanted improvement *before* we paid them, not after," said Mrs. Harding. By the March 14
meeting Curley and Quirk felt that they had gone as far as they could acting
as facilitators and observers in this informal role. At the same time, frustrated, the management attorney suggested that perhaps the chairman of
the JLMC should get personally involved. In reporting to the Committee,
Quirk and Curley recommended that Committee people use their peer
relationship with some of the parties to the negotiation in an effort to cause
each side to be more realistic and flexible and thus to gain some movement
by the parties. They also recommended that the Committee authorize and
commit itself to a stronger role in mediating the dispute.

Peer Interactions

As the JLMC assessed the situation, it reasoned that since some of the
concerns among the members of the town's negotiating committee were
their perceptions of substantive fire fighting capacity as well as financial
questions, the involvement of some of its own experienced members in
informal discussions with their peers from the town might be helpful. As it
evolved, in mid-March the Committee decided to ask Dusty Alward of the
Fire Fighters and Jay Gordon, a management member, to get involved.

Jay Gordon was to contact his counterpart, the finance committee person
on the town negotiating team. Gordon was a management member of the
JLMC and was a long-time finance committee member in Framingham,
Massachusetts. He was president of the state Association for Municipal
Finance Committee Members. Gordon was a successful local businessman
with a dedication to public service. He had a reputation for fairness, tough-
ness, and openness in labor negotiations as well as other matters. Gordon
took a leading role.

Gordon contacted Ellen Harding, his finance committee counterpart on the negotiating team, as well as members of the Finance Committee. He later related the essence of his discussions with her and the selectmen and Finance Committee members:

> The point I kept hammering home was that they were doing the citizens a great disservice. They were paying for fire fighters and not getting a good job done. I stressed that they had to train professional fire fighters, that a training program would have to be instituted, and that they had to provide competitive pay. Management has a responsibility to manage. As a result they had only themselves to blame for the poor service. You have to demand it, set a standard, provide an incentive.

Subsequently, it was decided that Alward would try to address the management team. Since it was an unusual step Alward got in touch with the president of the local to clear it with him. Chandler assented, and Alward and Gordon went to see Best on the morning of March 22. Alward told Best that he was not there to negotiate but to express his willingness to go to the floor of the local and press for a settlement if it seemed that the differences could be worked out. Best recalled:

> He gave me a lecture and talked about morale and management shortcomings and noted that both sides in the town bore responsibility for the state of the fire service. He told me he wanted to encourage a settlement but that without full parity it would be hard to sell the union. He thought he could sell them 80% parity (management's offer) in year 1 and year 2 of the three-year retroactive contract, but needed dollar for dollar in year 3.

Reportedly Alward went out on the streets of the town that afternoon and asked passersby their views of the fire fighters. He recognized that the selectmen couldn't easily vote to fund an agreement they thought the townspeople would oppose. To his surprise, the resounding response was that the fire fighters in Seabury were "no-good slobs, not civic oriented." He was shocked, but saw that the negotiating committees were simply reflecting community sentiment.

Shortly, David Stevens, a young, energetic fire fighter, took the union presidency away from "Bud" Chandler. Longevity was no longer a main issue for the union. Rather parity became the major issue for the fire fighters for the prospective portion of the contract. Based on this and Alward's persuasion, the fire fighters would give up longevity for parity, and take full parity only in the third year of the retroactive contract.

Alward went to the floor of the fire station for a union meeting that evening and, "putting my reputation on the line," convinced the membership that his proposal was the most money they could hope for, even though the earlier award had provided for more. Reportedly, he told them: "I can sell this, but if you want more, I don't think we can get it. The town doesn't think you're doing a good job and they're angry about it."

Hearing about the meeting, one management observer said: "He really

did put his reputation on the line and went far out of his way to tell it like it
is to his own people."

The fire fighters had finally accepted the package as presented by Alward, with parity in the third year and no longevity. The older fire fighters,
led by Chandler, were upset by this. Nevertheless, both Alward and the
fire fighters assumed the package would be accepted by the management
team since the fire fighters felt that they had made a major concession in
giving up longevity pay.

Shortly, he presented a proposal to the management negotiating team.
Alward told them that he realized that the fire fighters were only considered "truck drivers; and everyone thought the call men did the real work."
Alward then told management what a professional fire department ought to
be and that the town deserved a professional department but that they had
an obligation to manage the department, that there was a mutual responsibility. By describing the consequences, he informed them that poorly
equipped and poorly trained fire fighters can ultimately cost the town more
than they would save on lower wages and poor equipment since the town
would end up paying injury or death benefits to fire fighters in addition to
the direct costs of manpower replacements, the indirect training costs, and
the lost property—and lives—that resulted from poor protection. Then he
presented to the town management team his new proposal, for which he
had used his personal influence and relationship to the fire fighters local to
obtain: a rock-bottom offer. Alward said he would help to improve the
department through training, advice, and other means.

Best later reported that this presentation "made a dent" in the perceptions of the management negotiating team. Harding said that she was "impressed. Initially, we just resented paying the money. Now there was a
perception that we might get a better fire service."

Selling

Over the next several weeks, a series of individual and group meetings took
place between the involved JLMC members and staff and the town
negotiating committee. The purpose of these meetings was to discuss Al-
wards proposed package. By now the JLMC had a number of its members
heavily involved in those discussions. Paul Barber, a JLMC management
member, and a selectman from Duxbury as well as vice-president of the
Massachusetts Selectmen's Association, spoke frequently with Susan Simmons, the Seabury selectwoman who was on their negotiating team. Barber
was well known among selectmen around the state. He was both likeable
and persuasive. Jay Gordon took an active role and spoke further with Ellen
Harding, the selectmen, and finance committee members; Dick Brown
talked frequently with Edward Best. Each pair discussed the impact of the
proposal in terms of their particular areas of expertise and responsibility.

Best and Brown had—despite their first phone call—by this time established a good working relationship. Similar relationships seemed to be building among the other counterparts. Harding recalled some conversations with Gordon:

> We spoke a lot on the phone. We talked a lot about finance committee business. There was a movement to establish regional associations and we talked about Seabury becoming involved in that. He was aware of the problems with binding arbitration. We had a good relationship, since he was very knowledgeable.
>
> We'd always have discussions about the Seabury situation towards the end of the conversation, but never terribly specific. Generally, Jay talked about the need to reach accommodation.

The JLMC felt that Alward's proposal was reasonable and that it could be palatable to the town officials as they learned more about alternatives and experiences elsewhere in the state that were even more costly. Further, if the ongoing head-on conflict with the union could be calmed, there might be less resentment. With Alward as a buffer and Bergen and Chandler out of the picture, perhaps some of the personality conflicts could be avoided.

After a series of peer discussions, the negotiating team and the management side members of the JLMC (Brown, Gordon, and Barber) and Bob Curley (the senior management staff representative) met together on March 27 at the Seabury Power Company. While the JLMC members hoped that the town's team would accept Alward's proposal, they basically sought to gauge how the town's negotiating committee was working, what the dynamics were, and what differences or concerns remained among them that might be overcome to reach settlement.

As the meeting began, Best sought to clarify the town's position. The town had some very bad experiences with the fire service and fire fighter negotiations. In fact, at least one of his predecessors had erroneously stated the cost of a contract. The magnitude of that error had led to a policy of thoroughly calculating the figures for every negotiation. The resistance by the selectmen and the Finance Committee to paying the fire fighters a parity wage was significant, he noted, given the history of the fire fighters and the town.

Dick Brown, anxious for a settlement, decided to press Best, who by now he had gotten to know: "Look, Ed, you're being inflexible and you're going to be unemployed in six months if you maintain that position. You're going to have to get agreement on this or you'll be torn apart." Ellen Harding, who felt that interactions with the JLMC had been productive, defended Best, in whom she and the others were gaining confidence by the day:

> You're unfair and don't understand our situation. I'm not going to sit by and let you go on like this. We have a long history of difficulty with the fire department and its taking some time to digest the information. Neither we nor our Selectmen or Finance Committee are going to be pushed into anything we don't understand

and don't know the exact costs of. Remember, they haven't heard Dusty and seen the possibilities for improvement. Besides, we have to consider our ability to successfully recommend any package to the town meeting.

Paul Barber of the JLMC intervened at this point:

> Well, let's calm down and look at the realities of the situation. You've won the court case. On a statewide level, you've won the war. It was an important ruling and will help town managements deal with the minimum manning issue on a statewide level. Don't give it all away now over a small battle, a small amount of money. Remember, you're going to have to bargain with them again next year. You can try to beat them badly now, but you'll take it from them next year. If you win big, expect to lose big. Don't kick them when they're down; be magnanimous, and use it in the future."

Others from the JLMC dealt with some of the specific objections that had been raised to the proposal, many of which had been advanced in the earlier, individual discussions by the other members of the Seabury team and had been incorporated into Best's opening remarks. Not wishing to leave major hostilities between the Seabury team and the JLMC members, Curley, who had the confidence of the Seabury team, then spoke, apologizing for any injustices done to Best, but maintaining the need for continued negotiations and movement.

It seemed clear to the JLMC that the town was moving towards resolution and that momentum should be kept up. After all, the union had finally established a position they would agree to and, with Dusty's assistance, were held there for the moment. Best said he would call the JLMC within three days to notify them of the town's decision on the Alward proposal. Jay Gordon apologized for Brown's remarks and sought to calm things down. The JLMC seemed to back off Brown's strong position.

Within a day after the meeting Best was convinced that Alward's package was probably as good a settlement as they could hope for. Best had been doing his homework. Based on contract settlements and arbitration awards in other towns in recent months he knew that Alward's proposal was reasonable and as good or better than they could expect in arbitration. "I knew we'd lose in arbitration." Rather than go through the hassle of more hearings and court battles, settlement at this point seemed prudent. Later, one of his negotiating team recalled: "I think he came reluctantly to that conclusion, but the fact that the fire fighters had held still for so long with a negotiating position convinced him to take it while he could."

Internal Consensus

During the next weekly case meeting of the Joint Labor-Management Committee Best's promised call came through saying that the negotiating team had not yet agreed on the package. Alward was very upset, and felt that he had been double-crossed. "That coward!" he stormed. "I staked my reputation on that package, used my prestige in the fire station and the men have already bought it!" Following the case meeting, Brown called Best.

Brown: What the hell are you doing? It's a settlement. Dump your team if they won't buy the package!

Best: I can't—I need them as a buffer for the town meeting and between me and the Board of Selectmen and the Finance Committee. We've just got to do more work with them. They're the elected representatives and they're as much a part of the process as I.

A second meeting between the JLMC and the town's negotiating team was arranged. On April 5 Barber, Brown, Gordon, and Curley again met with the management team at the Power Company. In an aside as the parties approached the conference room to commence bargaining, Best reiterated to Brown his personal approval of the proposal. Still, he thought, there was the rest of the negotiating team and the constituents on the Board of Selectmen and the Finance Committee—not to mention the town. While the Committee and the Board might be shown Best's research and comparative calculations, the historical and political considerations added a dimension, beyond analytic comparison, to their thinking. Best had walked into the middle of this; he had been there less than a year and still remembered the split vote that appointed him. Not only that, but since his appointment, the man who was runner-up for the job had been elected to the Board of Selectmen. How far out front could he get? Best was in the middle and there was a lot of pressure on him. He was "mad at the JLMC, mad at his committee, mad that Alward was mad, and mad that the situation wasn't resolved."

Brown recalled: "Ed needed to get the bargaining team fully on his side. He was gaining support daily. If things went a little further his way, he could probably sell them the Alward package and get past all that history. I took a risk by provoking them, hoping to get them to say 'Hey, wait, we support George; lay off.' If George then said 'I support the settlement proposal,' there was a better chance they'd be swayed by his judgment and we could end the dispute."

Brown, who apparently had a plan, murmured to Best on the way down the hall, "Watch this . . ." Showing his hope and his frustration. Best replied "Watch *this*!" They entered the meeting room and the door closed.

The JLMC began: "Really, we're not trying to force it on you and we're sorry if it seemed so last time. It really seems reasonable in light of what other towns are settling for and other arbitration. Given the probable outcome and alternatives we think it's not so bad. You're arguing over $8,000. Our chairman will have to resolve it if you can't settle it and whether you 'win' or 'lose' it will cost in legal fees and in future battles. Let's settle it in 10 days, get rid of the aggravation. Dusty has sold it to the fire fighters and its the first time they've stuck to a concrete proposal. Dusty can help in rebuilding the department and in finding and training a new chief." Brown lit into Best again, as he had in the last meeting. Best then began an angry attack on Brown and the JLMC, shouting, "Who the hell are you, and who needs you, cramming this deal down our throats? My negotiations team votes NO! And we won't settle!" He went on for another moment and then stormed out for a brief period. "I knew I had to leave at that point. I thought that sticking up for my team and telling the JLMC about our collective pet peeves with them would rally my troops and maybe do some good, but I didn't really know how it would turn out." During his absence, Harding and Hannen again defended Best.

Since the last meeting things had begun to move a bit for the town's team. As Harding put it, "We were inching along." The numbers had been calculated and further executive sessions held in the interim by Simmons and Harding with the Selectmen and Finance Committee. But for some details—and past history—they were nearly prepared, if reluctant, to agree.

Best rejoined the group shortly, offering coffee all around. "He was always leaving the room for coffee. Ed was the coffee maker," one said. When he returned someone suggested they take the Alward proposal seriously, he replied with a guarded "OK," not sure what had transpired, or where his team was. "Let's look at it. It seems to make sense." The proposal was discussed in detail. By 11:00 p.m., with all parties exhausted, there was relative consensus.

Settlement

The next day, Best called Alward, finally locating him after several calls, to tell him the package was sold. "I owed him that call. He had acted as a buffer and had indeed put himself on the line." A few nights later Best and his negotiating team briefed the Board of Selectmen and the Finance Committee on the proposed settlement and their reasons for recommending it. They concurred.

Over the next several days separate negotiations resolved the police contract and provided a concrete basis for settling the last year of the retroactive fire fighters' contract and a basis for the prospective portion of the contract, since parity was part of the fire fighters settlement.

Three weeks later the second and prospective contract was agreed upon by the parties and on May 12 the contract was signed. At a town meeting later in May, the cost items were funded upon the recommendations of the Finance Committee, the Board of Selectmen, and the Town Manager, thereby making the two contracts effective.

*   *   *

Epilogue

Best, the town manager:

> "I think relations have improved with the fire fighters. At least we have an understanding of their problems."

Harding, the Finance Committee member:

> "I still have a lingering feeling that the JLMC twisted our arms a bit too hard. But without them I guess we'd still be negotiating. And the fire service is much improved."

Bud Chandler, the defeated local president:

> "I may be retiring, but I'll stick around to stir things up a bit. You need something to force good, honest negotiations. If you've got a legitimate request, you should get a legitimate reason before it's turned down."

Dave Stevens, the new local president:

> "The problem's not solved, just ended. Morale is low because there seems little hope for change. Keeping tax dollars down is more important than wisely spending tax dollars."

March 23, 1979: The JLMC received from the Seabury fire fighters requesting intervention in their contract negotiations. When the letter was mentioned during the weekly case meeting, John T. Dunlop, the chairman, looked up in surprise and said, "What? I thought we straightened that out already!" Realizing that the second of the two contracts the committee had "straightened out" a year ago was soon to expire, since its first year was in essence retroactive, he shook his head at the apparent continuation of contention.

April 9, 1979: The request for intervention was canceled; the parties had reached agreement on their own.

Chapter 6

CASE ANALYSIS: APPLICATION
OF JOINT COMMITTEE TOOLS

The cases in the two preceding chapters provide examples of the Joint Labor-Management Committee at work in resolving disputes. Each case emphasized different sets of tools employed by the Committee. Some of the tools are the traditional tools of mediation and arbitration, while others seem to have developed more directly from the membership structure, statutory powers, and philosophy of the Committee. This chapter will describe and examine the tools used by the Committee in seeking to resolve these two disputes.

The Barkfield case illustrates mediation and related techniques in a relatively typical dispute: one within a community unschooled in labor relations and with a weak and impractical labor relations structure. The Seabury situation is characteristic of a more complex dispute, one that required more creativity, flexibility, and sophistication on the part of the neutral agency—the Committee—than typically may be available; therefore, more original methods were used. Both cases were handled by the JLMC early in its existence, while its mandate and methods of operation were still developing. These cases remain illustrative of the Committee's case handling, even though the Committee's techniques, judgment, and authority have matured since then.

Many of the mediation techniques used in Barkfield and Seabury are not unique to the JLMC, for such dispute-settling agencies as the New York City Board of Collective Bargaining have some similar features.[1] Although varieties of many of the tools used by the JLMC—joint mediation, for example—are found in other forms of dispute resolution, such tools nevertheless are discussed here because of their place in the context and overall functioning of the Joint Labor-Management Committee. The JLMC, because of its structure and operation, appears to gain unusual entrée into disputes. It seems able to combine and alter common varieties of mediation and has some expanded capacity to focus dispute settlement on longer-term concerns in the bargaining relationship or service delivery.

The discussion is intended to describe a committee mechanism's capacity to approach some of the practical problems inherent in public sector collective bargaining and dispute resolution, to identify those tools and procedures of particular value, and to suggest some ways that the JLMC might have better allocated its efforts and resources in pursuit of its objectives. Part of the discussion will examine aspects of committee structure that make such tools available and affect their use. Essentially, this chapter describes the categories of tools available to a joint committee as an agent for dispute resolution.

Early, Informal Involvement

The Peer Network and Credibility

Although not called for specifically in the statute, the Committee's membership includes a wide and well-connected range of labor and management officials. In both the Barkfield and Seabury cases, the information network afforded by the membership alerted the Committee to possible problems and opportunities for settlement. As a result, the Committee was able to offer mediative and other assistance early enough to prevent hardened impasses and to take steps to improve the bargaining relationship.

The Committee became involved officially in Barkfield at the request of the police local. Originally, however, it had learned of the case from a management member familiar with that part of the state, who informed the senior management staff representative and an alternate Committee labor member of the problems. At about the same time the president of the Barkfield Police Alliance sought assistance from the same alternate Committee member, whose role he had heard about informally through officers in other towns.

The joint membership of the Committee, and the related fact that it came to the attention of at least one of the Barkfield parties through informal channels, aided mediators in winning the trust of the parties—an important prerequisite to successful mediation. The police had heard about the group, and their union president asked to meet informally with the alternate member, who was a policeman. Later, the management representative was introduced by the alternate member to the police as a close colleague. Early involvement and trust in the joint neutral had been established through informal peer relationships, and the police asked the Committee to become involved. The management side's acquiescence was gained only by a peer selectman vouching for the JLMC's and the staff's good intentions. Formal jurisdiction could have been exercised, but the probability of the parties trust and cooperation might have been much lower.

In the Seabury case, the Professional Fire Fighters of Massachusetts knew well of the ongoing problems existing in the town and was able to provide information to the Committee that convinced its members to get involved before the parties reached a serious impasse in the new round of negotiations. As in Barkfield, the JLMC sought to become informally involved, hoping for the cooperation of the parties in the mediation efforts. On the labor side, the Fire Fighters' hierarchy and Alward's influence therein made it relatively easy to gain the local's permission for the Committee to come observe. On the management side, however, it was not so direct.

The Committee, owing to its information network and its peer connections and perspective, was able to gain access to the problems in Barkfield and Seabury at earlier stages than they might have otherwise. Through early involvement, the Committee, as a neutral, could better provide perspective to the parties. Also, it could help the parties continue to seek solutions during frustrating periods when inexperienced bargainers might have been inclined to throw up their hands in anger and simply declare an impasse. With credible and expert help persuading the parties to continue the process, breakdowns in bargaining could be circumvented. The Barkfield and Seabury cases exemplify the value of early involvement of the neutral, as well as the ability to use the Committee structure and flexibility to gain access and confidence of the parties at those early stages.

Observation

At the same time it seeks early involvement in problem disputes, the JLMC tries to limit involvement to the minimum necessary to aid the effort toward settlement. This principle was particularly well illustrated in the Seabury case. The Committee first sent a single representative who did little but observe. Only later, when a greater degree of intervention seemed necessary, did the observers begin to sit in on caucuses of the two parties, where at first they only observed, and later provided advice. The opportunity to observe a dispute early on is useful in that some data can be acquired—insight into the character of the parties or of the dispute and its issues—that will aid in making proper judgments about further involvement. The capacity to gain access through the peer network obviated formal jurisdiction and increased the odds of cooperative relationships between the neutral (both staff and members) and the parties.

Savings in Time and Legal Costs

The Committee's early entry into disputes with the parties' acquiescence or at their request is frequently eased by its offer of inexpensive, high-quality assistance. As some of the Barkfield selectmen later noted, saving money by using the Committee rather than hiring attorneys to represent them in negotiation or arbitration was attractive initially and proved to be so in the end. Since the dispute did not go through the legalistic LBO arbitration proceeding and a new contract was signed within six months of the expiration date of the old contract, costs for arbitrators and attorneys were minimal. (There is no arbitration cost to the parties when the JLMC itself arbitrates.) In contrast, in one case handled by the Committee, the union reported that when it had previously gone to arbitration under the LBO system, its counsel had prepared 139 exhibits, largely statistical, for presentation to the arbitration panel. Further, a year and a half was not an unlikely waiting period under last-best-offer binding arbitration proceedings. While it could be argued that the wage increase and scheduling changes included in the Barkfield award might have made up for the attorneys' fees that were avoided by the town, it is not at all clear that a last-best-offer settlement would have been much different or cheaper for the municipality, especially if we assume the last-best-offer of the police—considered by everyone to be underpaid—as the one more likely to have been chosen.

In the Seabury case the issue of saving on settlement costs was a bit more obvious. The union local already owed some $15,000 in fees to their attorneys and after four years still did not have a contract; the state-level Professional Fire Fighters organization was expecting to pay $30,000 for the legal appeals that were already underway. While no figures on the town's projected legal expenses are available, it would not be unreasonable to assume that parallel costs for the appeals had been and would be incurred. As both cases suggest, the savings on attorneys' fees for a small town and small union are likely to be on the minds of the parties early in the negotiating process. (Both cases involved towns of 10,000 population and locals with fewer than a score of members.) The less formal and quicker procedures of the Committee, therefore, presented attractive possibilities for dollar savings to the parties. With respect to time, the Seabury case had dragged on for years, with the prospect for further lengthy appeals to come. The Committee's processes, unusual and complex as they were in this case, resolved the matter over a four-month period at minimal legal or other costs to the parties.

In some cases, one could argue, an attorney's financial interests may be served by the continuation of conflict and poor bargaining relationships, whereas rapid settlement would eliminate many legal fees. Observers of the Seabury case pointed out what they perceived to be the union attorney's repeated alteration of the bargaining parameters—actions that were lengthening the process—and recall what appeared to be his lack of interest in the mediation proposed by the Committee staff. He was ultimately eased out of the process. On the management side, to be sure, the new city manager initially rejected the JLMC's offer of involvement, even though he had a clear personal and professional interest in settlement. Still, the process evolved to where the town's attorney was not directly involved in the final stages of negotiation and settlement, although he continued to play an advisory role in subsequent negotiations.

In these two cases, the Committee's track record for rapid settlement had not yet been established, and the resultant potential for cost savings may not have been a major attraction. However, the cost of attorney's fees and the desire to avoid the uncertain outcome and costs of LBO and litigation certainly were considerations, and as such, encouraged acceptance of Committee services, particularly in Barkfield.

Joint Mediation

The Trust Factor and Substantive Knowledge

In most instances a single mediator deals with disputing parties both in their separate caucuses and when they are facing each other across the table. A mediator may talk separately with each side about settlement options—proposals that the mediator keeps in confidence until or unless there is potential for agreement. In such a situation, the mediator will encourage each side to make its position known or will make a proposal, based on the confidential information he or she has acquired from separate talks with each side, that would seem likely to be acceptable to both sides.[2]

In Barkfield, joint mediation was used to achieve better results along this dimension than those that might have been obtained if one mediator had met separately with the sides. In this case, joint mediation permitted a depth of understanding for the mediator and a somewhat more rapid movement through the issues in early stages of mediation than could have been expected using a single, neutral mediator. The more rapid movement came from three factors inherent in the joint mediation process: (1) the trust more immediately established with each of the mediators, (2) the substantive understanding that can quickly be utilized, and (3) the ability to deal with both sides simultaneously.

The two mediators, working separately and each sympathetic to and familiar with his respective side's interest, obtained a more candid view of issues and positions than might a single, neutral mediator. Joint mediation allowed the mediating team to learn and to understand more readily the true positions of the parties, which is especially difficult to do in situations rampant with distrust and inexperience. Only after a series of separate meetings with each side were the two mediators able to identify the issues between the parties. The time necessary for a single mediator to gain the trust of both sides and make similar progress toward resolution might have been longer, given the degree of mutual distrust and the disarray that prevailed in Barkfield. Since the parties in Barkfield were both distrustful of outsiders, they might not have easily permitted such intensive mediation by a single neutral. Similarly, the management staff member's knowledge of police work was not nearly as substantive as was his labor counterpart's, and his ability to be effective on those issues—especially where the parties were inexpert, was greatly strengthened by the use of joint mediation.

Frequently, the JLMC will send a single staff member to observe or mediate. In Seabury, informal joint mediation efforts began precisely because the management attorney was uncomfortable with the presence of the sole Committee "observer" initially involved in the dispute. In fact, it was this necessity that first raised the possibility of joint mediation teams in the JLMC context. The Committee's structure allowed it to respond quickly to that problem by assigning an additional staff member who was trusted by management. The JLMC's response to Seabury management's distrust of the first Committee observer suggests also the improved bargaining environment possible when each side feels properly understood and represented. The addition of an experienced, credible, and helpful senior management staff representative to complement the labor representative provided a team that was seen as neutral, and the mediators were allowed to sit in on the respective caucuses of each side. In this way, information useful to mediation was gained, and the parties were assisted and educated in the process.

In Seabury, the management negotiating team found especially useful the sort of general advice it received from the management staff representative on the mediation team. His insight and perspective, gained from experience, was valuable to the less experienced members of the town's negotiating committee. While management in Barkfield was less pleased than its Seabury counterpart with the outcome of the dispute, their subsequent comments nevertheless indicated that they had also received useful advice from their representative on the Committee staff.

The extensive involvement of Committee members in the Seabury case was brought about, at least in part, by the joint mediators, who from their closeness in position to each party could perceive the sorts of actions that Committee members might profitably take with their peers.

Joint and Representative Membership

Joint or team mediation requires that both mediators be acceptable to both sides. As the Barkfield case illustrates, the fact that the Committee is composed of an array of both labor and management people is an aid to gaining and retaining acceptability for the collective neutral. Parties to a dispute may more easily trust or submit to the judgment of mediators or arbitrators knowledgeable about the facts and history of the situation at hand and the substance of similar situations. The presence of knowledgeable staff on each side of the dispute also cuts time from the process that otherwise would have been spent educating a mediator or arbitrator unfamiliar with the local situation, unfamiliar with the substance and details of police or fire fighting work, and, perhaps, unfamiliar with the particular form or politics of local government. This joint expertise can permit fruitful mediation to begin very quickly, without spending an undue amount of time establishing the bona fides of the neutral. In addition, a more acceptable and practical result is likely.

Joint representative mediation, as used by the JLMC, allows the mediators to perform the usual mediative functions and also permits them to be advisers to each side. The substantive knowledge and the trust that prevail between people with similar backgrounds permit this advisory function, which strengthens inexperienced parties. Interestingly, in both the Seabury and Barkfield cases, neither mediator became a champion of actions favorable to one side. Personal trust and a respectful professional relationship between the joint mediators themselves are critical ingredients in providing a neutral process to the parties.

Peer Interaction

Persuasion and Perspective

Using methods that promote interpersonal dynamics similar to those operating through joint mediation, the committee mechanism permits another level and type of interaction: Peers of those involved in the dispute can assist or coax their counterparts as the situation requires. Barkfield accepted Committee assistance—in particular, the management and labor staff mediators—only after a selectman Committee member vouched for the two. On the management side, the board had more difficulty in accepting the neutral, but the Committee's membership was clearly instrumental in helping them to do so. The selectman member of the Committee, as someone known to the board and with interests like theirs, encouraged the suspicious Barkfield selectmen to accept the Committee's involvement, the involvement of the management staff representative, and—somewhat surprisingly—the involvement of the alternate Committee member, who represented labor.

The Committee's substantive knowledge and ability to understand the perspective of peer colleagues in the dispute were tools extensively used to resolve the dispute in Seabury. In the Seabury case, Dick Brown's entry as a Committee member illustrates how a member's stature in his or her professional and political affiliations can be important in settling a dispute. In Seabury, several organizational, political, and personality factors had created an intractable and unresolved situation that had persisted for three years. This long history of contention had left the bargaining relationship in disrepair, and nonstop litigation had been the major focus of the bargaining relationship. At the beginning of this period, a settlement agreed to by the negotiators had been rejected at the town meeting. To change this situation, the Committee relied heavily on its members to deal with their counterparts in Seabury.

To begin that process (after initial rejection), a management Committee member called his fellow town manager in Seabury to offer assistance. He described the situation and its consequences in terms a town manager could understand and relate to, given the nature of the impasse and its relationship to the town manager's job tenure. And he pointed out that it would cost the town nothing for the Committee's assistance.

After the senior management and labor staff representatives had brought the case as far as they could, they reported to the full Committee not only the status of the case but their assessment of the possibilities for settlement. The Committee then decided to use its members' informal influence to encourage a settlement by having members deal directly with their counterparts in the dispute. In that phase of the case, a former finance committee chairman and president of the statewide association in that field—a member of the JLMC—was asked to deal with the finance committee representative on the Seabury management negotiating committee, and talked often with her about cost effectiveness of fire fighting and related matters in her area of concern. Similarly, the selectman member of the JLMC worked with the selectwoman on the negotiating committee. In each instance, Committee members sought to deal with and promote with their Seabury counterparts a full understanding of the labor relations aspects of their mutual areas of expertise and responsibility.

Another Committee member, Dusty Alward, who was the president of the statewide fire fighters' union, became very active on the labor side. His interactions with the local union officials helped to alter their demands by placing those demands in a wider and more realistic context. These efforts resulted in a less expensive union proposal—one the town could swallow—with an added offer that the fire fighters would stop their court appeal should management accept the proposal. As the town negotiators came to believe, it also provided an opportunity to improve fire service and morale. Without JLMC involvement, the dispute might have been settled acrimoniously, with the management side seeking to be punitive rather than constructive regarding changes in the fire service.

To facilitate a settlement acceptable to both sides, the JLMC made an unusual move to push beyond the labor-management communication block: The Committee used its good offices to arrange an audience in which Alward, the fire fighter representative, could discuss with the management negotiating team the need for a professional fire department and present the proposed settlement package. This unusual peer interaction involving both sides made a critical difference in the position of the Seabury negotiating team. Both executive and legislative branch members in Seabury reported later that they began at that point to see management's responsibilities for improving the fire service, a perception that altered their view of the desirability of the proposed settlement. The union side JLMC representative achieved large changes in the union position, changes unlikely to have been accomplished had he not been clearly perceived as a representative of their interests. Such a peer relationship is not as likely or, perhaps, possible in situations in which a single neutral mediator or arbitrator is used.

In the end, both sides had significantly changed their initial positions as a result of the information and perspective provided by their peers and had accepted a settlement package that was a positive beginning toward an improved bargaining relationship and better fire service. Thus, the key Committee activity in the Seabury case was peer interaction and assistance. This process, over a period of time, successfully broke down rigid positions and perspectives—developed over years of bitterness—that no longer reflected the current needs of the community or those of the union. Informal peer interaction made progress toward voluntary settlement in a situation where more formal means might have hardened positions and led to an imposed third-party settlement.

The Role of Personalities

Peer interaction as a tool permits direct attention to the personal and institutional roles of those in a dispute. This capability can both assist in resolving a particular dispute and contribute to the longer-term improvement of the bargaining relationship, as personal and institutional relationships are improved.

A personality conflict, even if it has little to do with the issues at hand, can be damaging to the bargaining relationship or to resolution of specific issues, and thus impede settlement. On the other hand, personalities can often play an important role in the resolution of a dispute. In Barkfield, the contentious relationship between the chief of police and the board of selectmen appears to have affected the bargaining relationship between labor and management. The chief used his seniority and experience in town government and his not inconsiderable political skills to keep the board "buffaloed," as one observer remarked. In response, at least a few of the board members sought periodically to antagonize the chief, by overruling him on a personnel selection, by refusing to fund overtime, or by demanding special shifts from him.

The board's posture on overtime and other issues—partly a reflection of their poor relationship with the chief—specifically contributed to administrative and policy decisions by the chief in response to overtime and other issues that affected the officers. His challenging and inflammatory letters, written during the negotiations process, hardened the positions of both sides and made negotiations more difficult; board actions that were intended to show the board's power over the chief thereby affected the officers by their effect on working conditions. The impact these actions had on working conditions and earnings affected both the bargaining relationship and the specific demands made by the officers. The schedule demand, for example, which was resisted as expensive by the town, was an outgrowth of the previous harsh schedule and lack of overtime opportunities.

To achieve resolution of the dispute, the Committee might have paid more attention to this board-chief relationship, and the mediators might have been more active in this aspect of the problem. To be sure, the issue of schedule was mentioned to the board, but it was never pursued. The JLMC's representative membership provided an opportunity for peers to intercede informally and to focus attention on this problem or on the relationship contributing to

the difficulty. The Committee structure certainly provides a mechanism for dealing with internal personality problems, but the tool was
not well applied in the Barkfield case.

The Seabury case is an example of the better use of the Committee's ability to assess and act on personality factors. In that case, the
JLMC was able to work toward agreement by appealing to the
town's negotiating team; it focused individuals' attention on substantive issues and on the history of the dispute as they related to the
negotiators' respective professional interests. When Alward came to
a management meeting to talk about fire fighting and to present a
settlement proposal, his presentation was free of the sort of tense
personal relations that existed between the local union president and
the management team. The subsequent defeat of the union president removed the personality difficulties that were partly responsible for impeding settlement. Also, the influence of Committee
members and staff on specific actors in the process helped to bring
about removal of the union's attorney who, some observers believed, had been obstructing progress.

In recognition of interpersonal dynamics, we might refer to the
relationship between Ed Best, the Seabury town manager, and his
negotiating team and the apparent public altercations between
Brown, the JLMC town manager representative, and Ed Best. In
the wake of those actions and the reactions to it, substantive gains
toward settlement were made. While it's difficult to dissect the
specific effects of that interaction, it seemed to help move the town
negotiating team toward agreement. These incidents gave the
manager—who had been in office only a short time—an opportunity
to demonstrate his solidarity with the town, yet left open the possibility for movement, perhaps by enhancing his credibility. Also, if
Committee peers had not talked with the other members of the
negotiating team during negotiations, the town manager might have
been forced to maintain a somewhat more rigid line to avoid a public
position at odds with his employers' views. The Committee peers
helped to move the Seabury team in the direction that the town
manager had gone as a result of his own review of the facts—
movement he could not as easily engineer as a new manager in a
town with a history of resistance to fire fighter demands.

Credibility of Committee Peers

Joint mediation and peer interaction are made possible by the skills
and stature of the individuals who make up the staff and member-

ship and by the internal dynamics of a committee structure. Through the good peer relationships that had been built between the JLMC people and the Seabury town officials, the Committee peers sought a solution based on senior fire fighter member Alward's substantive settlement proposal. That management Committee members who had worked on the dispute had become convinced of Alward's plan illustrates the understanding and trust between labor and management representatives that had built up within the Committee. In that sense it was more than just Alward's proposal. This relationship was an example of the communication possible between labor and management in the municipality. The JLMC management members' obvious acceptance of Alward's proposal lent the proposal credibility, which helped the Seabury management team to maintain an open mind toward it.

Flexibility in Venue and Actors

As the two cases illustrate, the flexibility in the JLMC's statute and its membership and staff structure permit a wide selection of tools to fit the needs of each dispute, as the dispute changes, and as more is learned about it. This flexibility translates into options pertaining to (1) timing, (2) format, (3) place, (4) choice of Committee or staff person to become involved, and (5) degree of involvement. Obviously, a wide range of combinations and opportunities exist from which to adapt a committee approach to specific needs and opportunities.

Timing and Format

Barkfield is a good example of a situation where an increasing degree of formal intervention took place (as shown in Figure 3–1). A variety of Committee tools were used, ranging from informal staff contact with participants to an arbitration hearing. In its early stages, Seabury provides a good example of a case that moved along a continuum through a few stages of informal involvement—including observation and joint mediation—to a stage in which much different and unusual committee tools seemed better to fit its needs. These activities, or tools, included active development and explanation of a settlement proposal.

Place and People

A preliminary hearing was held in the Barkfield case after the staff mediators felt that their on-site mediation efforts could move the parties no further. Initially, the hearing was intended to provide a change in the bargaining forum; a hearing would formalize the procedure and give an impression that the case was coming to closure. Moreover, it introduced a new neutral into the process. In this different forum, the new actor had the advantage of the continuity of information and insight gained by the JLMC's staff involvement at the early stages and its continued presence during the hearing period.

The ability of the JLMC staff to brief senior members, the arbitration panel, or the single arbitrator accurately is a tool whose use obviates the need for the parties to laboriously posture for or otherwise educate the neutral. This may allow the JLMC to settle a dispute more rapidly, to the greater satisfaction of both sides, and in a manner that may contribute better to labor peace.

As was done in Barkfield, the staff mediators who have been involved in a case can brief the arbitration panel on the history of the case, on movement that has taken place, and on the true positions of the parties, matters of personality, and other stumbling blocks. The Barkfield case demonstrates, however, that this method of information exchange is only as useful as the relationships that are formed and the information gained by the staff. In Barkfield the utility of the staff-to-arbitrator briefings was limited by the staff's somewhat restricted awareness of the variety of personal needs and perspectives on the management side. The importance of the staff in this process of educating the arbitrators illustrates very well the value of both an information exchange and a working relationship between and among Committee staff and members and each party to the dispute.

In Seabury, Committee actors were added to the process as the need arose. For example, the first contact by the senior management member of the JLMC was rebuffed by Best, the Seabury town manager. A second JLMC member, who knew Best and held a similar job, telephoned him and was better able to "psych out" Best's needs and the way to approach him. Later, when the original Committee (labor staff) observer had some difficulty being accepted by the management side, a second observer, representing management, was added; Committee members were later brought in to contact other officials in a combination tailored to the composition of the Seabury negotiating team and to the circumstances of the fire local.

Degree

The introduction of new, and usually more senior, actors generally operates to increase pressure on the parties to settle. Introducing a new person with greater stature may prod along or even accelerate negotiations. The presence of a senior appointed Committee member (as opposed to a staff person) or a respected senior neutral lends added credibility to the process and thereby may affect its outcome, for the advice and suggestions of Committee members to peers carry added weight. A change in actors, as the involvement of Alward in Seabury suggests, allows the introduction of a totally different approach. The use of Committee members can be especially valuable in making progress toward resolution if obstacles to a solution are political or otherwise require the experience, contacts, or influence of a peer.

Hearings and Arbitration: Peer Bargaining

A form of joint mediation frequently takes place at formal hearings. When the Committee chair or vice-chair presides and the parties cannot come to agreement, Committee members frequently represent their respective sides in bargaining. Although not used very effectively in Barkfield, the Committee sought to use this peer bargaining technique as the basic tool at the formal hearing. Ordinarily, a hearing with the introduction of a new set of joint mediators (Committee level instead of staff member) and a neutral would represent a change of venue intended to move the parties forward.

This more formal forum is not intended as an end in itself, but primarily as a tool to promote yet another opportunity for problem solving by introducing a change in incentives, actors, abilities, and perceptions. In these hearings, Committee members on the arbitration panel expect to be able to exert some influence on their counterparts to renew negotiations after an apparent impasse. This renewal could take place at the hearing itself, and agreement, or agreement on procedures to pursue resolution, could be reached then and there.

The introduction of a person with the power to arbitrate seems, in other cases, to have altered the attitude of one or both parties toward bargaining or to have altered positions on some issues. And while the hearing stage in the Barkfield case succeeded in signaling to the parties that the situation would soon be resolved (as evidenced by their bringing formal letters stating their "final" positions), it did not serve, as intended, as another forum for bargaining since no "peers" showed up from the town. The selectmen were not represented at the hearing and thus could not react to the situation; nor could the neutral try any new approaches or ideas for resolution in their absence.

An additional consequence of a poor showing by Barkfield representatives was that the JLMC peers heard more persuasive arguments and got more information from the police. The problem is partially attributable to the selectmen's lack of knowledge about the Committee's procedures, information that is the Committee's responsibility to communicate. The Committee may also be faulted because it did not ensure implementation of its philosophy of active and equal participation of both parties in the process. Ordinarily, the discussion between the Committee peer and the management bargainers would aid the peer in impressing management's point of view on the labor peer on the panel. The selectmen's letter stating the management position—brought to the hearing by the Barkfield administrative assistant—did not exert the sort of constituent pressure on their Committee peer-advocate to negotiate constructively with his labor counterpart. In fact, the letter virtually created an impasse of its own: It declared a final position, leaving no leeway for the selectmen to amend their position as new information or new proposals came forth. This inability to make progress was precisely what the hearing procedure was intended to prevent. In the process, the acceptability of the arbitration award was also weakened by this shortcoming.

Maintaining Contact with the Parties

Key to Settlement Acceptability

A big problem in the last-best-offer arbitration process was the possibility that the award would be unacceptable to one of the parties. In general, the JLMC intended to increase the number of acceptable settlements by assisting the parties to settle through collective bargaining. The Seabury settlement was agreed on without a hearing or other formality and was acceptable to the parties after a process of peer interactions, explanations, and reflection. In Barkfield, the features of the ultimate award had been discussed among Committee staff and between the parties during the joint mediation process, although the management side was in less direct and intimate contact with the JLMC staff than was the union side.

In preparing the Barkfield award, the Committee staff kept in touch with the parties to ensure that the language of the proposed contract would not violate local practices and traditions or interfere with operations. However, more discussion occurred with the police side than with the management side, partly because the Committee staff had formed a better relationship with the police. On the management side, there were a larger number of factions, and the relationship between the Committee and the management group was not well developed.

Structural Difficulties

There were five management decisionmakers from Barkfield—all selectmen—none of whom could spend the necessary time on the case and none of whom was a spokesperson who could be the primary contact for the mediating agency. The selectmen's administrative assistant—the person with whom the Committee staff had the most contact—was constructive, responsive, and technically represented management's interests, but he did not have decision-making authority. Although there was sufficient communication with the assistant himself, his duties and institutional relationship to his principals was not such that regular contact with him would keep the selectmen well enough informed and persuaded. The structure of the town government and the interpersonal relationships among the selectmen and between them and their administrative assistant simply wouldn't lead to proper communication between the selectmen and the Committee. Were the assistant a town manager who was looked to institutionally by the selectmen for advice on such matters, the situation might have been different.

Ensuring Channels for Communications

Committee operations and procedures would have allowed a second level of contact to be attempted at Barkfield once it became clear that the staff was unable to develop sufficiently productive communication with the management side. The next level of Committee actors, with different and probably more influential local backgrounds and peer status, could have entered the picture. Committee members were not encouraged to take an active, informal role in the case or to use their own management knowledge or contacts at the later stages. The tools of change of venue were not effectively used to maximize Committee involvement and to ensure that the award was relatively predictable and acceptable.

When the Barkfield management did not show up at the hearings and mediation at the Committee level could not therefore take place, another opportunity to make the award more acceptable was missed. The information that came to light in the hearings and the direction of the discussion were not directly transmitted to management, and both parties therefore were not thoroughly and equally involved in the solution.

Since Committee principals did not have contact with the principals from the town during the course of negotiations—or even in the hearing process—they could not easily draw on any personal relationship or informal channel of communication. Committee principals missed the opportunity to get a better understanding of management's perspective and to give town principals a realistic set of expectations regarding the process or the outcome. When the award was finally negotiated between the Committee principals and approved by the neutral chairman, the Committee was ethically restricted from discussing with either party any matters concerned with the outcome, except for such technical matters as contract language. Thus, some of the selectmen seemed surprised by several features of the award.

Obviously, conscientious communications between a committee and both parties is necessary to take full advantage of a committee's ability to adapt its procedures to specific local conditions. But the need for a high degree of interaction also presents a potential limitation as a result of the JLMC's structure. The large case load and the volunteer, part-time nature of member participation may limit adequate, constructive, and proper communication between the parties and their Committee representatives. This problem must be counteracted by the presence of qualified, permanent staff, able to restrict member involvement to a minimum in specific cases yet able also to identify those situations in which member assistance will improve the outcome of a dispute.

Notwithstanding the clear indications that Committee contact with the Barkfield management side was less productive than with the labor side, it is unlikely that the features of the award would have changed dramatically. Had the Committee been more attuned to and aware of the amount of management feeling on certain issues, some alterations might have been made that would have satisfied the political difficulties of certain selectmen—for example, a more politically acceptable starting date for the new shift schedule. What might have changed significantly, however, were the perceptions of management regarding the acceptability and fairness of the award. Direct communication during the hearing stage might have given the selectmen more influence on the arbitration decision and would have made them more aware of the reasons for its outcome. Nonetheless, a committee cannot entirely make up for limitations of one of the parties although it has several tools with which to try.

Bargaining Experience and Relationship Building

A second set of reasons for maintaining the parties' involvement is to provide experience in bargaining and to open and establish channels of communication between the parties. Inexperience—or negative experience—has frequently left those channels closed. Thus, even if the JLMC chooses ultimately to arbitrate, it will generally seek to have first narrowed the differences as much as possible. This policy encourages both sides to "practice" their bargaining skills, beginning whenever possible with the least contentious of the issues under dispute. At a minimum, the Committee approach is to obtain agreement from both sides on the manner in which the dispute is to be settled.

Narrowing the Differences

The Committee's policy of narrowing the number and range of issues is part of its effort to improve the outcome of collective bargaining by improving bargaining relationships. The Committee continually encourages direct bargaining to establish the notion that negotiation of the major dispute is possible. The Seabury case is an example of good use of this function. In Barkfield, the fact that participants were able to settle most of the small issues through negotiation led to some improved capacity to settle their own differences. In the latter case, the staff mediators (approved by the Committee) performed as much mediation as they thought possible and sought agreement on as many issues as they could through fairly conventional means. The mediators introduced a list of issues and divided it between "agreed-on-matters" and "matters still in dispute." Keeping a list in view of the parties, the mediators kept the parties focused on the issues and began to control the negotiations so that differences could be narrowed. (An example of such a list is reproduced in Exhibit V of the Barkfield case.)

When both parties were present and a "neutral" was in control of the bargaining, writing everything down in black and white, both sides were kept honest and a certain discipline was enforced. In this way, the neutrals educated the parties in good-faith principles by holding them to interim agreements made, for good-faith bargaining is facilitated by living up to intermediate agreements. In the previous, less structured negotiating atmosphere in Barkfield, the parties often changed their minds or introduced new facts or conditions, a practice that did little to establish the necessary trust for bargaining. Although the management side indeed later voiced its displeasure with the outcome, their acceptance of and participation in the process led them to sign, ratify, and live with a settlement agreement, most of whose features had been discussed at great length and were actually agreed to at some point. Some spokesmen on the management side felt, partly as a result of their recent experience, they could handle negotiations the next time.

Separating resolved from open issues concentrated bargaining attention on the issues yet to be resolved. As the "resolved" list gets longer and the "open" list shorter, a sense of progress is provided; and as agreements can be counted and identified, the lists then encourage a sense of momentum. While not novel to mediation, this important technique was used by the Committee to structure the process and maintain a role in identifying and resolving the issues in dispute.

Sensitivity to Sovereignty

Maximizing Local Participation

One of the reasons that the Joint Labor-Management Committee was established was management's objection to union or third-party determination of spending or distribution of a community's resources. As an illustration of the Committee's institutional view, when it decided to become more formally involved in Barkfield, it began by sanctioning the informal mediation efforts already started—a symbolic gesture of interest and potential authority—rather than bringing the matter immediately to an arbitrator and thus removing the decision from the parties. The Committee did not take any formal steps at that early stage. Their efforts were fruitful, according to the parties, in that many issues were eliminated or settled, and in the process bargaining actually took place between them. Although ultimately the specifics of the large-money items—wages and scheduling—were decided by the Committee in arbitration, they were decided with a municipal and a police representative on the arbitration panel and within parameters that had been nearly agreed to by the parties before personality conflicts and mistrust blew up the near-agreement. The Committee, which perceived that increased local control over the outcome was desirable, attempted to maximize local participation in narrowing the issues and devising the settlement.

In connection with sovereignty, an interesting aspect of the Barkfield arbitration was that it did not seek to settle all the issues. This choice was a deliberate Committee tactic to adapt its actions to the political and institutional undertones of the dispute. The award acknowledged local sovereignty by making the issue of police duty on the ambulance service subject to what was called a "prescribed procedure." The parties were instructed to work out the details of a settlement by a certain date, but to work it out themselves.

The police chief had argued that the Committee could not settle the ambulance question because it involved the job description and was therefore subject to the exercise of a management prerogative. Nevertheless, it was important from a collective bargaining standpoint to settle the ambulance issue if the bargaining relationship was to stabilize or improve. The ambulance question also related to overtime (for EMT training) and to the pay issue, issues over which the police had threatened to cease ambulance duties. Recognizing this, the Committee sought to achieve resolution but did not itself become embroiled in the management rights issue, not did it seek to make the resource decision for the town. Rather, it tried to lay some groundwork by setting up a process and forum for constructive communication for dealing specifically with the ambulance problem apart from the many other issues. The parties themselves eventually worked out a solution in their joint interest, without the further intervention of a third party. However, the failure more thoroughly to involve the management side in the process that determined other aspects of the award somewhat weakened the sensitivity to sovereignty that might have prevailed in this case.

The Public Interest

In addition to the management rights issue, an overriding question of political philosophy was involved: As a matter of policy, the Committee eschews judgments regarding levels of public service—decisions that should be reserved to the community as its sovereign right. Yet while the Committee wished to avoid making political judgments, it did wish to encourage communication on all subjects affecting the collective bargaining relationship—not just aspects directly relevant to a settlement award, as might be true in a more usual arbitration.

This sensitive form of participation is both a strength and a danger in Committee activities: Unlike conventional arbitration proceedings, the Committee encourages discussion between the parties of issues that affect the bargaining relationship but which otherwise are issues of local "sovereignty" or "politics." Its membership and statute permit this sort of activity. The Committee's help in creating procedures for addressing the ambulance issue in Barkfield demonstrated its ability not only to avoid taking a political or public position on certain issues but also to assist in resolution of substantive problems outside the normal realm of an arbitrator.

Through the flexibility, contacts, knowledge, and pressures that a neutral—in the collective form of a joint committee—can bring to a situation, issues can be addressed more broadly than in a normal mediation or arbitration procedure, where the purposes, goals, and resources (for example, expertise and contacts) may be much narrower. The neutral agency's ability successfully to address broader issues while not interfering with local sovereignty seems to hinge largely on the continued good judgment and experience of its membership and an operating philosophy and membership that encourage collective bargaining.

Arbitration as a Tool

The Joint Labor-Management Committee issues an arbitration award when one of three circumstances pertains: (1) remaining differences are truly irreconcilable, either on substantive, personality, or political grounds; (2) the Committee has not used well—or chooses not to use—the requisite mediating resources available to work out the remaining differences; and (3) there is agreement, but it is in the political interest of one or both parties for an award to be issued.

Political consideration and personality factors significantly affected the willingness of both the Seabury and Barkfield managements to agree to a settlement package. Both groups were concerned— properly so, as political officials—that their communities might worry about the increased costs of providing police or fire services. Possibly, both management groups were particularly sensitive since these towns operated under a town meeting system of government in which most budget issues were subject to public debate. Anticipation of public input and opinion, however, is an important component of most municipal decision-making processes in the United States.

In Seabury, the feelings of the townspeople, aired in open debate during a town meeting on a settlement, caused the contract negotiation to reach an impasse several years before, and years of negative public perceptions of the fire department had since passed. Subsequently, the town negotiating team was greatly concerned about, and largely reflected, the public's negative attitude toward the fire fighters. In this case the Committee used its peer structure to help the team to consider a "reasonable" proposal and to see the continuing political and economic costs of the impasse, as well as the possibility of better management of the fire service. At the town meeting that followed the acceptance of the agreement by the negotiating team, the Seabury team, educated in the facts and alternatives and committed to resolution and improvement of fire services, was able, in turn, to recommend convincingly that the public ratify the agreement. If the negotiating team had been unwilling or unable to do this, an alternative remained: Through an arbitration award, the negotiating team could have been insulated from a politically unpopular agreement.

In Barkfield, the differences among the selectmen did not permit them to present a unified position to the public; some selectmen recognized the need for a significant increase in police salaries, as did the chief of police. There was little argument on the substance or merit of the issue, but political concerns over costs were precluding settlement. Interestingly, since the case was ultimately arbitrated along lines that the parties had previously indicated would be acceptable, there is reason to suspect that the selectmen's refusal to settle was affected by their expectations of how the public would perceive the settlement—that is, how the public perceptions might affect their political fortunes—as well as by their concern for an equitable settlement with the police. Possibly this is a common problem in public labor-management relations.

The JLMC, under the statute prevailing at the time, permitted use of conventional interest arbitration, which elsewhere frequently formed the basis of a dispute settlement system. In this case, the selectmen in essence avoided full political responsibility for the outcome of the dispute. The JLMC mechanism provided room for political posturing, while still forcing discussion and settlement on most of the issues. In other cases, the JLMC has served these two needs by taking public responsibility for awards that had been, in fact, approved by all parties. This is an example of the common tool of interest arbitration put to situation-specific use by the Committee.

Mediators as Educators

Most of the tools discussed above, including joint mediation, peer interaction, maintaining involvement, and arbitration, require a large component of "education." The various settlement tools and types of interactions used provide information, perspective, or the advice of experienced people to parties in dispute. This sort of education can affect the outcome of a dispute by affecting the participants' perceptions of issues or the conduct of the bargaining process. In the longer term, it can also affect the bargaining relationships and bargaining abilities of participants. The Seabury and Barkfield cases illustrate a series of such educational activities, where a third party does not seek to impose a solution but seeks instead to create a process by which the parties themselves can find a solution. In Seabury, especially, the JLMC used education to alter positions or perceptions.

Probably, a much wider range of issues can be explored and resolved by persuasion and dialogue through an open process than by the simple use of arbitration authority. Thus, the capacity to engage in multifaceted educational functions suggests another category of JLMC activities. The JLMC tries to encourage improvement in four areas: (1) the knowledge and ability of management actors, (2) the legislative-executive relationship, (3) the internal relationships on the labor side; and of course, (4) the relationship between management and labor.

Improving Management Knowledge and Abilities

Barkfield management, as a result of elective job turnover and the lack of negotiating experience, lacked the significant personal relationships, traditions, or other elements of a stable bargaining structure to help maintain communications or otherwise move to solve the issues in dispute. Absent, for example, were an established set of relationships among the Barkfield board members that would have allowed informal cooperation and traditions that would aid the process of accommodation within the board. Instead, the lack of an active spokesperson and the diversity of the board allowed disagreement and posturing to slow the process. By always negotiating as a group, the board sought to avoid sending conflicting signals to the union or making conflicting promises. Nonetheless, the result was greater confusion; there was no one management representative responsible for preparing for negotiations. Where the necessary expertise and internal relationships have not developed within one side or the other and the bargaining team members cannot agree among themselves, the only position left is a negative one, which makes progress difficult. Such was the case in Barkfield.

One notable problem that awaited the mediator's arrival in Barkfield was the lack of constructive bargaining-related communication on the management side between the chief of police, who was the relevant line executive, and the board of selectmen. The chief appeared to believe that "amateur" selectmen meddled in his business and made demands for police services for which they were unwilling to appropriate the necessary funds. He felt also that the selectmen spent little time discussing or understanding the police business on which they made financial decisions or judgments. The selectmen, in turn, seemed to feel that the chief was an "entrenched bureaucrat," and they took actions through their legislative power that might, in fact, have been aimed at trimming the chief's power as much as they were aimed at the operational issues at hand. The result, of course, was to muddy the bargaining relationship and exacerbate police feelings about several issues, including scheduling, overtime, and EMT training for the ambulance crew.

Legislative-Executive Relations

The second educational function engaged in by the JLMC relates to the public sector legislative-executive split in authority, which affects labor relations as it does other municipal functions. In Seabury the separation of powers and the consequent diffusion of decision making between the executive and legislative branches of government precluded obtaining timely unity on the management side. The situation in Seabury illustrates to a certain degree the differences that may prevail between the executive and legislative members of management, although it surely is not an extreme example. The results of such diffusion can harm the credibility of the management negotiator—as it did in Seabury when the Trent contract was turned down—and often makes negotiation more complex for the union leader, who then, in effect, has two parties to deal with. If the legislative ratification process turns down a contract, the union may have difficulty internally in settling for anything less than the original agreement with the executive. The political risk to a union leader of doing so can complicate subsequent attempts at settlement. However, the formal separation of powers can be bridged by constructive informal relationships—as was done in Seabury through the establishment of a legislative-executive negotiating committee—or by a formal procedure that ensures coordination. When the Seabury negotiating committee was split, the JLMC was able to provide assistance in bringing it together.

A primary method the JLMC uses to educate management and improve their ability to work as a team during bargaining is peer assistance. This form of "education" was used in the Seabury situation, where a Committee member who was a town manager went to considerable effort to communicate with the Seabury manager. However, even after the manager became convinced of the desirability of the settlement that was proffered, the legislative members of the management team were not similarly persuaded, although they were moving toward the settlement offer. So JLMC members talked individually with their peers on the legislative side, providing some longer-term perspective and comparisons with other fire services and fire contracts in the state. In trying to pierce the town's long-standing low regard for the fire fighters, the JLMC peers additionally sought to discuss management's responsibilities in training and other aspects of running a good fire department. Another, more common, approach taken by the JLMC in both was to use joint mediation, in which a staff member works directly, almost as an adviser, to management.

In Barkfield, the police chief and others referred to the newly constituted personnel board as one that, as a standing committee, would be better able to handle personnel and labor relations matters in the future. This approach may well help in dealing with problems that arise because of turnover. However, the separate matter of the relationship between the board of selectmen, the town meeting, and the personnel board itself requires definition and coordination similar to that among the governing entities in Seabury. Thus, the creation of a new entity to maintain some management continuity in spite of high election-induced turnover must include an awareness of the relationship of that entity to other management actors.

The JLMC was able to educate participants to help bridge the gaps in substantive perceptions between Seabury legislators and the executive. Through the JLMC members' personal experience with legislative and executive conflicts, and experience with disputes in their own areas, the Committee was able to provide peer assistance, which helped bring the two parts of management together. For example, the selectmen and finance committee representatives were reminded that court appeals are drawn out and costly, with no guarantee of success, and that during the period of uncertainty over outcome, their capacity to manage a useful fire service would be affected. Outside peers could more credibly discuss acceptance of a negotiated settlement in the face of the town's negative perception of and antipathy toward the fire fighters. The ability of the JLMC to bring fire fighter member Alward to speak to management was a key in moving the negotiating committee toward settlement, for the newly appointed town manager would have had more difficulty persuading his team without Alward and other JLMC peers. The town manager was helped in obtaining unanimous backing from the town legislators for a settlement recommendation to the public at the town meeting—a unanimity that, perhaps, took political pressure off individual selectmen to oppose the settlement.

Within Labor

The third category of educational activities undertaken by the JLMC—activities concerned with internal relationships on the labor side—is demonstrated by the Committee's dealings with the fire fighters local in Seabury. Union members were arguing among themselves about whether priority should be given to the longevity pay issue—a major bargaining dispute between labor and management—or to wage parity with the police. By the time the Committee became involved, the original position of the fire fighters, which stressed longevity pay, was no longer a priority issue, due to turnover in the fire department, for the majority of the union members. It still was a significant aspect of their demands, however, probably owing to the continuing leadership by an older fire fighter and the continuing presence of the attorney from earlier negotiations, although the younger members were more interested in wage parity. Alward's influence on several fronts helped resolve this internal dispute.

The Committee's ability to help clear the confusion and effect the presentation of an unambiguous proposal hinged directly on the efforts of its joint membership and their expertise. First, a Committee member who was a state fire fighters union official was able to involve himself in this and other internal issues as no outside neutral could have done. Second, he was instrumental not only in developing a union proposal that addressed the real priority concerns of the local (assisted by the electoral defeat of the local president, who favored longevity pay), but he also successfully "educated" the fire fighters to assume a realistic view of the outstanding settlement barriers. Such internal problems can be tackled by the Committee because the diverse experience and contacts of its various members provide an opportunity to "fit" a specific member to a problem where his influence, credibility and knowledge can have an impact.

Labor-Management

The fourth educational challenge to the JLMC pertains to the relationship between management and labor. Internal accommodation on each respective side is a prerequisite. For this reason, management in both Seabury and Barkfield had difficulty dealing with, much less agreeing with, the union. The same principle applied in Seabury: No positive answer could be given to the union until the management side agreed among themselves. Thus it was important, first, to help each management group to reach internal agreement. The JLMC was more successful in Seabury, where they worked more assiduously at that aspect of the problem.

In Barkfield, in contrast to the management side, the police—although somewhat inexperienced—seemed to be reasonably well organized, focused on their roles, and doing their homework. The preparedness of the union, however, was insufficient by itself to yield a settlement because communication of their views to management was extremely difficult, given the lack of established roles or informal relationships between labor and management. For example, when the patrol officers tried to reopen negotiations with the board just prior to Committee involvement, they relied on a formal channel, a letter that was to be transmitted through attorneys. Through an error or misunderstanding, the selectmen never received the letter, and there was no informal channel of communication between any member of the union negotiating team and the management side that could have been used to help restart negotiations—at least not without a significant sacrifice of pride by one side or the other.

When the Committee mediators arrived in Barkfield they found that considerable mistrust had built up between the two sides. Bargaining had been impeded in the absence of accurate information about and understanding of the issues, as well as by the parties' attitudes toward bargaining (initially, the selectmen did not wish to make trade-offs) and toward each other. The joint mediators were able to restart face-to-face negotiations and thereby provide experience with bargaining and open direct channels for discussion.

In Seabury, the long history of labor-management contention and the continual turnover in the town manager position slowed bargaining progress. No continuous attention had been paid to these problems; for a period of over a year, no bargaining had taken place. To deal with the short- and long-range impacts of these difficulties, the Committee relied heavily on individual staff and peer assistance and separate meetings with each party, combined with constant communication between the members of the mediating team to define the issues and pinpoint areas of disagreement and possible accommodation.

When working with inexperienced groups, the Committee mediators can impose practices that begin to move the process and build trust, so that agreement on one can help negotiations to progress to the next issue. This process not only resolves one issue at a time but creates a perception of movement where only frustration existed before. In addition it teaches the inexperienced parties something about bargaining. Narrowing of issues can also take place under conventional fact-finding procedures, but the bargaining relationship is not easily strengthened by this approach, for the parties do not receive practice at bargaining with one another. Guided by experienced Committee neutrals, this process can transform an impasse into a process of narrowing differences and strengthening the bargaining relationship on the way to a settlement.

Cooling Off after the "Joy of Settlement"

Another tool for improving the bargaining climate is illustrated by the Committee chairman's insistence that a prospective contract be negotiated in Seabury in addition to the retroactive contract on the table. This move was intended to provide a period of peace during which a better relationship would have a chance to develop, rather than beginning a new round of contention. The use of a prescribed procedure in Barkfield to settle the ambulance issue *after* the other issues were settled allowed that very emotional and complex question to be handled in the absence of the contention that surrounded an open contract. Frequently, when faced with a history of contention and poor labor-management relationships, the JLMC will seek to bring about face-to-face bargaining and settlement or otherwise effect a period of stability.

Ongoing Education

Management in the public sector, both executive and legislative, must cope with particular structural stresses affecting their bargaining capacity. Because mayors, selectmen, or council members are elected every two, three, or four years, a management bargaining team frequently will change—perhaps not completely—at these intervals. Because of the turnover of elected and appointed officials in public organizations, it is often very difficult to establish productive relationships within the management team (and with counterparts on the labor side), to gain a substantial amount of experience, or to focus on long-term consequences of negotiations or settlements. There is a constant need, therefore, for educating newly elected or appointed government officials on labor relations matters, especially if they are determined to participate in the bargaining itself. (Even in cases handled by professional negotiators, turnover of elected officials can result in policy changes or in approach to labor-management matters.)

The educational functions performed by the Committee and its staff to improve these relationships were critical to the settlement of both the Barkfield and Seabury cases. In particular, the importance of educating local officials in the often unfamiliar realm of labor relations may well reflect the need for permanent institutional provision of such information and service. Since it is unlikely that elected officials, especially part-time officials, will in all cases see the value of or take the time to educate themselves on such matters, a JLMC sort of informal assistance, through a peer network, at times of immediate need may be among the most effective educational methods.

Summary

The Barkfield and Seabury cases illustrate a number of principles in the use of a JLMC-type mechanism. The broadly based membership structure of such a mechanism and its numerous procedural options offer ways to achieve early settlement between parties to a dispute, as well as the development of constructive long-term bargaining relationships. The degree of a committee's success in reaching these goals, however, is not only dependent on its structure and procedures but also largely on the quality of its staff and membership and on its own internal dynamics and policies.

As seen in Barkfield and Seabury, successful intervention of a committee is highly dependent on the skills of the staff as assessors and as mediators, and on the availability, integrity, judgment, and peer influence of committee members. Ultimately, it is the skill and judgment with which available tools are matched to the problems and the wise use of a committee's authority and informal contacts that can lead two disputing parties toward settlement and improvement in the bargaining relationship. Good choices must be made—in committee appointments, in staff hiring, staff assignments, and the format and degree of staff and member involvement in a dispute—to put to advantage the mechanism's flexibility and potential.

Interpersonal relationships on a committee also are critical to JLMC success. Expeditious and accurate definition and narrowing of issues, for example, depend to a great degree on communications by and between the senior staff representatives and with committee members. Respect for and trust in each other's skills and judgment is a prerequisite to this sort of communication. The diverse professional backgrounds, influence, and knowledge of staff or committee peers can cause a large degree of movement by the parties toward settlement and can benefit the bargaining and operational relationship between the parties. Thus, the composition of a committee's membership and staff brings about the creation, availability, and application of the tools. The committee chair must be alert to these relationships and dynamics, as they are, indeed, the root of the mechanism's strength.

The Barkfield and Seabury cases also point out some limits to the effectiveness of a JLMC's work. In Barkfield, Committee contact with the management side was arguably inadequate. However, the time Committee members have available for interaction is often scarce. An unusually large number of actors or issues in a particular dispute, such as in Barkfield, or of a large case load, precludes extensive time commitment on any one case. Yet the very time invested by Committee and staff members was a key element in the settlement and the subsequent improved fire service in Seabury and what brought the parties as close as they came to resolution in Barkfield.

In Barkfield and Seabury, tools were chosen that seemed to fit the substantive, interpersonal, and political aspects of the situation. While one can question the choice, timing, and application of Committee tools and strategy to the specific circumstances and events in the two communities, the important point is that the Committee had flexibility to choose from and invent a wide variety of tools.

The Committee's options for choosing methods to bring Barkfield management into the dispute settlement process were not exhausted. On the other hand, it used extensively its flexibility to advance toward acceptable settlement in Seabury. The character and range of this flexibility is vastly different from the options available in more rigid interest arbitration schemes. This flexibility, however, requires the exercise of good professional judgment: Because of the options such flexibility permits, there is opportunity for errors in judgment as well.

In general, these two cases illustrate a JLMC's capacity to draw on and apply a spectrum of methods and tools. That capacity derives from the degree of statutory flexibility, the specific personal and professional traits and talents of the staff and membership, and the investment of their time and their choice of options—all related to the obstacles in the bargaining situation. The array of committee-induced tools is large, can be situation-specific, and can permit changes in technique as each situation requires. Used well, these tools can be used not only to resolve an impasse but to leave the parties better able to solve their own problems in the future.

Endnotes

1. The New York City Board of Collective Bargaining has two labor, two management, and three neutral members. For descriptions of the membership and procedures, see "New York City Charter 54, Office of Collective Bargaining (as amended by Local Law 1 of 1972) and Revised Consolidated Rules of the Office of Collective Bargaining, New York City and Amendments," Office of Collective Bargaining, 250 Broadway, New York, New York 10017.
2. For a discussion of characteristics of a mediator and mediation, see Simkin, *Mediation and the Dynamics of Collective Bargaining.* On this point, see Chapter V, especially pp. 94–106.

Chapter 7

RESULTS OF THE JOINT LABOR-MANAGEMENT COMMITTEE EXPERIMENT

As an experiment in dispute resolution, the Joint Labor-Management Committee could be assessed in many ways. It is, of course, important to specify the criteria by which judgments are made. Rather than to serve as an economic study, the purpose here has been to examine principles of collective bargaining and public policy as they have been combined and applied to improve labor-management relations and to develop alternative approaches to dispute settlement.

This chapter will assess the performance of the JLMC against the expectations of its creators. Thus, the objectives described in Chapter 3 will be used as benchmarks: (1) Is there, in fact, more problem solving and structural change under the Committee approach than under last-best-offer arbitration? (2) Is there more bargaining, mediation, and local responsibility in settlements? (3) Are settlements more practical and acceptable to the parties and the public? (4) Is it cheaper to reach settlement? (5) Is there faster resolution of impasses, less litigation and bitterness, and fewer risks and surprises to both parties? (6) Is weak management strengthened as a party to bargaining? This range of questions will be examined here, while discussion in Chapters 8 and 9 will concentrate on the factors that account for those results and whether they might be applied in other jurisdictions.

Other, perhaps more discrete, factors could be analyzed in an effort to draw conclusions about JLMC performance. For example, a

171

different sort of study might examine the size of settlements, contract ratification by membership and legislative bodies, or contract enforcement issues such as grievances or the impact on strike activity.[1] Although some of these factors are included in the following discussion as part of the larger picture, specific analysis of these sorts of categories is not undertaken. As stated in the introduction to this volume, this study is focused on the institutional, political, and interpersonal dynamics in public labor-management relations.

The performance questions can be approached by both quantitative and qualitative means. Several dimensions of its performance can be quantitatively examined by comparing the record of public safety dispute settlement since the JLMC's inception with the record of the pre-1978 period when last-best-offer arbitration and its related statutory framework existed alone. Qualitatively, using the case examples and other observations of the mechanism at work, those less quantifiable results of the Committee's impact on bargaining relationships and outcomes can be compared with the expectations and intentions of the Committee's founders.

Absolutes rarely contribute to resolving an impasse and are unlikely to be attained for quite a while in the practice of public sector bargaining. So, in discussing these elements, and recognizing that solutions to collective bargaining problems are negotiated examples of compromise or accommodation, the underlying criteria will not be, "Is this the optimal way to handle public safety disputes?" but rather, "Is this a good or better way to handle public safety disputes? Is it appropriate to circumstances that typify public sector bargaining (and the specific jurisdiction examined) and does it yield results more satisfactory to the parties than the system used before?"

Implicit in the controversy surrounding the creation of the Joint Committee were complaints by both sides about the existing forum for dispute resolution and about the state of labor-management relations generally. Later, in more explicitly setting forth the mechanism's objectives, both labor and management wished to avoid some effects of the last-best-offer mechanism that had been in place. The JLMC also wished to improve the substantive outcomes and relationships resulting from municipal police and fire fighter collective bargaining.

These and other objectives, as briefly presented in Chapter 3, can be thought of in two categories: positive and negative. The "negative" objectives are those that were intended primarily to *alter* practices or results perceived as negative, which had arisen since or as a result of the LBO impasse resolution procedures. The "positive" objectives are those that were intended to improve, in the longer term, the quality and results of collective bargaining, dispute settlement, and labor-management relations.[2]

The negative objectives are those most subject to quantitative comparisons. Where data were available, an attempt has been made to present and interpret those data pertinent to each objective. The positive objectives are less measurable, certainly at this early point in the JLMC experience. This discussion will examine the limited data that were available and germane and will relate some anecdotal or qualitative information to assess progress toward accomplishment of those less easily measurable objectives. (It might be noted for future study that the JLMC now has had nearly four years of experience, approximately the same experience as with the earlier last-best-offer statute. Thus some comparisons beyond those permitted by the data in this study might usefully be made.)

Quantitative Measures of Performance: Differences from Last-Best-Offer

Intended to improve on the performance of the last-best-offer mechanism, the following are the Committee's negative objectives:

1. To elicit faster resolution of disputes.
2. To effect more frequent use of mediation than arbitration for settlement.
3. To lessen risks and uncertainties to the parties.
4. To reduce the amount of litigation and resultant contention.
5. To yield less expensive resolution of disputes—that is, lessen the expense to the parties.
6. To increase the amount and degree of direct bargaining.

Faster Resolution

The first objective is the simplest to examine. A comparison can be made between time required for resolving a dispute under the pre-1978 system and the time required for resolution following the establishment of the Committee. Two sets of data are referred to in this and the following sections to examine time taken for settlement: (1) data compiled by the Committee's research director and (2) data independently compiled and verified for this study.[3] (These data cover only the first two years of JLMC experience.)

In performing the independent verification, first the raw data were verified by inspecting the Committee's minutes for consistency between reported case disposals and their compilation in Committee tabulations, and by independently reviewing the records of the Board of Conciliation and Arbitration. As both sets of data depend heavily on the Committee's data compilation, significant efforts were made to verify its accuracy and utility for measuring differences between the two periods. Some discrepancies between the data sets were found, and some minor differences in definitions produced some differences in the data used to calculate each set of results. Although these differences account for variation between the two data sets in terms of specific percentage changes, the magnitude and direction of the changes between the period before and the period after the Committee's inception were essentially the same for both data sets. The general conclusions of the independent study parallel the results of the Committee's own analysis and go further to test the statistical significance of the trends and conclusions suggested.

In September 1980 the Joint Labor-Management Committee issued figures demonstrating its improvement in settlement time over the previous system of dispute resolution.[4] These data are reprinted in Table 7-1. According to Committee figures, under the pre-1978 procedures administered by the BCA the average time for resolving a dispute after impasse was nearly seven months. Since JLMC establishment in January 1978 through August of 1980, just under five months elapsed on the average between impasse and settlement, but this single figure obscures the fact that settlement time continued to drop after the Committee got underway: In fiscal year 1980, after the Committee had one and one-half years of experience, average settlement time was reduced to just over three and one-half months. Cases that went all the way through the BCA's procedures to last-best-offer arbitration took an average of just over fifteen months during the pre-1978 period. In comparison, where the Committee required "formal" action—such as a hearing, peer bargaining or some form of arbitration—time to settlement averaged six and three-quarter months.[5]

One especially informative difference between the Committee's data and the analysis done for this study is that this work compares the *period* before January 1, 1978, when only the BCA existed, with the subsequent *period* during which both BCA and the JLMC were in operation. Committee data in Table 7-1 aggregates BCA data through June, 1979 and compares the performance of the two agencies. Since the BCA was still in existence and handling some public safety cases after 1977, and especially because the two mechanisms began to work in concert, the settlement data of each process after 1977 cannot be viewed realistically as independent of one another. Although it seems tempting to compare the Committee approach to the BCA and its LBO-dominated system, it is not appropriate to do so; some of the results since between 1978 and 1980 in police and fire fighter bargaining may be related to the agencies working together, to the threat or availability of LBO, or to the impact on the BCA of the Committee's less formal proceedings. The parallel operations of the two agencies, moreover, may have affected the behavior, quantity, or quality of the case load that each received. Therefore, the independent numbers prepared for this study compare on a combined basis the *period* prior to the beginning of 1978 with the two-year period since.

For example, it may be that the JLMC is now handling the more difficult cases owing to its general policy of sending cases for outside handling (either to the BCA or other mediators) when it perceives that the Committee's special characteristics will not be needed. This policy may keep the more difficult—and, therefore, frequently more lengthy—disputes within the Committee and elongate the average time to settlement in a statistical comparison with the BCA. For these reasons one might expect to find the Committee now resolving cases *less* rapidly or with *more* intervention than the BCA on a comparative basis in the post-1977 period. This trend is demonstrated in Table 7-2. In 1979 average days to resolve a dispute by the JLMC was not appreciably faster than the BCA; however, the combined average time for settlement is significantly less than before the Committee's 1978 beginning.

Figures 7-1 and 7-2, respectively, show visually the relative time required for resolving all police and fire fighter disputes at impasse before 1978 and after. The results before 1978 are in Figure 7-1, and post-1977 data, composed of combined results of the BCA and JLMC, are in Figure 7-2. Visual comparison quickly shows the change in the number of days taken to resolve a dispute during the two periods. During the latter period, proportionately more cases were settled in a lesser number of days. After getting these results on a combined basis, some tests of statistical significance were performed. At the 5 percent level of confidence (using a median test),

Table 7-1 Police and Fire Fighter Bargaining Impasse Activity

Overview of Board of Conciliation and Arbitration (G.L. CH 1078, Acts of 1973) July 1, 1974–June 30, 1979. (Labor organizations representing both police and fire departments are entered in both the police and fire headings.)

A. Stage of Settlement

	Total # of Impasses	Settled Prior To Appt. of Factfinder	Settled Prior to Factfinder Report	Settled Upon Issuance of Factfinding Report	Settled After Factfinding Report	Settled By LBO Award
Fire:	274	101	35	52	30	56
Police:	381	145	86	71	30	48
Aggregate:	648	245	118	121	60	104

B. Average Settlement Time (Months)

	Pre-Factfinding Report	Factfinding Report	Post-Factfinding Report	LBO Award	Overall
Fire:	3.31	8.81	9.24	15.17	7.41
Police:	3.04	8.48	8.95	15.32	6.07
Aggregate:	3.18	8.79	9.10	15.24	6.69

Overview of Joint Labor-Management Committee (including overlap with BCA) January 1, 1978–September 1, 1980

Cumulative Case Activity

Date	# of Cases	Informal Settlement	Formal Settlement	LBO Award	Pending Cases
9/30/78	28	10 / 35.7%	4 / 14.3%	1 / 3.6%	13 / 46.4%
1/31/79	80	30 / 37.5%	11 / 13.75%	1 / 1.25%	38 / 47.5%
5/31/79	91	44 / 48.4%	18 / 19.8%	3 / 3.3%	26 / 28.6%
9/30/79	124	54 / 43.5%	24 / 19.4%	5 / 4%	41 / 33.1%
12/31/79	136	62 / 45.5%	28 / 20.6%	5 / 3.7%	41 / 30.1%
3/31/80	160	73 / 45.6%	36 / 22.5%	5 / 3.1%	46 / 28.75%
6/30/80	200	95 / 47.5%	41 / 20.5%	5 / 2.5%	59 / 29.5%
9/1/80	221	111 / 50.2%	45 / 20.4%	7 / 3.2%	58 / 26.2%

Average Settlement Time (Months) as of 9/1/80:

a. Pursuant to G.L. Ch 150e, Acts of 1977:

Informal	Formal	Overall
4.54	7.85	5.85
n = 59	n = 39	n = 98

b. Pursuant to G.L. Ch 154, Acts of 1979:

Informal with Jurisdiction	Informal without Jurisdiction	Informal Removed from BCA	Informal Referred to BCA	Formal JLMC Only	Formal Removed from BCA	Overall
3.57	1.73	3.29	2.90	6.78	6.59	3.63
n = 22	n = 17	n = 10	n = 3	n = 8	n = 5	n = 65

SOURCE: Joint Labor Management Committee for Municipal Police and Fire Fighters. Published in *Massachusetts Business and Economic Report*, Vol. 8. No. 2, Fall 1980. Management Research Center, School of Business Administration, University of Massachusetts, Amherst, Massachusetts 01003.

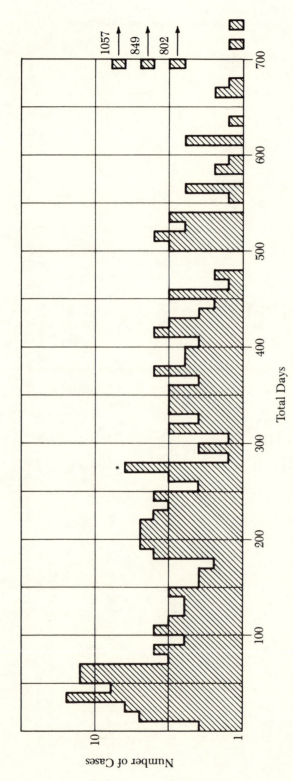

Figure 7-1   Dispute Resolution Time in Days for Each Case (1974–1977) (BCA).   Illustrating the use of the plot, at this (*)
point eight cases were resolved in 271–280 days during the 1974–1977 period.

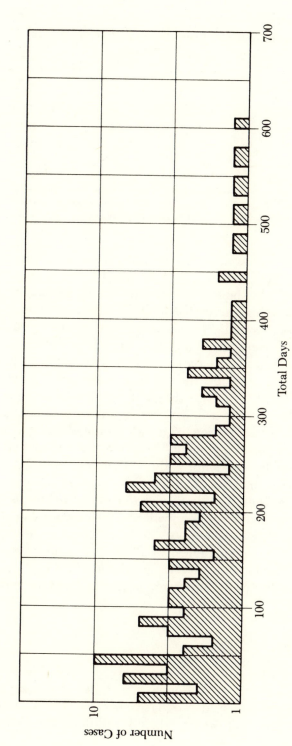

Figure 7-2 Dispute Resolution Time in Days for Each Case (1978–1979) (BCA AND JLMC).

Table 7–2   Average Number of Days Taken to Resolve Disputes

Year	BCA	JLMC	Combined
1975	285.4		
1976	277		
1977	247.3		
1978	196.4	153.2	177.8
1979	90.4	106	100.7
1974–1977	265.3		
1978–1979	172.6	131.7	150.9

SOURCE: Joint Labor-Management Committee and Board of Conciliation and Arbitration files. Chart from independent compilation of JLMC and BCH data by Wm. H. Mattfeld, September 29, 1980.

while the Committee *alone* did not process cases significantly more rapidly after 1977 than did the BCA after 1977, the *combined* JLMC/BCA results show reductions in time for resolution from the previous period that are significant at the 5 percent level, even with the less favorable numbers used in this independent examination.

These results were tested further using matched pairs of bargaining units that had filed impasse petitions both prior to January 1, 1978 and after. The results showed that municipalities that had disputes settled under the two different systems had reduced, after January 1, 1978, their average time from impasse declaration to settlement by anywhere from 65 to 145 days, with an average reduction of 105 days, or 41.3 percent.[6] This test, while it does not control for other variables or identify other factors that may be involved, strengthens the conclusion that the new structure and process have significantly lessened the time to settlement of police and fire impasses. Overall, both studies, with some differences in degree—largely explainable by differences in definitions and assumptions—demonstrate a reduction of nearly half in the overall time necessary to settle disputes in public safety since the Joint Labor-Management Committee and its procedures were introduced into the process and environment.

More Mediation

Using the data developed for this study, we are able to examine directly the degree of mediation used both before and after January 1, 1978. Cases were considered to have been settled in mediation by the BCA if settlement occurred before the BCA sent letters to the

Table 7–3 Cases Resolved Through Mediation

Time Period (Calendar Years)	BCA	JLMC	Combined
1975	31.8%		
1976	32.0%		
1977	39.2%		
1978	63.6%	60.6%	62.4%
1979	84.8%	54.7%	66.3%

SOURCE: Independent compilation of JLMC and BCA data by Wm. H. Mattfeld.

negotiating parties that announced the initiation of fact-finding. JLMC cases settled prior to its announcing an intention to appoint a mediator-arbitrator were considered to have been settled in mediation or at a prior informal step.

Table 7-3 shows that prior to 1978 less than 40 percent of public safety impasses were resolved through mediation; since January 1 of that year more than 60 percent of the cases have been resolved that way.* It also shows the dramatic increase after 1978 in the proportion of mediated settlements by the BCA. According to the data, the JLMC did not resolve as large a proportion of cases in mediation as the BCA during the period shown. Again, this finding may reflect the Committee's handling of the harder-to-resolve cases which it seems to do as a de facto matter of policy. In addition, some arbitration awards reflect agreement between the parties but are issued at the request of parties who, for political or other reasons, prefer that the Committee issue an award. The Committee estimates informally that about one half of its formal (arbitration) decisions represent such agreements, thus inflating its reported arbitration statistics and reducing the recorded number and percentage of mediated settlements. Periodically, arbitration BCA awards also reflected informal agreements, although it was not reported to be as regular an occurrence.

The directly measured results (not adjusted for estimated number of officially arbitrated awards that were actually mediated) of the combined activities were confirmed by standard chi-squared tests,

---

* Fiscal 1980 and 1981 data were not available in time to be independently verified for this study. JLMC FY 1981 data show JLMC received 71 petitions, of which 61 percent were resolved by the JLMC alone through mediation by June 30, 1981. In addition to the 43 FY 1981 cases resolved, 39 additional cases outstanding from prior years were resolved. Of the 43 settled cases from FY 1981, only one case required issuance of an arbitration award.

which indicate as much as a 60 to 80 percent increase in the proportion of cases resolved through mediation since the JLMC began its work. (The true proportion of mediated cases would be higher.) Of course, factors other than the Committee's existence and procedures—such as management's past experience with arbitration (recall that municipalities lost 2 to 1 in LBO arbitration before 1978)— also may have contributed to the increase in settlement by mediation, as may have the development of more experience with bargaining and consequent improvement in the bargaining relationship.

These data on mediation can be related to the data on time to settlement. It appears that the critical factor in reducing the average time to settlement is the resolution of a greater proportion of disputes prior to the time-consuming arbitration stage. The new practices have not simply shortened the time taken with each settlement tool but they seem to help parties avoid the lengthier arbitration proceedings. The increased use of mediation thus seems closely related to faster resolution. As one would expect, not only has the time to settlement been shortened but as a result of the means employed to do so, more cases are resolved by face-to-face bargaining, generally aided by mediation.

Fewer Risks and Uncertainties: Lessening Surprises in Settlement

While it is not possible to compare directly the degree of risk and uncertainty faced by the disputing parties before and after the JLMC's establishment, inferences from the statistical results on settlement time and mediation are suggestive. A comparison of these data suggests, first, that due to the variety of procedural options available to the Committee, the parties may feel greater initial uncertainty about the process and what it will require of them. Second, to the extent that both parties participate through increased mediation or peer representation in the resolution of the dispute there is, in general, less risk of a surprising outcome than in last-best-offer proceedings. Since the parties have continuing involvement and input into the process, risk and uncertainty of outcome is lessened due to the availability of fairly specific information virtually throughout the process. Third, because of more rapid settlement, the period of time is shorter during which the new contract terms are unknown to the parties.

More specifically, a 60 to 80 percent increase in mediation and the use of arbitration machinery (which to some degree is actually another negotiation process) have probably lessened the amount and degree of uncertainty that pertains during impasse regarding the probable settlement. Awards that are negotiated through the peer bargaining system seem to involve less risk and surprise than a last-best-offer settlement or other arbitration awards, particularly when the Committee structure and membership dynamics keep the peers working on the settlement in touch with their counterparts in the dispute. In terms of uncertainty of outcomes, many of the surprises observed seem to have occurred when the peer relationship in a peer bargaining arbitration was not well formed or well used. These activities enable the Committee to improve each side's perception of its chances of "winning" or "losing" on a specific issue. When properly operating, this approach makes it less likely that the parties will take, at the final step, outlying positions or be surprised at the result. Under LBO a surprising outcome was often the result of unrealistic calculations of risks, especially on the part of the cities.

In spite of a reduction in settlement surprises under the JLMC mechanism, some parties—and frequently their attorneys—have complained of uncertainty regarding the procedures to be followed. The less formal, flexible, and unfamiliar Committee procedures leave some confusion regarding next steps in the process or how it will end. Some of this uncertainty may dissipate as Committee practices become better defined and better known to the labor-management community. Still, the varied tool kit of the Committee doubtless will leave some uncertainty in terms of specific processes and, to a lesser degree, end points. Conceivably, the uncertainty regarding the JLMC procedures to be used in any specific dispute may, if used skillfully, serve to promote direct bargaining and voluntary settlements by parties less willing to risk that form of the unknown. On the other hand, as a practical matter JLMC procedures for settlement are rarely determined without consultation with the parties. Greater communication in this regard could ameliorate the remaining uncertainty with respect to both outcomes and procedures.

Overall, the shorter time to conclusion and the more direct connection of the parties to settlement through bargaining and mediation suggest that the degree of risk and uncertainty over outcome has been reduced, although procedural uncertainty may have been increased under Committee jurisdiction.

Less Litigation

The Committee's performance against its objective to reduce litigation was not measured for this study because data were not easily compiled on the number of LBO awards challenged through litigation. It was reported by Committee members and attorneys for various parties that litigation following an LBO award was not atypical. In contrast, since 1978 only one suit has been filed challenging an award by the JLMC, and that dispute was subsequently resolved informally by Committee action. Subsequent to that event the Committee has, whenever possible, required parties to an arbitration to sign waivers of appeal, a practice whose legality has been questioned by some but not challenged formally. The trend is decidedly away from litigation, but the magnitude of the change awaits further research.

Cheaper to the Parties

Prior to 1978 the primary costs to parties at impasse were legal fees incurred as a result of the quasi-legal, prescribed procedures leading to last-best-offer arbitration. Although incidents of "lost" wages in prolonged disputes occurred for a time due to a loophole limiting retroactivity to the existing budget year, this practice was later precluded by statute. Retroactivity is now the norm in Massachusetts as it is in most states which permit arbitration. Since LBO hearings typically required evidence to be presented formally to fact finders and arbitrators, parties were usually represented by counsel. Police unions, of course, also retained counsel, as did many towns and cities. Both parties frequently retained outside counsel for negotiations as well as for these dispute settlement proceedings.

The less formal proceedings of the Committee are less likely to require an attorney's assistance, and the parties are encouraged to deal directly with each other. The reduction in litigation, the near halving of time from impasse to settlement, the increase in mediation and direct bargaining, and the altered forms of arbitration have combined to reduce the direct and indirect costs of attorneys' time and that of other outside personnel and institutions previously involved. Under the LBO statute the parties paid for the arbitrator's time. Under the JLMC, if the dispute is arbitrated by either the chairperson or vice-chairperson, the Committee absorbs the cost, although the cost of outside arbitrators is still shared by the parties.

Table 7–4   State Budget for Dispute Resolution

Fiscal Year	BCA*	JLMC
1977	$277,991	
1978	308,000	$ 45,000
1979	330,808	150,000
1980	364,953	227,130
1981	381,000	408,155

*The BCA also provides mediation services and grievance arbitration to private industry.

SOURCES: BCA and JLMC.

Transcripts have been used on only one occasion in a JLMC hearing, reflecting virtual elimination of that cost element. Overall, mediation via the Joint Labor-Management Committee is a cheaper way for the parties to resolve a dispute. Apart from expenses to the parties, public monies have been expended by the BCA and the JLMC. Total budgets for recent years are shown in Table 7-4.

The BCA and JLMC budgets suggest that some costs of dispute settlement may be transferred to the state under these procedures, although one could argue that the state, the citizens, and the parties gain as a result of the reduction in conflict (and its direct and indirect costs), improvement in relationships, and bargaining outcomes more acceptable to both parties.

More Direct Bargaining

Under the Massachusetts' LBO procedures prior to 1978 it was widely perceived that frequently only *pro forma* bargaining would take place before an impasse petition was filed.[7] By waiving fact-finding, as the amended LBO statute permitted, the parties could go directly to arbitration after mediation. Since an increased proportion of disputes handled by the BCA and the JLMC have been settled at the mediation stage, it is clear that a larger proportion are settled by a process that includes bargaining between the parties—that is, the increase in mediation since 1978 suggests that more bargaining between the parties is taking place.

The nature of the Committee's case handling practices virtually guarantees that parties to every impasse must bargain more than they were compelled to under the BCA procedures alone. Even the most difficult cases are subject to one or more forms or levels of mediation that are available, even as successive impasses are reached. (See Chapter 3 for a description of these practices and alternative forms and tools to induce bargaining.) Increased bargaining also results from those instances where the Committee fosters direct bargaining simply by sending an assessor or observer or promoting peer interaction. (This sort of case is included in the tools and "informal" categories at the bottoms of Figure 3-1 and Table 7-1, respectively.)

As noted earlier, a significant proportion of arbitration awards are actually settled through joint mediation between the parties or through a mediated peer bargaining process which more nearly approximates a bargained outcome than would most forms of arbitration by an appointed third party. In peer bargaining, by engaging a volunteer representative of each side to bargain by proxy, the result is more like what the parties would have reached themselves had personalities, politics, or other non-substantive impediments not interfered. Although the result may better represent the interests of the two sides, it may not itself especially contribute to the development of the bargaining relationship. Yet, many features of a bargained settlement are likely to prevail under these mediative and peer-bargained arbitration arrangements.

Another way of examining the changed amount of direct bargaining is to gauge whether more parties are able to resolve their disputes without the aid of a third party. The previous discussion points out that such a third party increasingly is a mediator rather than an arbitrator or a fact finder. A related question is whether more parties are settling contract disputes without resort to *any* formal impasse procedures. Although on the surface there appears to be a slight decline in the number of impasses reported annually since the beginning of 1978, an accurate year-to-year comparison of the number of impasses is not possible without a more careful review of contract expirations. Nevertheless, tests on the data developed for this study do not show the decline as statistically significant. Possibly, these data are examined a bit early in the Committee's existence to gauge its impact on the sort of structural change in bargaining practices and relationships that would lead to significantly fewer reported impasses.

The lack of significant decline, then, may be due among other possibilities to continuing inexperience with direct bargaining, perhaps a result of management turnover and the political fluctuations that make stable bargaining relationships difficult to build and sustain. Possibly, more experience with direct bargaining over one or two bargaining rounds will cause an increased amount of direct bargaining to take place in the future and reduce the need for resort to impasse procedures. A comprehensive matched-pair analysis comparing the same city and union over several bargaining rounds could shed some light on this point in a few years.

Although there has not been a statistically significant reduction in the number of reported impasses in the first two years of JLMC operation, it is nevertheless clear that increased mediation, the Committee's practice of introducing bargaining into the format of arbitrations, and other policies have been associated with more settlements occurring through bargaining between the parties than occurred prior to 1978. Arbitration awards that are actually jointly agreed to—and most are—represent a form of reduction in *real* impasses, in the usual sense of the word.

Summary: Quantitative Measures of Performance

Overall, the Joint Labor-Management Committee, as the dominant alternative for settling disputes in public safety (and as of December 1980 the exclusive form of public intervention), has made progress in ameliorating many of the problems that were perceived during the pre-1978 operation of the LBO related system of dispute resolution. Settlements have been faster by nearly one half.[8] Significantly more settlements during the post-1977 period have come about through mediation rather than arbitration. Face-to-face bargaining has been increased, yet more may be attainable. The reduced settlement time and the increased degree of contact between the parties seem to lessen the parties' uncertainty and sense of risk during the process, although the flexibility of the process itself causes a degree of uncertainty. Indications are that parties are saving money, while the state's direct expenditures have increased. The JLMC system is producing less litigation than LBO and therefore avoids the resultant costs, tension, lack of communication, and uncertainty. The number of impasse petitions and requests for assistance have remained about the same for the period measured, while significant reductions have taken place in the degree of third-party intervention in the bargaining process.

Qualitative Measures of Performance: Further Improvement in Dispute Settlement

The framers of the Joint Committee also had some goals that they regarded as positive objectives—aimed not at ameliorating serious shortcomings with the existing process but rather at improving bargaining skills and relationships and at improving day-to-day operations of police or fire services. These positive goals were:

1. More mutually acceptable settlements.
2. More settlements in the joint interests of the parties.
3. More local responsibility for settlement of disputes.
4. More problem solving.
5. More practical settlements.
6. More structural change in bargaining relationships.
7. Strengthening management's bargaining skills.

These categories are highly interconnected and are, in general, less susceptible to quantitative analysis or to early indications of results, although some preliminary indication may come from the data discussed in the previous section. Gathered through case studies, through discussions with labor and management officials and politicians, and through observation of features and effects of settlements, the evidence on these objectives is largely anecdotal and impressionistic.

A significant relationship does seem apparent between achievement of these positive objectives and prior achievement of the negative objectives. For example, the greater the degree of direct bargaining and successful mediation, the more likely settlements will be in the joint interest of the parties and acceptable to them. Similarly, to the extent that direct collective bargaining can result in more information exchange and bargaining experience than can arbitration, as direct bargaining increases there is more likely to be stabilizing change in the bargaining relationship. Also, as useful information is exchanged between the parties, the opportunities for problem solving—and thus for structural changes and improvement in services—will be greater. Since several of the positive objectives seem similar in their character, a number of them are combined for this discussion.

More Acceptable Settlements in the Joint Interests of the Parties

Several factors suggest that an increased proportion of collectively bargained police and fire settlements may be acceptable to the parties under the JLMC process. First, the decrease in last-best-offer arbitration suggests that since 1978 there are about thirty cases fewer per year in which one party by definition finds the settlement unacceptable; the lack of litigation further suggests the degree of settlement acceptability. While the reduction in litigation may be partially due to the Committee's practice of requiring a waiver from each party before it will take a case for arbitration, the parties' willingness to sign the waivers indicates lesser interest, for whatever reason, in opposing settlements—even those that are arbitrated.

Second, the increased proportion of mediated settlements under the JLMC forces the parties' involvement in the settlement process and outcome through bargaining, which provides an opportunity for more thorough discussion and compromise on the issues. And where there is an exchange concerning each side's priorities, settlement is more likely to reflect those priorities. The lower number and proportion of arbitrations and higher number and proportion of mediations suggest that more settlements are now in the joint interest of the parties.

To examine acceptability, one can also observe the views expressed by some of the parties regarding JLMC arbitration. Some arbitration awards issued by the Committee, even when peer bargaining was used, have produced dissatisfaction with the substance of the award. Such dissatisfaction often seems to arise in instances where an extreme position was maintained by one party—usually the one that later complains—and/or from an insufficient degree of contact between the parties or between one of the Committee peers and the dissatisfied party. However, in those instances where one or both parties find the outcome unacceptable, it is difficult to know whether the dissatisfaction is more or less severe than that which might have existed following LBO awards. However, some parties claiming dissatisfaction with the substance of Committee awards have nevertheless found the Committee helpful in achieving settlement and have conceded that the award seem fairly arrived at.

A key to the acceptability of the awards is therefore the more widespread acceptance of the *process* for dispute settlements, especially in comparison with that of the predecessor mechanism. That the JLMC mechanism itself is accepted in the two communities contributes importantly to acceptability of individual settlements that are products of the mechanism. We might recall the comments of a local union president and fire officer from whose department an engine company was taken out of service after Committee arbitration. He said, "We knew the chairman was a fair man. Our Committee representative has full confidence in him."

Overall, the reputation of the JLMC's neutral process, the related increase in mediation, and the concomitant increase in the amount of bargaining seem to have led to greater acceptability of settlements. This acceptability is indicated by the general lack of formal or informal challenge to settlements, by the continuing agreement on the process, and most fundamentally by the way in which agreements are typically reached, where the parties themselves help to fashion the outcome.

Local Settlements

As stated above, the Committee believes that face-to-face discussion will produce the best results for both parties by exposing the true problems in the dispute. The Committee therefore has been interested in increasing the local parties' degree of responsibility for settlements, not only for reasons of settlement acceptability, but also because it believes that with local agreement there is more of a commitment to make that settlement work.

One indication of greater local settlement activity would be a reduced number of declared impasses. The data in Table 7-1 do not show a significant decline in the number of impasses following committee establishment. However, the data show that a large number of impasse settlements are achieved without formal Committee or BCA involvement. (Sixty-eight percent of completed cases were informally settled after JLMC establishment, in comparison with thirty-eight percent of cases prior to 1978.) In these cases, the Committee has played a smaller role than would an arbitrator or, frequently, a mediator. For example, a phone call might be made, an observer sent, or informal mediating performed. Although intervention at some level is common, the lesser degree of intervention since 1978 suggests that more responsibility is being taken by the parties in reaching settlements.

By encouraging local settlement the Committee has sought to leave matters of local policy, particularly where service levels or resource allocation issues were at stake, to the community itself. (Resolution of Barkfield's ambulance service issue in Chapter 4 is an example of this policy.) In addition, the amount of bargaining in both JLMC mediated and arbitrated settlements puts the discussions and settlements themselves very much in the context of local conditions and priorities. While it is not possible to measure directly, greater local responsibility for and commitment to settlements appears to result from the increase in bargaining and acceptable settlements.

Problem Solving, Practical Settlements, and Alterations in Bargaining Structure

To the extent that positions taken or impasses reached reflect difficulties in the operation of a public service or related work practices, it frequently will be important to resolve that difficulty to resolve the impasse. Alterations in services have on some occasions taken place as a result of discussions fostered by the Committee and the mediative and substantive assistance it provided. To the extent that such substantive expertise is applied and the parties are led to productive discussions, relatively more practical settlement options that address the real problems can be considered.

A deeper look can be taken at such service delivery or work practice problems in the more flexible, less formal, and more substantive interactions allowed by the Committee's statute, structure, and practices. The Barkfield case provides an example of two operational problems—scheduling and ambulance services—that greatly affected the parties' day-to-day relationship and their ability otherwise to reach agreement. Resolving the operational issue may make it easier for the parties to reach agreement by removing a seemingly insoluble problem or by demonstrating that the parties can indeed make progress in their discussions. In some instances, however, it may not be possible to evaluate until the next bargaining round whether the operational problem has been solved. In Seabury an improved fire service was a partial result of the settlement. In both Barkfield and Seabury the parties emerged apparently better able to resolve their own disputes, thereby suggesting an improvement in their bargaining skills and relationship.

Practical settlements and problem solving frequently involve alterations in service delivery practices. The Committee has frequently shown an ability to help the parties address schedules, manning levels, facilities usage, capital investment, and other down-to-earth problems. The flexible JLMC mechanism and its knowledgable members together appear able to influence service improvements by causing the parties to focus on the substance. Probably long-range structural change in service delivery is related to the Committee's ability to cause positive changes in the bargaining relationship. The parties need to be involved in productive discussions in order for practical ideas for change to emerge.

There are numerous examples like the two case studies contained in this volume where structural problems in the bargaining relationship have been discovered and altered or where attempts at alteration were made. However, it is difficult to gauge the full impact of the Committee's work on the structure of bargaining relationships until several bargaining rounds have gone by, allowing for the impact of elections and other turnover on stability in the relationship. Some proxies for a measure of this improvement in relationships might be a reduction in number of impasses reported, decreasing frequency, or intensity of third-party involvement.

Strengthening Management

The Committee attempts to deal with many of the factors that tend to weaken management's ability to be effective in collective bargaining. Poor management quality, inexperience, and conflicts among town officials often weaken management as a party to bargaining. Through personal contact by Committee staff and members with municipal officials, the Committee seeks to educate the management side regarding labor relations practices, as previous chapters have described. To the extent that turnover in municipal management is a fact of life, the existence of a structure like the Committee may permit mediators who are knowledgeable in the field (and often about the history of the parties) to re-educate the newcomers year by year, both in specifics and in general principles of labor relations. Each side is encouraged to call the JLMC's management or labor representatives for general advice, even if not involved in a dispute. Short-handed on staff and time, the Committee has not been able to expand its informal, peer-educative functions as much as intended. Most management education occurs during mediation or dispute settlement through the first-hand involvement of peers in dispute settlement.

Unlike the predecessor arbitration process, the JLMC thus provides a vehicle to strengthen the sometimes weak management side and thereby improve the bargaining relationship. Two knowledgeable parties are more likely to come to terms than are two uninformed parties. The Committee's commitment to education, therefore, has the potential to mitigate the inherent weaknesses of the management side which arise from turnover of elected leadership, the separation of powers, and overall lack of labor relations experience. The strengthening and equalizing of local bargaining abilities perhaps may lead to more local settlement of disputes.

Overall, one cannot say conclusively that municipal management has been strengthened during the Committee's first two years, although casual observation and the case studies in this volume demonstrate that individual management teams have been educated during specific disputes. The Committee furthermore has recently completed an internal study which suggests that even when an impasse is declared, management generally is now in a stronger position, with fewer outstanding issues, than was the case earlier in the Committee's existence.[9] The Committee, in its peer and mediative roles and as an informal clearinghouse of labor relations concerns, seems to provide at least a service and a support for management that never before existed. Committee and senior staff members can assist management in ways that a more usual neutral agent could not. Committee assistance to the management side (also available to the labor side) provides a mechanism that, at least in individual disputes, can strengthen the abilities of the management side to carry on a productive bargaining relationship.

Leadership turnover common to public management can retard the development of stable relationships and improved bargaining practices in a community. This inherent difference from private employment relations may be a fundamental barrier to parallel maturation of public sector bargaining practices. Re-educating public management on issues, practices, and personalities, therefore, may be basic to the evolution of improved public labor relations. It may be that a joint neutral system can address this need more appropriately than can those existing institutions which provide only labor–or management–oriented training services. The joint approach of a committee, representing both viewpoints, seems capable of more realistic education and can avoid creating additional antagonism that is sometimes a by-product of one-sided advisory services. Thus, the educational function of a committee must be considered not a secondary offshoot of its mediative functions but a critical service needed to increase over time the number of mediated or unaided settlements and to improve bargaining relationships.

Meeting the Positive Objectives

The positive objectives are not only more difficult to measure but they may prove more difficult to achieve in public bargaining, where more external factors and forces can influence the process. Nevertheless, indications are that the increase in bargaining and the existence of a central, skilled, and respected agency is providing avenues for more mutually acceptable bargaining outcomes than was possible under the more rigid and legalistic arbitration system that previously prevailed. Improvements have been made both in bargaining relationships and in service delivery under this approach. As basic Committee operations have become more regular and as experience with the mechanism grows, more attention can be and is paid to these longer-term objectives and related activities.

Summary

While further and more comprehensive study could be made in an evaluative piece following a few more rounds of bargaining and years of JLMC experience, quantitative examination of its impasse resolution activity suggests that the performance objectives of the Committee have been partially met by faster, less expensive and more mediated settlements. Time to settlement has declined by nearly half, and the proportion of mediated settlements has nearly doubled. An increase in good-faith efforts to solve issues in dispute, mutually acceptable outcomes, and local commitment to carry out settlements also appear, on preliminary review, to be influenced positively by the Committee's presence. Thus, the JLMC seems generally to have succeeded in improving upon the results of conventional and last-best-offer impasse procedures.

Uncertainties with regard to JLMC procedures are troublesome but may dissipate with experience, and the remaining uncertainty may be partially offset by the value of procedural flexibility. However, the Committee's flexibility in determining procedures could have drawbacks should the parties not be kept sufficiently informed. Through its peer network the Committee has informal tools available to prevent most confusion on the part of those involved in a dispute, but its volunteer membership limits its use of such tools.

The possibilities for improving services and bargaining relationships, strengthening management, and promoting other long-term changes have been illustrated by JLMC activities thus far. Until recently, time spent on evolving and stabilizing basic practices has prevented thorough attention to these long-term objectives. Nevertheless, progress has been made. Now that the Committee has had a few years to become established, further study of its ability to tackle entrenched and inherent difficulties in public sector bargaining would be of value.

Endnotes

1. For some studies of these dimensions in various settings see Lipsky *et al.*, *The Impact of Final Offer Arbitration*; Kochan *et al.*, *Dispute Resolution Under Factfinding and Arbitration*; Stern *et al.*, *Final Offer Arbitration*.

2. These "negative" and "positive" objectives were articulated formally on June 15, 1979, in remarks by John T. Dunlop, the neutral Chairman of the Joint Labor-Management Committee, and Demetrios Moschos, Management Chairman of the Joint Labor-Management Committee, to the Massachusetts City Councillors' Conference, Brandeis University, Waltham, Massachusetts, sponsored by Brandeis University and the Institute of Politics, Harvard University.

3. The statistics relied on in this section are from an independent study by Captain William H. Mattfeld, September 29, 1980, while a candidate for a master's degree in Public Policy at the John F. Kennedy School of Government, Harvard University. The author notes and appreciates his patience and analytic skills applied creatively to some very unwieldy data. The author and Mr. Mattfeld gratefully acknowledge the cooperation and skills of Paul F. Cody, Research Director of the Joint Labor-Management Committee for Municipal Police and Fire Fighters.

4. John T. Dunlop, "Commonwealth of Massachusetts Joint Labor-Management Committee for Municipal Police and Fire," *Massachusetts Business and Economic Report* Vol. 8, No. 2 (Fall 1980), Management Research Center, School of Business Administration, University of Massachusetts, Amherst, Massachusetts.

5. As defined by the Joint Labor-Management Committee, formal settlement refers only to the issuance of an interest arbitration award. Informal settlement refers, then, to Committee participation ranging from "observer" status to cases in which jurisdiction has been taken, mediation supplied but no third-party award issued.

6. To be more precise about the meaning of the interval describing reduction in time to settlement, it may be stated in statistical terms: One can state with 95 percent confidence that the true average reduction in time to settlement lies within this 65- to 145-day interval. Since the data that was used represented only part of the whole population, the mean reduction of 105 days represents only the average reduction for the sample used and not necessarily for the population as a whole, whose average reduction should be between 65 and 145 days.

7. There has been much discussion in the literature on compulsory interest arbitration regarding the "chilling" or "narcotic" effect of such impasse proceedings on actual bargaining. Clearly, there was a perception that such was the case in Massachusetts. Many discussions and analysis of this general problem are available. See Geare, "Final Offer Arbitration"; or Peter Feuille, "Final Offer Arbitration and the Chilling Affect," 14 *Industrial Relations* 302 (October 1975); or Stevens, "Is Compulsory Arbitration Compatible with Collective Bargaining?" among others.

8. According to the JLMC's annual report for FY 1981, overall average settlement time for cases resolved in that year was 3.70 months. Average settlement time for those cases in which the Committee did not formally take jurisdiction but was

involved in settlement was 1.60 months, and for those cases in which the JLMC voted to take jurisdiction, 4.73 months.
9. Unpublished internal study by Paul F. Cody, Research Director, Joint Labor-Management Committee for Municipal Police and Fire Fighters, 1981.

Chapter 8

ADVANCING CONCEPTS IN PUBLIC BARGAINING: STRUCTURAL IMPROVEMENT AND THE ROLE OF POLITICS

There are several elements of the Joint Committee experiment that attend to especially troublesome aspects of public labor-management relations. These are highlighted here for use in application and conceptual development in the field. Chapter 1 outlined a number of factors that differentiate public and private labor relations and that help explain public sector bargaining problems. This chapter examines how well the JLMC considers a number of those factors and whether its concept and mechanism represent an improved approach to public sector dispute settlement.[1] Two important functions of a joint committee approach will be addressed in this regard: (1) the extent to which it can provide some stability to a given public bargaining environment so that the parties can better focus on problem solving, and (2) the extent to which the effect of politics on bargaining behavior is appropriately factored in and otherwise kept out.

One impediment to public bargaining is the relative lack of broad-based experience with bargaining and dispute settlement. In contrast to the current state of private labor-management relations, many practices and assumptions in public bargaining are still in flux. The right to unionize and to bargain are still questioned in many public jurisdictions. Impasse procedures, in particular, are being debated, both where such procedures do not exist and where they

197

have been enacted. The prevalence of strike prohibitions and other sovereignty-related issues impels the search for alternative closure mechanisms, yet the lack of consensus on alternatives frequently leads to dissatisfaction with and change of the existing procedures. Thus the parameters of the bargaining relationship are frequently unstable.[2]

The lack of agreement on proven techniques for public bargaining and dispute settlements results in frequent alterations in the laws, rules and practices governing collective bargaining in many jurisdictions, leaving one party or both baffled or upset with the new arrangements and seeking to use influence to change arrangements to suit their predilictions. In the public environment, where experience has not yet encountered the bulk of the problems and where tools and approaches have not yet evolved to fit these problems, productive labor-management relations is often difficult to achieve.

Therefore, an important aspect to address in assessing the JLMC's contribution is the capacity of a mechanism like this to introduce and maintain a stable legal and procedural framework for public bargaining and dispute resolution. One important aspect of this stability is the mechanism's capacity to balance labor and management's relative power to influence the process. Another feature of a stable bargaining framework is its ability to permit changes in practices to evolve incrementally as experience highlights necessity, rather than introducing large and discrete changes which tend to generate their own controversy and instability. Yet another is the extent to which management's sovereignty concerns are addressed in conjunction with the desire for collective bargaining.

A second and related area to consider in assessing the JLMC mechanism's contributions to the field is its ability to recognize and handle the presence of politics in public affairs.[3] Political aspects of the public bargaining relationship and environment necessitate looking beyond the tools developed in private employment settings. Politics affects the bargaining environment as laws are passed and procedures are changed. It also affects the outcome of individual disputes and perceptions of the parties concerning the impartiality of the neutral body. Finally, politics importantly affects the tensions and relationships within the management side. Techniques and mechanisms for resolving public sector disputes must, therefore, recognize and confront these political and related differences from private employment.

Structural Stability in the Bargaining Environment

Frequent additions to and constant changes in public bargaining laws occur as one or the other dissatisfied party challenges by various means laws, regulations, and awards. These challenges can cause new laws to be promulgated or otherwise influence—often unilaterally—prevailing practices and rules. Improving the stability of such an environment might be defined as creating a situation in which (1) both sides find they have reasonable influence over the parameters governing the labor-management relationship, (2) the rules, practices, and traditions are known, and (3) the most important needs of each side are taken into account. Without such equilibrium in power and influence, bargaining and dispute settlements are made difficult by bitter feelings, political and judicial efforts to alter the parameters, and confusion over proper behavior and procedures. A stable environment would be one in which neither side would feel unduly compelled to use its political influence to alter the basic structure of the system or the rules that define the relationship and procedures.

The stability that has characterized the bargaining environment since establishment of the JLMC appears to have arisen from four general principles: (1) joint development of the mechanism and participation in its operation; (2) equilibrium of access and power to influence decisions regarding elements of the mechanism and handling of specific disputes; (3) a broad and flexible legislative basis (in this case a state statute) that allows adaptation to developing experience and changing needs without requiring hostile public debate, participation of outside parties, or legislative action; and (4) preservation of key aspects of bargaining and sovereignty. These four factors seem to improve (over other methods) a joint committee's ability to promote a more stable set of bargaining relationships and environment.

Joint Participation

Joint membership reflects the concept that stability can be better promoted by agreement between the sides than by actions of the political system alone or with a disproportionate influence of one side on the political process. The first four years of the JLMC's existence indicate that the two sides can be entrusted with the power to determine their own fate. They make rules, process cases, and propose and impose settlements that have, with one exception, never been appealed or seriously challenged.

The JLMC experience indicates that joint participation in development of the structure and operation of the process can result in a blending of seemingly opposing viewpoints and needs. At the time of JLMC creation, for example, labor's prime interests were to obtain closure on contract disputes. In contrast, management sought, at a minimum, more equal treatment than it perceived it had been receiving under last-offer binding arbitration, and it more generally wished to avoid third-party involvement. A joint mechanism was sought to mesh both sets of interests, as each side was prepared to pressure the political system to act in its singular interest. By joint agreement on a procedure for development of a dispute resolution mechanism, a system was developed that reflected each side's priorities.

The concept of joint responsibilities facilitates adjustment to changing needs and developing interests. For the first four years the JLMC has made a number of adjustments reflecting fluctuating needs, varied interests, and simple experience. Indicative of the mechanisms' capacity to meet these needs and interests is the development of a variety of tools and staffing arrangements and the fact that, to date, no significant pressure has been exerted by unions or city and town management (as had been during the previous decade) on the state legislature or executive to alter materially the dispute resolution statute for public safety employees.

The question that remains to be answered over time is whether the joint structure is capable of preserving such a tension-based balance. Thus far, turnover in key Committee individuals has not damaged this balance. When each party is satisfied that a mechanism is capable of meeting its needs, attention and energy are directed toward making the process work. Thus energy is not expended on arguing, challenging, or changing laws or awards but is devoted to the existing process, in a forum in which each side has sufficient access, power, and trust in the system to make use of that system.

The representative manner in which the Committee was established and its internal operating dynamics have stabilized to some degree the power relationship between labor and management. Because the joint mechanism was created and is run by both sides, each side has been able to influence internal procedures and the system can incorporate the changing needs of both parties. Thus, neither side has an immediate interest in altering the parameters of bargaining and invoking the uncertainty and resentment that characterized the earlier 1970s. This stability, however, can be threatened by radical, rapid change in the external environment, as seen during the debate and passage of Proposition 2½. Careful maintenance of communication on these issues has helped to keep the environment stable. A breakdown in the Committee members' capacity to exchange views would alter its capacity to adapt to such external changes—or to internal changes of similar magnitude.

Equilibrium of Access and Power

Joint participation is a key to stability, and in labor-management relations such participation must include an acceptable degree of influence over outcome on the part of each side. Joint participation cannot exist where the power relationships are greatly unbalanced. For example, in time periods or jurisdictions in which only consultation rights existed or in which no neutral dispute resolution procedures were in place, management had the bulk of the power to settle disputes. They could do so by refusing to bargain in good faith or operating a simple "take it or leave it" strategy. To alter the environment in their favor, employee groups sought to use their political clout with the legislature by lobbying for dispute resolution mechanisms that would force the process to a conclusion. In Massachusetts this was accomplished through the introduction of last-best-offer arbitration. Management saw this approach as tipping the balance toward undue labor influence in the process, and it spent lobbying and legal energy to block or alter the LBO procedure.

One reason for management's willingness to rely on the Committee mechanism and drop its efforts to return to pre-LBO, management-dominated conditions was its perception that the Committee assured it more nearly equal influence with labor on cases and policy. The Committee's establishment seemed a reasonable alternative to provide management with an important, equitable voice in final settlements. Management's positive experience with the JLMC resulted in its withdrawal of opposition to binding arbitration as long as the JLMC could control its use.

This mutually beneficial redirection of energy and the resultant group dynamics and relationships within the JLMC have served to moderate and channel some of the political power of the public

employee groups in directions that provide solutions satisfactory to
both parties. The effect of the JLMC on the balance of public employee and management political power has been extremely
significant in promoting a stable and constructive labor relations
environment.

A positive example of the Committee's success in promoting stability and redirecting energy toward problem solving is the Seabury
case of Chapter 5. Unhappy with a binding arbitration award declared by a third-party arbitrator, the town filed an appeal with the
courts. The appeal stopped the bargaining process; no bargaining
took place for at least a year while a fight was waged in court. Instead
of working toward a settlement, the parties awaited the outcome of
the court case. (Although the court decision would affect the entire
award, the arguments centered on *one* item: whether minimum
manning was a bargainable issue.) The court decision was bound to
anger one of the parties by either throwing out or upholding the
entire LBO award. In contrast, when the JLMC became involved in
the case, it worked out between the parties a solution tolerable to
both sides, taking into account the political and substantive realities
of the entire package on the table. The approach appeared successful
to the degree that energy was spent resolving issues in dispute
rather than in arguing about legal parameters. In addition, a degree
of learning and improvement resulted in the bargaining relationship
and in the quality of service.

Broad Enabling Legislation

A third feature of the JLMC has also contributed to the stability of
the police and fire bargaining environment in Massachusetts: the
Joint Committee's flexible legislation, which permits it to alter
practices to fit changed or newly discovered circumstances in the
bargaining environment without requiring renewed legislative debate. This feature both smooths and accelerates changes in impasse
practices. Without joint participation and a balance of power, such
flexibility could have negative results.

Under a flexible statute, the still-evolutionary nature of public
bargaining need not require protracted political debate over proposed changes in practices. As experience or problems accumulate
within a jurisdiction, parties need not tolerate increasing levels of
frustration with existing practices and then experience a radical
change in procedures; new techniques or smaller changes in re-

sponse to experience can be implemented by internal joint decisions of the committee membership. For example the development of hearing formats, conditional bargaining, peer bargaining, and other techniques were not contemplated previous to the Committee's actual operation. Changes in impasse practice, it appears from Committee experience, can evolve with limited associated turbulence under a legislative framework broad enough to accommodate development and change.

The passage of Proposition 2½, which excised the Committee's power to mandate funding of arbitration awards, removed arbitration as a tool but left intact the Committee structure. To continue its work under these new conditions, the JLMC has adapted by using, to an even greater degree, its representative membership and their peer relationships to foster bargaining and problem solving. In particular, work with the legislative branch of municipalities has intensified. A severe test of the Committee's effectiveness without the power of binding arbitration may be ahead, but the flexible statute, continued commitment of the parties, and the many forms of influence toward resolution allowed by the group's mandate and structure may help preserve some stability in the period ahead.

The Costs of Change. Without the Committee, Proposition 2½ would have resulted in a void in dispute settlement practices, which would tend to focus top-level attention away from disputes and problem solving and toward a new political fight. Without the JLMC's flexible mandate, legislative action to put new machinery into place would have been required. Another political battle, with its attendant uncertainty of outcome and negative effect on individual bargaining relationships, such as stalling, court challenges, and other tactics, would contribute little to labor peace or productive public safety operations, which during this period of fiscal restraint would be difficult enough to maintain. In contrast, the Committee's internal and statutory flexibility seems to keep the labor and management communities talking and seeking ways to resolve disputes. A less adaptive arrangement during this or a similar stressful period could force one party or the other back to the legislature, the courts, or other arenas of confrontation where change can be sudden, unpredictable, or antithetical to the interests of one or both parties.

Beneficial Aspects of Flexibility. An important side benefit of an adaptive mechanism is that the parties have time and energy to develop productive bargaining relationships. Without the need for constant legal battling or adaptation to new laws, new institutions, new actors, and new procedures, the parties can focus more time on bargaining and on issues. With fairly constant parameters, the temptation is reduced to stop negotiating while waiting for the court to throw out on appeal a ruling statute or award.

A broad statutory base gives the parties the means to avoid protracted public and political discussions and sudden or unwanted changes in the laws governing disputes. If coupled with a joint representative mechanism, this flexibility allows dispute resolution practices to evolve with greater attention to problem solving and with less disruption. The field of public labor-management relations is also served in that adaptable mechanisms facilitate experimentation and evolution of improved techniques and tools.

Sovereignty and Collective Bargaining

As discussed in Chapter 1, management, citizens, and political scientists have often cited sovereignty as grounds for objecting to third-party decision making in interest (or even grievance) disputes. The JLMC responded to this concern by providing a means of settling disputes that keeps the power from a third party and, through the Committee's practices and membership structure, distributes it to those who must live with the settlement or, at a minimum, to group representatives who are elected officials or their direct appointees. Any outside arbitrator appointments are made only with joint consent of the JLMC membership, and outside arbitrators are carefully briefed by members and/or staff. The volunteer and representative members have critical influence over virtually each case decision.

Joint approval of the enabling statute and management participation in policy formulation and the settlement mechanism has allowed management to become a full participant in resolving disputes and in determining labor-management policy. Thus, the issue of sovereignty has been handled to the satisfaction of most nearby management observers; through the JLMC, a management Committee member affects importantly every policy and case decision. Still, labor maintains its influence as an equal party to bargaining and settlement both through the emphasis on bargaining between the parties and through peer bargaining in arbitration.

In contrast to systems in which third parties resolve impasses, management is fundamentally involved in this crucial range of fiscal decisions. For labor, the more rapid closure of disputes meets one of its most important criteria. With both sovereignty concerns and bargaining concerns largely satisfied, the argument is stilled over which philosophy or method should dominate in determining terms and conditions of public employment. The silencing of the debate between advocates of sovereignty and advocates of bargaining contributes much to the equilibrium and consequent tranquility and stability in the bargaining environment.

Politics: Factoring It In and Keeping It Out

In discussing both the stability of the bargaining environment and the broader need for improved understanding and ability to practice public sector labor relations, an important question arises: Does this mechanism assist our handling of politics in public labor-management relations and its impact on bargaining, settlement, and implementation?

The effect of politics on the evolution of public labor relations practices and on the settlement of individual disputes has long complicated the discussion and practice of the art. Additional knowledge of and practice in dealing with this complication could contribute to better structuring of dispute resolution practices, better handling of specific disputes, and more satisfaction with the outcomes on the part of the parties and the public. Thus, the connection between politics and the nature of the bargaining environment shall be examined here. Some conclusions will then be drawn about the Committee's attempts properly to factor in this special dimension of the public sector.

Distinctions from the Private Environment

Public sector labor relations seem in many instances to be carried out according to someone's *idea* of private sector labor relations; the grandstanding, get-tough-at-contract-time mayor seems to be taking a page from labor relations of a bygone era—or at least some of the more truculent episodes in modern private sector labor history. This approach does not solve all problems in labor relations and collective bargaining. Some of the important differences between public and private circumstances have implications for successful public bargaining and dispute settlement. To the extent that this Massachusetts experiment factors in those differences, it may contain some useful lessons for designing and carrying out resolution of public sector labor disputes.

It is both well known and widely accepted that in the private sector internal union politics often plays an important role in labor relations, the dynamics of negotiations, and ability to settle. Although there are political influences on private management behavior, corporate officials are not elected in the same way as union or political leaders. Politics—in the sense of elections, checks and balances, and resulting activities—therefore is not ordinarily a factor in private management.[4]

In the public sector, internal union politics remain a factor in bargaining behavior and traditions, but the fact that management is elected or appointed by elected officials suggests critical differences between public and private management behavior and labor relations practices. As Chapter 1 notes, elective politics in public management alters its basic ability to negotiate and settle labor disputes in a number of ways: First, changing political leadership affects the stability and quality of the bargaining relationship, can reduce continuity, and can prevent expertise from developing in the management chair.[5] Second, the existence of elections requires that management officials be sensitive not just to their sense of fairness or the bottom line, but to public perceptions.[6] In addition, unions support some candidates and oppose others, complicating bargaining—particularly at election time. Third, the separation of powers means that a legislative body is likely to be involved in second-guessing and pressuring the executive, sometimes negotiating itself, and usually in ratifying a collectively bargained agreement. The viewpoint and/or the power of the legislature may constrain the flexibility of the management negotiator.[7] Also, there are frequently a variety of elected officials—often in conflict—who are involved, such as mayors, town council members, finance committees, personal boards, and the like. Fourth, because of the political activity of unions as lobbyists, campaigners, and voters in local elections, relationships between the unions and the legislators will affect the executive-legislative relationship. For example, union leaders under some circumstances may formally or informally bypass the management negotiating team and seek means to influence legislators.[8] Fifth, and further complicating these factors, is the relationship of state-level politics and state regulations, statutes, and other programs (such as state aid to municipalities or civil service rules) to the statewide political activities of union or municipal groups in nonbargaining matters.[9] Also, a critical difference, of course, is the traditional effect of labor groups in lobbying for bargaining rights and other parameters in the labor relations environment. With the increase in restrictions on local government revenues, this state-level relationship may be even more crucial. Typically, employee organizations are active in such arenas.

Politics: In or Out?

Keeping partisan political influence out of decisions is critical to making proper and fair decisions and maintaining the trust of the public and the parties. Perceptions of political neutrality in dispute resolution will improve bargaining behavior. For example, a party's views of the LBO process affected behavior and generally will encourage bargaining rather than stalling or the seeking of other forums.

Different from partisan politics in influencing third-party decisions, the day-to-day politics of the community, which determine the character of its executive and legislative branches, and the community's elections are a part of the normal and accepted workings of a municipality as an employer. Participation of local unions in municipal politics is also part of normal activities in most jurisdictions. These are critical facts of life in the public thicket; in seeking to resolve disputes realistically in public employment, one must take these facts into account. Cost calculations and the ability to pay cannot by themselves bring the parties to accommodation, for either party can be influenced by or may seek to influence an outside force such as the media, the legislature, or the populace. This predisposition to involve external political forces must be recognized and dealt with.

Keeping Politics Out: The JLMC Appointment Process. Seeking to ensure that the mechanism would be isolated from partisan political influences, the creators of the Joint Committee designed a statute that does not permit the governor or the legislature to influence the nomination of members or the selection of the neutral. The law mandates that the governor appoint members who are nominated by the constituent labor and management groups, thus increasing the commitment of the parties to the process, since they alone determine the quality of its membership. Similarly, the neutral chair and vice-chair are selected jointly by the members. Both groups can less easily (or are less likely to) criticize or bypass the process when they have responsibility for all appointments to the group. This method of appointment carries the risk that a bad nomination might be made by one of the parties. However, such an action would have direct negative consequences to that parties' interests. This relationship between the power to appoint and being directly affected by the consequences of any mistake in this regard provides a greater incentive perhaps for careful, less politically motivated nominations than one might find under an appointment process controlled by a legislature or governor.

Thus far, no significant difficulty with this arrangement has surfaced, although it is unclear whether an unsympathetic governor could influence nominations should he or she choose to do so. Apparently, the political channels of both sides have at different times assisted in maintaining a good relationship with the chief executive's office in and ensuring independence of the committee. (One staff member to a high-ranking politician inquired about some "job vacancies" on the Joint Labor-Management Committee and was briskly informed of the statutory appointment procedure and the proprietary feelings of both union and management about Committee membership. The matter was promptly dropped.)

The success of this appointment procedure depends not only on respect from the governor and legislature but also to an important degree on the organization and internal discipline of each side. Without the statewide organizational structures of both sides, agreement on nominations might be difficult. The need for internal consensus is a potential obstacle in the appointment process, inasmuch as internal differences within the fire fighters, police, or local government advisory committee could have caused delays and dissatisfaction. The Massachusetts JLMC has experienced only some minor difficulty in this regard.

Keeping Politics In: Nominations and Membership.   The nominating and appointment process, on the other hand, is one aspect of the committee's structure that keeps two important political considerations *in* the mechanism: The process is responsive to the parties' internal politics and thus encourages their commitment and ability to make it work. By encouraging the groups to accommodate their internal political differences in order to nominate someone representative, the process tries to keep internal group politics from entering the dispute resolution process.

Next, local electoral and legislative politics represent political considerations important to dispute settlement. These can be molded into the process by the membership composition of a committee. Representing a spectrum of officialdom on the management side, members as a group can be perceptive of and knowledgeable about electoral politics, the political relationship between executive and legislative branches of a municipal government, and related political matters. Similarly, the practiced political antennae of the union side add to the group experience and information about dealing with political relationships. Through its members' experience and sensitivity and by its informal operations, a committee can be kept aware of most political differences, electoral issues, and other considerations that may be affecting the behavior of either side in a dispute. This characteristic of the membership structure provides an informative adjunct to the normal mediative abilities of a neutral agency.

Political Factors in Bargaining Decisions

A municipality sometimes sees an advantage in binding interest arbitration because the responsibility for a politically unpalatable decision could then be blamed on the third party. Use of LBO arbitration allowed a mayor or manager to take an extreme public position in opposition to the union and/or to cost increases while taking little responsibility for the outcome. A political point may be made, but bargaining and operating relationships often suffer. Internal union politics in some instances can prompt similar grandstanding behavior under the security of third-party responsibility. Notwithstanding problems in the bargaining relationship, there can be political incentives for both sides occasionally to seek settlement through the arbitration process rather than through bargaining.

By using policies and tools to encourage bargaining at each successive impasse, a committee can work to prevent the inclination to take rigid positions for political purposes. Rather, it seeks to keep parties talking to enable them to solve problems locally and to take responsibility for settlements and outcomes. As politically experienced individuals, however, committee staff and members understand the exigencies of politics. Committee arbitration awards have been, therefore, periodically issued because of the political need of one or both parties, not always because of a lack of agreement or voluntary settlement. While in some circumstances the parties may make inflammatory public statements for political reasons, under joint committee practices they are normally engaged in bargaining and settlement.

Using Political Ties

Through a committee's peer structure, a mayor in a negotiation, for example, can be approached by a committee member who is also a mayor. The member-mayor can provide some credible perspective on the connection of the dispute to other political considerations. He or she may suggest some ways of accommodating both political and negotiating priorities, such as altering the term of the contract so that it does not expire at a politically critical time.

The Committee membership, consisting as it does of members from both legislative and executive branches of management, also finds itself frequently resolving differences between legislative and executive actors in a municipality. The Seabury case is a relatively dramatic example of these activities. This sort of peer assistance, which recognizes political relationships, is one of the important tools afforded by a joint committee with a peer membership structure.

With the apparent removal of arbitration power as a result of Proposition 2½, greater use will probably be made of Committee ties that bring an executive and legislature into a closer working relationship in labor-management matters to ensure that a municipal legislature will fund a contract settlement. With the fiat of binding arbitration no longer available, mediation and persuasion will have to prevail to an even greater degree than before.[10] The experience of Committee members and their observations of other communities where this executive-legislative relationship works well can help resolve the debilitating differences that sometimes arise between the two branches over funding labor costs. In those states and localities facing reduced resources, avenues for such accommodation may be particularly useful. Such avenues will also be of use in jurisdictions where arbitration is not available.

Internal Politics

The presence on a committee of individuals with ties to their respective communities poses at least one problem for factoring in the politics of collective bargaining. In resolving an individual dispute within a joint committee, something inequitable or inappropriate could conceivably become part of a settlement as larger or unrelated political issues influence some members' behavior. For example, it may be critical to the internal politics of either the labor or management side that its representative on a committee strongly favor the constituent's position on an issue in dispute. In the interest of maintaining that representative's credibility with his or her constituency and therefore his or her strength as a committee member with influence on that constituency, members of the other side might yield on that item even if it were somewhat contrary to their own constituents' interest. Since most settlements are actually mediated between the parties, the possibility of this sort of situation is minimized, but it could arise in difficult cases involving peer bargaining, for instance. Also, the presence of experienced staff-neutrals, the balance of power within a committee, and the general commitment of the members to strengthened bargaining and long-term stability are intended to prevent the development of trade-offs harmful to any party.

A less serious trade-off might occur in expediting the scheduling of hearings or mediation sessions where it may be important to a labor or management member's credibility to show action in a particular case. Similarly, because the same group handles all disputes, a committee member may be willing, in the interest of settlement, to influence constituents to concede on an issue in exchange for the general assurance that the group will provide the member a concession, either in that dispute or another. Were there no opportunity to accommodate internal political interests from case to case, a single issue might fester and prevent settlement in each of a series of unconnected cases and might unwittingly harm the credibility of a member over the long term. On the other hand, injudicious handling of such trade-offs could result in actual or perceived improper influence. The Committee has gained from experience in this area. It's a delicate point of ethics and, like most such points, must be resolved both in a general context of proper public conduct and practical problem solving in the public interest. It represents the usual dilemma of means and ends. In this instance the dilemma relates to a short-term decision with slight consequences to an individual or party but with larger implications for resolving problems or maintaining a process for doing so in the broader community.

Interlocking Political Interests and Dispute Settlement

Politics and political alliances are often very relevant to a particular local labor dispute, to the development of a bargaining relationship, and to the resolution of disputes. For example, where a local union may be in the habit of appealing to the local legislature over the head of an executive, a committee, by helping management to unify its legislative and executive parts and to work more effectively at bargaining, can minimize the use of this "end-run" practice and thereby strengthen the bargaining process. Or, if it seems useful to settlement, a committee labor representative can urge the local union to deal head-on with the executive branch. With the management and labor sides of a committee working toward common goals and strategies, indirect political efforts to alter wages and working conditions can be redirected in favor of face-to-face bargaining.

Issues which may affect more than one municipal dispute also can complicate labor-management relationships. Simple weekly communication between the two sides at case meetings decreases the opportunity for misunderstandings to arise and enmities to develop over broader political issues. The two sides of a committee are therefore better able to work together not only to resolve individual case problems but also larger issues that might affect them—issues such as civil service reform and questions associated with reductions in revenues and the desire for some fiscal relief from the state. By providing a statewide focus where none existed before on certain matters affecting labor-management relations, the Committee has increased the capacity to devise mutually acceptable alternatives, or at least to maintain a dialogue. As this volume goes to press, the JLMC is discussing regionalization of public safety services. By necessity, a topic such as this that affects the interests of several municipal jurisdictions cannot be handled in the context of an individual dispute; rather it must be dealt with at a high level of organization and political authority.

Sharing Political Power

Although a unified management was not single-handedly responsible for the emergence of the Committee and the sweeping aside of binding arbitration, management was unified in collecting signatures for a referendum to repeal binding arbitration and in negotiating with the fire fighters over the substitute for arbitration. Accordingly, the strength of this unity put pressure on the fire fighters to negotiate and compromise, but management's unity and accommodation with the union was expressed to the legislature through the political power and channels established by the fire fighters over many years. It was the fire fighters' clout in the legislature that ultimately gained an alternate mechanism to the binding arbitration that management had been seeking to replace.

Similarly, the Committee's first requests for budgetary support were handled in the legislature by the fire fighters' lobbying channels. Management had significant input in the budget process and was able to have its interests served, but through the fire fighters' political channels. Management thus succeeded because it developed personal and professional relationships and respect through the Committee mechanism, which had identified common interests and for which both sides shared some common commitment. More recently, management channels have been used as well.

This sharing of political power has stabilized and strengthened labor relations in several ways. First, the Committee provides a respected state-level focus for municipal public safety labor relations that had not previously existed. Second, a variety of issues concerning the overall structure and process of statewide public safety labor relations can be discussed, influenced, or settled. Third, it serves to focus management dialogue—previously splintered—and gives a united group of management members a voice to influence state level labor relations issues.

Summary

As academics and practitioners in this field seek to advance the state-of-the art and our understanding of it, those aspects of the JLMC that explicitly deal with the developmental and political aspects of public labor-management relations seem to be worthy of note. In many instances the parties and the environment in public labor relations will require nurturing before practices and talents are sufficiently developed to regularly produce generally stable relationships and outcomes. One must also distinguish between those aspects of politics that must be screened out and those that are necessarily a part of labor-management interactions in the public sector. To the extent that the several distinctions from private employment can be factored into revised or new approaches to public labor relations, perhaps a more effective and satisfactory set of dispute resolutions and bargaining techniques can be evolved and applied. While inspection of the Massachusetts experiment may provoke other lessons or problems, stabilizing the environment and handling politics are two which, in the light of experience of the last two decades, seem worthy of attention in seeking to advance the field.

The JLMC has exemplified a flexible statute and structure that allows the continued maturation of bargaining and dispute resolution practices without significant disruption to existing practices. As a result, rather than using Massachusetts public safety dispute resolution efforts as a target of change and resentment, energy has been spent on improving communication between the parties, resolving individual cases, and building bargaining relationships.

Different sorts of mechanisms that permit evolution and avoid conflict can be envisioned; that is, mechanisms of the parties' own making, with recognition of real needs and safeguards against real suspicions, and not anyone else's idea of how things should work "if politicians and union leaders would behave properly." A broad enabling statute allows for adaptation to changing circumstances without extensive political posturing and debate and permits practices to adapt internally to changing needs and circumstances while avoiding the uncertainties associated with statutory regulatory and administrative reform.

The JLMC represents a creative if imperfect response to the sovereignty question. Committee membership includes appointees who have been elected in their jurisdictions, and local management authorities, together with their labor counterparts, play a significant role in developing settlements. The public interest seems to be better represented in this joint structure than through arbitration, for these joint processes allow for greater accountability through elected officials volunteering as Committee members.

One disagreement in public sector bargaining, and dispute resolution in particular, has been over whether it should resemble collective bargaining or public policy making. A major contribution of the JLMC experiment is that it has created a way to incorporate critical features of each process. The joint approach incorporates more collective bargaining and a greater degree of public policy control than would exist under most interest arbitration mechanisms. It does so by handling sovereignty concerns through its membership.

The important role of politics in public sector labor relations has been incorporated into the Committee mechanism, as has the need to deal with political motivations and pressures on the parties in dispute. Inappropriate political influence over its membership and decisions has been largely avoided by the appointment process and the tension maintained by equal participation. This balance of political power also enables the Committee to use political ties to obtain information that in turn allows relevant political factors in a dispute to be acknowledged and considered with some perspective. Here again, it is the membership structure that permits these political factors and influence to be properly incorporated and to be effectively utilized.

The Committee has not only provided a consistent voice and united front for management but has also become the source of an unusual political partnership between labor and management. This partnership, which is still quite young, may prove to be particularly useful for approaching state officials on matters of common labor-management interests, such as employment and civil service issues and allocation of financial resources.

The joint membership of the mechanism forms the basis for the factors contributing to stability of the bargaining environment. Similarly, the membership structure and the conditions of appointment permit politics of a partisan nature to be screened out and allow political factors which impede settlements to be handled in a direct manner.

Endnotes

1. For a general discussion of public and private differences, see Walter Gershenfeld, J. Joseph Lowenberg, and Bernard Ingster, *The Scope of Public Sector Bargaining* (Lexington, Massachusetts: Lexington Books, 1977), Chapter 1. See also Harry H. Wellington and Ralph K. Winter, Jr., "The Limits of Collective Bargaining in Public Employment," *The Yale Law Journal*, Vol. 78.

2. Examination of the changes in bargaining rights and dispute resolution practices over only a few years suggests the frequency and rapidity of such changes. See selected issues of *Summary of Public Sector Labor Relations*, U.S. Department of Labor, for a simple comparison. For a discussion of aspects of these changes see B. V. H. Schneider, "Public Sector Labor Legislation—and Evolutionary Analysis," in Aaron *et al.*, *Public Sector Bargaining*.

3. For a discussion on several aspects of politics in public bargaining, see Lieberman, *Public Sector Bargaining*, Chapter 4, "The Political Nature of Public Bargaining." See also Bok and Dunlop, *Labor and the American Community*, Sector Bargaining." See also Bok and Dunlop, *Labor and the American Community*, Chapter 14, "Labor in National and State Politics," for a general description of labor's involvement in politics and Chapter 15, "Labor Unions and the City," pp. 427–34, and Chapter 11, pp. 316–17.

4. See Footnotes 1, 2, and 3, above.

5. Related to turnover as Slichter, Healy, and Livernash note, bargaining stability and outcomes are enhanced by a close relationship between the negotiator and decisionmaker. See Slichter *et al.*, *The Impact of Collective Bargaining on Management*, p. 926.

6. See Bok and Dunlop, *Labor and the American Community*, pp. 72–73, for a brief discussion of union elections.

7. See for a brief discussion, Lieberman, *Public Sector Bargaining*, pp. 71–72.

8. For examples of such political activity, see Albert Shanker, "Repoliticizing the Bargaining Process," in Franklin J. Havelick, ed., *Collective Bargaining: New Dimensions in Labor Relations* (Boulder, CO: Westview Press, 1979); or Bok and Dunlop, *Labor and the American Community*, p. 317.

9. One discussion of this issue can be found in "Collective Bargaining and Civil Service in Public Employment: Conflict and Accommodation" (Institute of Industrial Relations, University of California at Los Angeles, 1976), Tab C.

10. Power to arbitrate was effectively ended with an opinion issued by the Attorney General of The Commonwealth of Massachusetts on February 10, 1981. The Commonwealth of Massachusetts, Department of the Attorney General, John W. McCormack State Office Building, One Ashburton Place, Boston, Massachusetts.

Chapter 9

PRINCIPLES FOR DESIGNING
A JOINT MECHANISM

As suggested in Chapter 1, one major purpose of undertaking this study was to identify what, if any, aspects of the Joint Labor-Management Committee would have utility in other settings. Toward that end, we have reviewed certain aspects of the development of public sector dispute resolution in Massachusetts and elsewhere and described tools that can be applied by a joint committee to resolve disputes. Chapter 7 sought to measure performance and account for the JLMC's apparent strengths and weaknesses. In Chapter 8 we noted two specific contributions to the state-of-the-art in public sector dispute resolution—a state that requires some improved art to deal with the growth in conflict which may well characterize the public sector in coming years.

To round out our examination of the mechanism's usefulness, this chapter will set forth the general principles that seem to underlie the joint approach—principles that can be used to evaluate or design a mechanism appropriate to a variety of governmental and occupational setting. A comment frequently made in discussions of the Joint Labor–Management Committee is that its genesis and existence are unique, that it arose in Massachusetts from a series of special circumstances uncommon to other settings. The research and analysis that led to this volume suggest, however, that this is not true, and that there is a set of general criteria and conditions that would permit and sustain a joint mechanism of this sort elsewhere. In some circumstances the necessary conditions may be present; in others they may not. As in any collective bargaining situation, the characteristics and features of the parties' relationship and environment will affect the shape of the contract and the future of the relationship.

Analysis of this study or of the Joint Committee itself may contribute to the further development of concepts concerning public bargaining. For the purposes of advancing theory and practice, we shall take an analytic look at the key factors in the development of this approach. First, we shall summarize and examine the critical factors in forming and establishing a joint problem-solving mechanism for resolution of public sector disputes, including aspects of the political and economic interests of the parties and the broader interests of the community. Next, we shall look at the aspects of the structure and operations critical to a joint mechanism's success, including the membership structure and the role of the staff. Finally, we shall discuss certain features of internal policy and procedures that are important to successful functioning of such a mechanism.

Critical Factors in Beginning a Joint Mechanism

A joint mechanism will not arise in every jurisdiction where one or another party is impressed by the results of the Massachusetts JLMC or is otherwise seeking a better way to resolve disputes. Nor is it likely to arise and become workable simply because a member of a legislative staff finds it is an interesting concept. Rather, some important ingredients in the labor relations and political environments would have to coincide with the characteristics of the occupation and jurisdiction under consideration. Let us attempt to generalize about some ingredients and principles needed to support the successful beginnings of a joint mechanism to resolve labor-management disputes in the public sector.

Tension to Focus Attention

Some form of tension in labor-management relations would be important in establishing a new joint mechanism for dispute resolution; it would provide an incentive for change and generate and sustain interest in a new mechanism once it had begun. One form of tension might arise from dissatisfaction with an existing method of dispute resolution—or the previous lack of a closure mechanism. Another form of tension might arise from the mutual pain inflicted by a recent event or the apprehension at an impending crisis. A strike, a serious fiscal or service delivery problem, or even a political crisis might suffice.

Dissatisfaction with both the existing mechanism and the obvious alternatives brought the parties and the political actors together in Massachusetts. This tension kept them working together, searching for solutions at the early stages before they had developed any other shared purpose, experience, or relationships and before they had mutually experienced the "joys of settlement." Without need, discomfort, or tension felt by all the relevant parties, the necessary political and labor relations energy may not be marshaled toward forming a new means to resolve disputes.

Confluence of Interests

The parties' interests must overlap with corresponding interests of other critical actors, especially those responsible for legislative change. The specific interests and agendas of political actors can be different from, but their needs must be consistent with, those of the parties, so that there is reason to discuss ways of altering the statutory procedures for resolving public sector labor disputes. If the political actors see greater benefit in avoiding discussion or change, discussion will not take place in the law-making forum that determines the parameters of bargaining and dispute settlement.

If one side desires reform but the other does not, discussion of change is unlikely to begin. The interests of employers and unions in settlement may be divergent. For example, in the field of education some recent strikes have been costly for teachers in fines, lost wages, and negative public opinion. School boards, in times of fiscal stringency and tax revolt, have become more frugal and often have had public support for taking a strike and shutting the schools down. A means for accommodation may not be especially appealing, especially to those school board officials who enjoy favorable press attention during strikes. However, if the specter of closed schools were to become political anathema, there might be more interest in finding a way to avoid strikes and the management interests might be persuaded to seek some political accommodation with the teachers in search of a better way to resolve labor-management differences. Until then, the requisite confluence of interest will not exist such that (1) agreement could be reached between the parties on a new mechanism, or (2) the legislative actors would not find themselves in a lobbying crossfire between union and management interests.

The existence and timing of mutual interests must extend also to the diverse groups within both the labor and management sides; for example, some unions or municipalities might favor change and accommodation while others favor the status quo.

The political system, furthermore, must be ready to legislate. In Massachusetts, the legislature and the governor were in a political tug-of-war over the existing form of dispute resolution, and legislators were torn to some degree between their loyalty to municipal officials and taxpayers in their home districts and their political allegiance to the fire fighters. Consequently, they were ripe for a solution. All legislatures are periodically in need of proposals that have no opponents. This readiness for a simple and noncontroversial legislative action will vary, depending upon political and labor relations history and traditional relationships between labor, management, and the political system.

Fiscal restraints may produce some opportunities for a confluence of economic and political interests. Fiscal limitations may prompt discussions and searches focusing on new approaches to dispute settlement. This fiscal pressure may ameliorate political, historical, and substantive problems that might otherwise have prevented political or economic accommodation. The tension-producing event and the timing of a proposed solution must somehow cause the economic interests of the parties to converge with the political, economic, and other interests and constraints of the political and legislative system.

Agreement by the Parties

The agreement of the relevant labor and management actors allows the parties to work jointly at establishing the new dispute resolution process. A tension-producing event is critical to focus interest, but agreement to work together is necessary as well. Among other things, agreement by all affected parties to work together minimizes the destabilizing and trust-reducing effects of either side seeking advantages with its own legislative sponsors as the legislature considers a proposed change. In Massachusetts, had the final legislation been altered to favor one side or the other, the likelihood of both parties being committed to the workings of the process would have been greatly diminished. Agreement between the sides prior to entering the legislative process therefore is important in gaining an agreed-upon outcome and for minimizing suspicion and mistrust at the outset.

A process negotiated and agreed to by representatives of both the labor and management sides makes the process far more likely to reflect substantive realities and realities of bargaining practices. Similarly, negotiation and agreement on the process by the affected parties themselves will enhance the possibilities that its spirit and intent will be carried out; a document drawn up by relatively inexperienced lawyers or legislative staff is much less likely to be realistic. Similarly, a process carried out by subsequently appointed staff and officials is much more likely to be challenged by the parties as early interpretations are sought in favor of one side or the other. In contrast, with design and establishment carried on by the *same* set of individuals, the mechanism is more likely to fulfill its intentions.

To work most successfully such agreement cannot simply be among a few public-spirited members of the labor and management communities but must encompass all groups with legal or political standing or influence on the issue. Otherwise, political and legal challenges and other destabilizing actions may take place. Such actions could threaten the creation and, later, the viability of the mechanism since its real authority would be confused or undermined. For example, the LBO process, which preceded the JLMC in Massachusetts, was always opposed by management, partly because they had no voice in its inception and because its design and operation represented few, if any, of their concerns. Challenges to awards were encouraged by many in management who hoped that the 1973 LBO statute would be overturned or constrained by the courts. Were there agreement on the form and structure of that dispute settlement process, there might have been greater acceptability of settlements; attacks on the process and challenges to specific settlements, no doubt, would have been minimized. The JLMC has not been perceived as belonging to labor (as management perceived LBO) or to management (as labor perceived the no-strike/no-dispute resolution statutes of years before), and serious challenges to the JLMC have, therefore, been minimized.

If agreement between the parties on the form of dispute resolution is not achieved, a number of consequences are possible. Politicians may receive conflicting signals and be unable or unwilling to produce a workable and acceptable statute. Or the design of the mechanism may be faulty and the mechanism unworkable and/or unacceptable. Not only may there be disagreements during the legislative process, but the mechanism itself could later become a forum for squabbling among the parties rather than a forum for jointly resolving problems. Agreement among the parties on the process is crucial.

Political Clout and Skill

Agreement among the parties concerning the process in most instances must be followed by legislative action. Depending on the legislative and executive politics in the jurisdiction, the parties must have—or borrow—the clout and sophistication to guide the legislation, in agreed-on form, through and back from the relevant legislative body. If the law that emerges reflects the parties' agreement, it will more likely be a system that reflects the reality of labor-management relations and the needs and interests of the parties.

Ironically, to institute a system that avoids partisan politics in its operations, a sophisticated application of politics in its inception is imperative. Successful passage may require exhaustive work and delicate interpersonal skill in the legislative process to keep out nonconstructive political influence. It also requires sensitive political antennae to prevent philosophical, conceptual, or legal niceties from being added to the bill—additions that could unhinge agreement or interfere in subsequent rational operation of the mechanism. Politicians are often unschooled in the dynamics of labor relations, so it may be advantageous to leave the bill's substantive and procedural details to representatives of the two groups who have the necessary knowledge. In this regard, convincing the legislature that the public interest is being served may itself require considerable political sophistication. In concept, the joint structure and the participation of a respected neutral should allow the public interest to be well represented and the parties to be trusted to work out their agreement.

In addition to the need to resolve the political standoff in Massachusetts, passage was aided by the fact that the political system in general may have been more prone to prevent police and fire disputes from escalating than it might have been for other occupations. Because of this underlying sensitivity to public safety, there may be greater immediate political opportunity to be innovative in resolving disputes in public safety services and in other areas the public deems essential than in service areas perceived by the public to be less critical.

In another dimension of politics, if the joint mechanism is to apply to municipal disputes, not only must state-level politics be taken into account in obtaining passage of an agreed-on mechanism, but the politics of local jurisdictions and local disputes must also be considered in its design. Similarly, if a mechanism is to be designed for other levels of government, parallel political considerations must be factored into the structure, membership, and operations of a joint mechanism.

Where the parties do not have reasonably easy access to the key state legislative and executive actors it might be difficult to shepherd such legislation through, particularly if the issue is controversial. Therefore, whether through the parties or the neutral, some channel to the formal and informal aspects of the legislative system must be available. In Massachusetts it was largely the fire fighters and their lobbying muscle that eased the way, and the relationship of the statewide Massachusetts League of Cities and Towns to the governor also contributed to rapid review and acceptance of the compromise. In another jurisdiction the leading actors might be the police or perhaps the teachers. Elsewhere, a totally different set of political circumstances may require a wholly different approach. However the political constellation on such matters may appear, a commensurate degree of skill and influence must be present among the parties and the neutral to bring a joint mechanism to fruition. The strategy will differ, but the necessity of clout commensurate with the local political situation will likely be a factor. Lack of an appropriate degree of political acumen could be a major barrier to establishing a workable joint mechanism.

Strong, Respected Neutral

Participation of a strong and respected neutral during the establishment of a joint problem-solving process may be important for several reasons. First and most obvious, agreement on the process can be mediated by a nonaligned party if the parties are unable to agree on their own. Second, information concerning experience from other labor relations settings and concepts can be incorporated into discussions and decisions on the new mechanism. Third, a respected and intelligent neutral can most credibly represent the public interest to legitimize a joint recommendation to the legislature. Fourth, where necessary, important initial credibility can be lent by a neutral to the effort to alter a tension-filled and mistrusted system. The extent to which this "umbrella" role is necessary will depend on the labor relations and political environment that exists at the time and place. The stature of the neutral may help allay fears that an imbalance in power would result in an outcome favorable to one side or that the parties together would "run away" with the process. In Massachusetts, because of the bitterness and political enmity between the sides, a neutral of stature was indispensable. In another setting, with greater trust between the parties, the stature of the neutral may be less crucial, although experience and skill would always be required in mediating the discussions and in providing perspective on labor relations practices. Also, a neutral dedicated to mediation will best help the mechanism to promote bargaining and avoid third party imposition of settlements.

Finding and recruiting a neutral may, in some instances, pose problems. Where public labor relations are relatively extensive, neutrals are likely to be found in practice or in colleges or universities; elsewhere, such people may be hard to find. Possibly, in those instances, candidates with private sector experience could be brought in and their experience converted to public sector use, although the political "savvy" and knowledge peculiar to public bargaining and political life would clearly have to come from elsewhere in the group originating the change. For instance, in developing the Massachusetts JLMC, the neutral, John T. Dunlop, left state politics to the locals, although it was he who insisted that the parties stand jointly on the document they produced and not agree to any changes without joint consent during the legislative process. Even though the specific actors and alliances were not well known to him, Dunlop's government experience had left him aware of the dangers inherent in the political process.

In discussions about transfer of a joint mechanism to other political settings, occupations, or circumstances, Dunlop's presence is frequently cited as a unique and, therefore, limiting factor. Surely, he is a neutral of national stature and experience, characteristics that contributed to his utility in this situation. However, the characteristics that led to his role in guiding the process are simply those of a strong and respected neutral. First, he was acceptable to both sides on the basis of his reputation. (He knew none of the actors personally.) Second, he was known for solving difficult labor-management problems. Third, he had a reputation for not being easily intimidated by posturing or threats. Finally, his experience obviously would help him guide the parties through difficult periods and over difficult issues. Experience, neutrality, and courage are rare enough, perhaps, but there are neutrals in every part of the country who are possessed of those characteristics. In any successful dispute resolution task, whether it be an individual dispute or designing or chairing a mechanism, the neutral must be able to perform.

Some have argued that certain aspects of Dunlop's background uniquely gave rise to the format and practices of the JLMC. Surely, he brought experience from other joint committees and a certain philosophy to the table, but then so would another neutral of standing bring his or her experience to the table elsewhere, probably strengthening the concept of joint resolution. To the extent that the creation of certain of the devices is credited to Dunlop, the creation of those devices, then, is no longer needed. Just as Edward Land created the Polaroid idea, his presence is not essential to every manufacturing operation or innovation in instant photography. Nor is it clear that if he had not invented the process, someone else would not have done so—in a somewhat different form at some other time and place. George Taylor, a famous practitioner and professor in modern labor-management relations who pioneered the establishment of permanent umpires for handling disputes, was not the only person capable of carrying out the process, as experience has shown. Overall, Dunlop is not a necessary condition, but a strong neutral is. As evidence, a vice-chairman, Morris A. Horowitz, has for the past two years presided over a significant proportion of JLMC meetings and cases with considerable results and full respect of the parties, thus providing a "laboratory" where another neutral can be seen successfully at work in this setting.

Mechanism Tailored to the Situation

Every occupation or jurisdiction will have its own needs and possibilities for establishing an improved means of resolving disputes. The means must be consistent with the occupational, political, and "cultural" conditions that prevail. The reality that prevailed in Massachusetts (described in Chapter 2) will not exist elsewhere. Thus, a mechanism in another jurisdiction would have to be designed around the prevailing needs and circumstances.

To gain the agreement of the affected parties—necessary to acceptance of change and to subsequent operations—the mechanism must be responsive to the needs of the situation. To fashion a realistic mechanism, several considerations should be borne: First, the natural and statutory boundaries of the problem must be reflected in the solution. Second, the proposal must have the capacity to handle the most important substantive and political concerns of each side and of the relevant political actors. Third, the individuals participating in the mechanism's formulation must be appropriately representative of the affected parties and be substantively knowledgeable about the range of problems that must be considered.

A dispute resolution process must be created in such a way that the boundaries of the solution coincide with the political, geographic, and statutory characteristics of the problem. For example, in Massachusetts a statewide joint labor-management committee for public safety disputes could gain acceptance and be formed because the labor and management sides already were represented by statewide organizations that "matched" the groups experiencing the problem. These organizations could subsequently nominate representative members and, even during early negotiations on a new mechanism, have a sufficiently defined structure so that individuals could negotiate representatively and in good faith on behalf of each side. (The lack of police involvement in those early discussions could have been costly except for the fire fighters' historically close relationship and legislative influence with most of the police groups.) Altering the status of police and fire fighter dispute resolution required alteration of only one statewide statute, which covered only those parties involved in the discussions. By gaining the support of their close political allies (the fire fighters and the legislature, the municipal association and the governor), all the relevant political forces were wrapped in. Thus, the solution required no additional substantive knowledge, actors, or institutional relationships, simplifying the type of solution available and easing the process and possibilities for agreement.

The necessity of dealing with problems as they exist and developing a mechanism likely to solve those problems requires that an appropriate selection of knowledgeable and influential people be brought together. It is necessary to include in the initial discussion groups people with a range of interests and knowledge that will likely yield a practical and acceptable set of proposals. Collective bargaining agreements, while often containing features common to agreements negotiated elsewhere, are individually unique as applied to the needs of the parties at the time and place of the agreement. The same principle applies if a dispute resolution mechanism is to be workable and acceptable.

Reflecting the Boundaries of the Problem

The boundaries of the dispute resolution problem and of the political and bargaining relations will be important in defining the possibilities for a workable joint mechanism in another political jurisdiction or in another occupational setting. In each case the boundaries will vary and will affect the way a mechanism could be conceived, designed, and structured. Also, geography and related politics and traditions, degree and form of unionization, urban or rural concentration of bargaining units, and governmental structures relative to the problem may suggest the features of a workable mechanism.

Joint Mechanisms along Occupational Lines. It is probably simplest to think of an adaptation of the JLMC to handle disputes at the state level in another occupation, such as teaching. In Massachusetts, where there is already precedent for a joint mechanism, there are important occupational and political differences between teachers and public safety employees that heretofore have precluded a joint mechanism for labor-management relations in education. There is not, for the moment, a tension or tension-producing event that would bring the two sides together for discussions. Teachers' strikes have become expensive for the teachers and their union, while strikes tend to save money for the towns, who do not have to pay operating costs during the period the schools are closed. Therefore, a proposal for a JLMC-modeled mechanism for teachers has not been as attractive to administrators or school boards. In contrast to public safety issues, moreover, politicians in most jurisdictions are not these days on a "hot spot" regarding teachers' strikes (safety isn't threatened nor are lost school days currently a major political issue), so the requisite political support for a new way to resolve educational disputes is not apparent. Besides, without the parties' agreement, the legislators may be better off politically to leave the issue alone.

An additional problem in formulating a teachers' mechanism in Massachusetts is that the two major teachers' unions (affiliates of the National Education Association and the American Federation of Teachers) are rivals and might themselves have difficulty reaching agreement on a process. Thus, the requisite overlap of interests to gain consensus and political support is not currently in evidence, although other events, such as the passage of Proposition 2½ in Massachusetts, may help create the necessary tensions: The provisions of "2½" revoked the school boards' fiscal autonomy and thus subjected their spending to the approval of the local legislature. This additional obstacle to approving wage increases and other expenditure items could drive the unions together and find the school boards looking for allies with local political muscle (such as teachers' unions) who are interested in obtaining educational funding.

Representation for discussion and membership may be easy to structure if the parties could come together. Since there are associations of school board members and superintendents in the state and, despite the rivalry, since the two major unions represent most of the teachers in the state, a basis exists for a constituent network and representation on both sides. Strengthening the capacity to form a joint, representative membership structure is the fact that both unions have reputations for relatively good internal discipline and have traditions of statewide actions in labor relations matters and politics. Thus, the representation and boundary aspects arguably could support a productive mechanism—if there were joint agreement and if the legislative and other political actors were prepared to go along.[1]

Problems in Representation.   Municipal white-collar and blue-collar occupations present different issues in formulation of a joint mechanism, and in obtaining and maintaining representativeness. On the union side, representation for municipal workers would not necessarily be simple where there are many occupations, units, and, perhaps, different unions representing the relevant employee groups. In jurisdictions where only a few unions represent most of the statewide municipal work force, consolidated and acceptable representation might be possible. Also, where there exists a state level or jurisdictionwide association of unions that is or could become sufficiently stable, a joint mechanism with appropriate representativeness might be formulated. Without such an infrastructure, the necessity for representation and consensus could lead to an unwieldy committee. Thus, the questions of boundaries and the parties' infrastructure within those boundaries are important in finding and defining an appropriate area and structure for handling disputes.

In contrast to an alliance or amalgamation of occupational representation on one committee, a series of separate occupation-based groups also might be considered. Such a chain of committees could be established all at once, or more likely, over time. For example, some occupations with different traditions, history, or wage and work patterns than white-collar occupations—like sanitation or highway workers—might be handled separately. However, if occupationally organized joint mechanisms existed in a state, such separateness would require coordination; there would have to be a way of integrating wage and settlement relationships among different occupations within a town as well as considering the fiscal posture of the municipality in the deliberations of each joint group. Therefore, some way of coordinating and passing information between occupational committees would be necessary to keep the dispute settlement mechanism from contributing to instability of labor-management dealings, especially to "whipsawing" phenomena. The coordination problem might be overcome by something like an appropriate body of committee chairpersons who met periodically to keep each other informed of settlement patterns and developments and to coordinate across occupational lines within municipalities or other areas with important wage relationships.

Finally, it might be difficult to find enough experienced management members with sufficient available time to staff a series of committees, inasmuch as they would have to be drawn largely from the same population of potential management members. In Massachusetts limited management resources might pose a problem. Other states or jurisdictions may have a different complexion of management, thereby obviating the problem. In any event, attention must be paid to the availability of proper management—and union—membership and representation.

The membership structure must, among other things, reflect the local situation in such a way that all parties that may come in for dispute handling find they have a friend in court. This effect may not always require a direct representative, but rather a trusted member of a coalition of unions or towns or counties, respectively. The membership structure must somehow, in the context of local needs, customs, traditions, and feelings, be structured so as to maintain the interest and trust of the affected parties and to obtain acceptance of and a commitment to whatever process has been jointly developed.

Laws and Geography. Another type of boundary relates to existing statutes and their coverage of civil service or labor relations laws and customs. For example, statewide mechanisms have an appeal where statewide civil service laws exist, but are not as attractive where public employees are covered by a complicated series of separate legislative provisions and administrative practices. In a jurisdiction where local ordinances relevant to civil service or labor relations are independent from those of the state, or where the labor relations traditions or patterns differ significantly within an area, a single statewide joint dispute resolution mechanism might not be feasible or appropriate.

Differing traditions can be as important as written rules; California may be a good example. Although certain statutes provide statewide labor relations coverage, the state may be simply too diverse and geographically large for the interests of some labor or management groups in the northern and the southern parts of the state, for example, to converge and be represented in one unit. A joint committee may find it exceedingly difficult under such circumstances to use the informal communications that are an important aspect of its strength. The distances between and size of the groups may simply make communication and momentum too difficult to sustain even if customs were sufficiently similar throughout the state. The JLMC approach, however, can be modified to reflect regional realities.

As an example of one such adjustment, the JLMC constituents frequently have chosen the Committee's members and alternates with geographic representation in mind. Recognizing the low regard for Boston held by many in western Massachusetts and perceiving the need for more awareness of regional customs and issues, the JLMC sought a staff member from that part of the state. A staff mediator is employed who resides in western Massachusetts and who commutes to Boston for case meetings and other occasions. Such regional staffing and membership considerations improve peer acceptance in dispute handling.

Another example of the importance of traditional boundaries is the City of New York, which operates its public labor-management relations rather separately from the rest of New York State. In the city, most public labor relations problems are handled by a joint mechanism through the Office of Collective Bargaining. The self-contained nature of the city's public labor-management relations allows a separate tripartite approach, which takes into account its own occupational, jurisdictional and political relationships.

Wage, Occupation, and Other Relationships. Can a tension-producing event that is localized, yet crosses occupational lines, serve to bring the parties in a jurisdiction together? For example, general labor troubles in recent years in San Francisco have caused some leaders to wonder whether a joint mechanism might avoid strife for a broad spectrum of public employee occupations. There are some central questions related to this thought: Could a mechanism be set up that is capable of representing and communicating with the wide variety of municipal occupations? Does the representational infrastructure exist, or could it be formed? Could members and staff with sufficient and substantive expertise and credibility to deal with diverse occupations be found and recruited? Would the occupational homogeneity of a San Francisco joint committee upset wage or other relationships with locals across the bay in Oakland? How might the Oakland relationships be handled?

If the requisite political support for a joint committee could be formed in San Francisco, the county, city, and state legislative requirements would have to be congruent—or altered—so that they would not hamstring the effort. This hypothetical example illustrates the complexities in matching events and problems with political and legal jurisdictions as well as with representational questions and wage relativities. Nevertheless, despite the additional problems involved in setting up a joint committee across occupational lines, the concept and mechanism appear broad enough to incorporate these complexities in jurisdictions with a proper infrastructure and a need to develop a new approach.

Critical Elements in Structure and Operations

The foregoing section concentrated on important considerations in establishing a new joint mechanism for handling disputes. Let us now examine aspects of structure and operation that most seem to contribute to positive results from a joint committee mechanism.

Local Conditions and Traditions Reflected

Just as local boundaries and traditions must be reflected in the formation of a successful mechanism, the operation of the mechanism must continue to recognize these factors. The membership, staff, operating rules, and relationship to other agencies and activities must take into account local traditions, expectations, legal structure, and other realities. Operating practices, protocol during meetings, and mediative and other activities must continue to be sensitive to these relationships and traditions. For example, to avoid conflict in the Massachusetts JLMC police members do not have a vote, nor do they seek to influence debate on fire fighter cases, and vice versa.

Maintenance of protocol and traditions may contribute, through lack of confusion and good relationships, to smooth working of the mechanism. Without continuing attention, especially at the outset, to local history and traditions, the internal relationships of the groups can suffer from mistrust, and the external activities may be stymied for lack of internal sensitivity. While a new mechanism may properly wish to alter certain traditions and expectations, immediate reactions and long-term consequences to those alterations must be anticipated if the desired change is to be achieved over time.

The Neutral

Just as the selection of an appropriate neutral to assist in formation is critical, a neutral's reputation and skills can mitigate the effects of otherwise serious fallout from any misperceptions or misunderstandings that may arise in the course of operations. As a mechanism begins operation, the neutral is in a position to build dynamics within a committee that will foster agreement and problem solving—as would a neutral mediating a dispute—to help to develop policies and practices, and to remind participants of long-term labor relations consequences of actions under consideration. Providing this sort of perspective as well as a credible and neutral channel for bringing other problem-solving procedures and information to the group are important aspects of a neutral's responsibilities once a joint committee commences operations.

Membership

In any joint mechanism the membership structure will be a central element in maintaining the mechanism and satisfactorily resolving disputes.

Representative Acceptability. The representative membership is helpful in promoting acceptance of decisions and processes of the joint mechanism, especially when a novel or controversial technique or decision is evident. Ongoing representation in policy or case decision making, whereby the parties can feel they have a friend in court —especially if dissatisfaction or mistrust characterized the environment—helps to create and maintain an acceptance of the mediative and other efforts that take place. This acceptability is especially important in view of the variety of settlement processes that may be used. The representation can also aid in the acceptability of settlements. While blind acceptance of settlements or processes may occur, communication with one's "representative" can help to allay fears and provide information about the process or the settlement itself. Acceptability and trust in the mechanism are more likely to produce attitudes conducive to rapid problem solving.

Marketing. Representative membership is especially useful in the early period, as it "markets" a process that is new and different or in settings where *any* intervention in perceived management prerogatives is resented. It is also useful where an alternative mechanism to dispute resolution remains in place, as with last-best-offer arbitration by the Board of Conciliation and Arbitration in Massachusetts. In a comment that reflects successful representative marketing, the head of the Massachusetts Municipal Association said in reference to using the JLMC for help: "We make our people go there." As a result of its participation in creating the Committee and its role in appointing the membership, the Municipal Association encourages its municipal constituents to approach the JLMC to solve problems constructively rather than to engage in other practices (such as litigation) that might prolong disputes. The membership composition, by utilizing ties to their constituents in different professions and geographic areas, can play an important and continuing role in promoting the use and acceptability of the mechanism and its decisions.

Internal Leverage. If the membership is composed of leaders from the relevant communities, influence can be exercised on constituent behavior in a dispute. These leaders have access to and can get attention from parties in a dispute. They can use persuasion rather than compulsion. These characteristics allow side conversations during which education (or even chastisement) regarding bargaining behavior can take place in relatively non-threatening ways. A mayor can tell another mayor, for example, about the effects of bargaining on an upcoming election that no college professor credibly could. A police officer can tell another officer what sort of arbitration award is likely if the dispute is not settled, and he or she is likely to get a better response than would a lawyer, appointed to "med-arb" the dispute, who said the same thing.

The internal discipline and infrastructure of each side help determine the ease and strength with which such tools can be used. Also, the members and staff's willingness to communicate with their peers in a dispute is critical in wielding influence and educating peers in a dispute.

Volunteers. Voluntary service of committee members is controversial because of the time constraints under which volunteers must necessarily operate. In general, however, voluntary committee work in conjunction with regular municipal responsibilities encourages bargaining in several ways. First, it maintains the individual's continuing interest in settlement. Busy members with other jobs do not earn their money by continuing conflict; it is in their interest to end conflicts and to leave the actual development of solutions and detail work to the parties themselves.

Second, in the same way that volunteer membership encourages local responsibility and local settlement, volunteers who are active members of either the labor or management community will not want responsibility for a settlement that either party will not accept or cannot live with, so they are likely to encourage bargaining and other responsible behavior by the parties.

Third, the volunteer committee members, because of their ongoing ties and day-to-day responsibilities in the labor or management community, are constantly mindful of the interests of their constituents in a dispute—although they will have a wider perspective than the local leaders. This dual responsiveness helps to balance the discussions and emphasis of the members as they handle a dispute, particularly in peer bargaining. The balance helps maintain each side's confidence in the mechanism's neutrality and at the same time promotes confidence that one's interests are being well represented.

The lack of labor-management relations experience on the management side and the multiple duties of management officials could hinder the attraction of skilled management members who can devote sufficient time to the tasks involved. Simple recognition of time and availability problems can lead to active recruitment and selection of individuals more cognizant and tolerant of these demands.

Getting good people to serve under these circumstances is not simple. Some status or other motivating benefit must be attached to the position to attract otherwise busy people to become volunteer members. The opportunity to create something new and useful seems to have attracted many to the initial Massachusetts' JLMC; yet, following turnover in membership, people of stature in the two communities continue to be attracted. It has been suggested that members are attracted by the opportunity to learn about more sophisticated aspects of public labor relations. Perhaps the opportunity to influence broader, statewide issues, such as impact of fiscal constraints, civil service reform, regionalization of services, or broader collective bargaining policy is attractive as well. The presence of obviously talented and recognized people as committee members at the outset is especially important to establish stature and credibility—which can make later membership attractive—and to develop realistic policies and operating procedures.

Substantive Knowledge.   The selection of active labor and management people provides not only representation but also channels and background to obtain the all-important knowledge of specific local situations and issues, the parties' needs and concerns, and the political dimensions of the dispute. Members who are sophisticated about politics are probably most effective at keeping other, extraneous sorts of politics out of labor relations decisions.

The representative membership provides substantive knowledge for use in mediation. The combination of ties to the parties and familiarity with the range of issues permit more ready access by a mediator to the real issues and the true position of the parties. These qualities of the neutral frequently permit rapid removal of simple or false issues or unrealistic positions. A well-selected array of members could bring to bear technological, political, administrative, or financial expertise, as well as lessons learned in other towns on the many problems obstructing settlement. This background plus the volunteers' concentration on settlement is an important combination to help keep the parties focused on the facts and on solving the problems at hand.

Internal Tension, Neutrality, and Sovereignty.   The dynamics of membership must produce a balance between cooperation and tension so that the public interest is well served along with the welfare of the employees. The natural differences in labor-management interests in an atmosphere of accommodation allow problems to be resolved by the joint membership rather than having disputes "won" or "lost" as under LBO arbitration. When both sides of the joint mechanism have intimate knowledge of the needs of their constituents, the neutrality of their collective action is promoted by each side's use and presentation of its information and position. The neutrality depends equally on the neutral chair's capacity to foster a trusting and constructive set of relationships between the members, as well as on the natural tension created by expression of opposing viewpoints.

In a joint mechanism, with each side of a committee representing a constituency, a tension is created that permits both the public interest and the employees' interests to be served. On a voluntary committee operated like the JLMC, elected and appointed representatives of the taxpayers' interest deal with elected representatives of the workers. Sovereignty is recognized in that fiscal and service-related interests are protected by management representatives in all decisions. Bargaining, however, is the dominant process. While, arguably, the purest form of sovereignty—which would require direct unilateral decision making by elected public representatives—is not maintained, the presence of elected and appointed representatives of taxpayers in the JLMC form of arbitration reflects a much greater satisfaction of both sovereignty and bargaining principles than does arbitration by neutrals appointed by more usual methods. This combination of sovereignty and bargaining, which is related to the means of appointment and character of the membership, greatly strengthens the political and practical acceptability of the joint mechanism.

Multiple Tools. One result of joint representation is the emergence of many tools not ordinarily available to a single neutral. For example, it permits joint mediation, which is especially useful where there is little trust and/or experience among the parties to a dispute. Peer bargaining is also made possible by a joint membership. A joint membership structure can be used to create a multidimensional or collective neutral (including members, senior and junior staff, and neutral chair and vice-chair), which can then employ an array of responses to different kinds of disputes or to changing parameters of an existing dispute. While poor representation or a lack of experience or integrity might eliminate the advantage of this multidimensional neutrality, a joint mechanism expands the range of tools for dispute settlement beyond that which is generally possible in a unidimensional neutral or neutral agency.

Relationship to the Political Community. Since most public sector dispute settlement mechanisms are politically determined, the capacity to maintain ties to and support of the political superstructure is important. Therefore, such maintenance must be a conscious part of operating a joint mechanism.

Each side on the committee, if properly representative, acts as a lightning rod for its own constituents and prevents significant complainers from going to the legislature on their own. Thus, political intervention is avoided and the bargaining environment is kept stable as the parties confine their efforts to bargaining.

Method of Appointment. Those who resolve disputes must be perceived not only as neutral in a labor relations context but also as nonpartisan; the parties must have confidence that each dispute will be heard and judged on its merits. The method of choosing members, therefore, must preclude partisan politics from influencing the membership or, ultimately, decisions. Of course, the appointment process must have the capacity to produce knowledgeable and representative members. Where there is no infrastructure for channeling appointments that are acceptable and representative on the part of each side, the strength of the membership structure will be reduced unless an alternative and equally satisfactory selection procedure is arranged.

Quality of Members. To establish and operate a mechanism with potential to resolve disputes, the membership must be composed of people with experience, ability, and interest in labor-management relations as well as with standing in their respective communities. A membership with broad contacts and perception can be most helpful in the widest variety of cases. It would be sensitive to the consequences of one settlement on situations elsewhere, so as to minimize problems that could lead to instability in other wage or bargaining relationships. The personal integrity and professional quality of the members themselves can serve to promote credibility as well as results.

Since the objectives and external parameters will differ from jurisdiction to jurisdiction, the membership selection process and structure should reflect the needs of each geographic, political, and occupational circumstance. In selecting members it is important to keep in mind specifically what the membership must do for the endeavor to succeed—that is, who it must represent, what substantive expertise is required, and what obstacles may be faced. This relationship of the membership structure to the situation at hand will be critical—perhaps determinative—to the success and utility of a joint mechanism.

Staff

The system's reputation, credibility, capacity to improve bargaining relationships, and ability to make productive use of members' time for dispute resolution depend heavily on the staff. A strong staff is especially important at the outset to contribute to the establishment of good mediative and communications practices and the development of a reputation for effectiveness. The mechanism is most aided by staff who are skilled analysts as well as practitioners of labor-management relations.

Multiplying the Efforts of Members and Others. A strong and sophisticated staff will multiply greatly the impact and use of a volunteer member's time if it solves most problems and brings others as far as possible toward solution, judging the best time and way to employ members' talents, contacts, and stature. A critical function of staff members is to brief other neutrals—committee members, outside mediators, or arbitrators—prior to hearings, negotiations, or other meetings on the status of the dispute. Their ability to do so effectively depends on their ability to deal effectively with the member, the chair, or the outside neutral, and on their sophistication in interpreting and handling the problem.

As an example of staff interaction, the briefing prior to a hearing or similar event that introduces new neutral actors is an important point in the hierarchy of available tools. The usefulness of a hearing can be limited by the staff briefing: If inadequate, the new neutral actor or actors waste time by seeking information that is already possessed by the neutral institution. Such a nonproductive or repetitive procedure frustrates the parties, who have already invested significant time in providing that information to the staff and does not lend credence or acceptability to the processes and decisions of the neutral body. The resultant negative perceptions may weaken confidence in the institution or cause an unwillingness to heed even the advice of a party's own representatives on a joint committee. The staff must also function well in relation to the parties in dispute, since they handle much of the ongoing contact and almost all of the initial contact with the parties. Surely they must be perceived as neutral to remain acceptable to both sides.

Joint Staff.   One controversial element of the JLMC has been the joint staff. The existence of a joint staff—one senior labor representative and one senior management representative—can play a large role in expanding the effectiveness and availability of the members. While a joint, rather than a classically neutral, staff may seem at first glance to detract from the staff's and institution's neutrality, the experience of the JLMC suggests otherwise; staff representatives acting alone have been generally accepted as neutrals. In difficult cases, where mistrust and inexperience of the parties abound, the use of joint mediation can "neutralize" the staff representativeness and can also strengthen the mediation and education process, for in such circumstances it provides each side with a trusted colleague and a channel of communication to the other side.

The full-time use of joint staff to support volunteer members provides each group of principles in a committee (labor and management) with a day-to-day expert and a person to serve as their delegate and advisor. The respective labor and management backgrounds of a joint staff permit these senior staff members to engage in many of the same activities as committee members as a result of their political and substantive knowledge and capacity to win the confidence of the respective sides in a dispute. By performing such functions, the staff permits better use of members' time.

As a participant in caucuses or in advising or admonishing one side or the other, a joint staff parlays the advantages that the joint nature of the mechanism itself brings to the bargaining process and to mediation, even more than could a highly competent neutral staff.

Certainly, the ability of the two senior staff representatives to collaborate is important in the successful operation of such an arrangement. It is imperative for smooth operations that each side of the joint mechanism finds acceptable the senior staff representative of the other side, as well as its own. Thus, poor choice of the joint staff could negate these potential advantages.

As much of an advantage as may exist in having senior staff perform many functions similar to those of a committee member, the fact that they are not members should be underscored. To preserve the principles of internal political representativeness and the related tension that allows peer interaction to stimulate bargaining and to assist in maintaining a semblance of sovereignty, it is important that voting members on cases and policy are chosen by the constituencies.

Credibility and Competence.   Perceptions of acceptability also relate to competence of the staff. If the parties trust the competence, neutrality, and integrity of the staff, they will be more willing to come voluntarily to the institution for help and to accept its processes and decisions. If trusted and seen as competent, the staff can become an institutionalized but informal source of advice and assistance to parties preparing to bargain or having difficulty negotiating, without the necessity of formally requesting assistance or declaring an impasse. Similarly, a credible and competent staff able to win the confidence of the parties can do a lot of educating in the course of mediating a dispute.

Quality.   Much of what has been said about the staff in earlier chapters suggests their qualifications. While it is possible and desirable to train junior people—as is being done with several neutral staff—a successful joint mechanism requires some senior staff with maturity, experience, and judgment. Those qualities will assist it in maintaining the necessary relationships and interactions, while retaining the institutional reputation for neutrality and competence. In this public environment, the staff should be knowledgeable about politics as it affects the behavior of parties in dispute. Of course, their knowledge of labor relations dynamics and their instinct for mediation will be the most critical. Those with experience can more easily find and create alternatives to bargaining processes that are going nowhere or are headed for a blow-up. Similarly, it takes some sophistication to let things blow up with some certainty that the pieces can be picked up.

With political, interpersonal, and labor relations instincts, the staff will recognize when members should become involved and in what role. Proper use of such judgment will allow cases to be more fully handled by the staff and will make possible more time-effective use of members' contacts, skills, and stature. Given these delicate and indispensable staff functions, simply reassigning some civil servants as investigators and mediators will not likely achieve a staff with the requisite skills and relationships.

Recruitment. As in many endeavors, good staff may be difficult to attract and retain, and it is important to think about the problem in a particular jurisdiction as the mechanism is formed. Too often, planners and policy analysts simply assume that the necessary skills are available at any place and time and at the price the local civil service system is willing to pay. In establishing a competent, neutral organization, that formulation is surely too simple. Apart from the all-important assessment of their qualifications and sophistication in labor-management relations, the senior staff and other staff must be acceptable to the members as a group; the members, therefore, not the civil service board, must have control over staff selection.

However, acceptance of the staff by the members is only a minimal condition of success. The staff will ultimately have to be acceptable to parties in dispute—a difficult quality to assess through written examination. Talented individuals must be attracted and paid a market wage. Frequently, this means hiring in an employment category outside of the more usual civil service categories. Independent hiring authority can eliminate cumbersome paperwork, antiquated or unreasonable salary or qualification restrictions, and associated delay and penuriousness, all of which may cause otherwise desirable candidates to go elsewhere. Similarly, the flexibility to fire staff members must exist; should staff members lose their acceptability or neutral reputation, they are of no use. Here again, normal civil service strictures may not be appropriate.

To attract staff and to maintain and focus their energies, it is important that they be engaged in a way that permits them independence and otherwise uses their ability effectively. Talented people will find a JLMC-type of endeavor enjoyable and rewarding only if there is the opportunity to learn, create, and exercise their independent professional judgment in the pursuit of solving problems. The opportunity to work with senior labor and management people and neutrals of stature and experience may also prove attractive. The same features can attract good junior people. In any event, the capacity to attract and retain high-quality and effective staff should be a conscious part of any endeavor for a dispute settlement system. Where the principals are volunteers, the quality of staff will be especially important, as well as careful consideration of the working arrangements and relationships between committee and staff, because more usual arrangements may not fit.

The staff is a critical link between the objectives of a joint mechanism and actually resolving disputes. A poor job at the staff level can elongate a case, cause bitterness between the parties and toward the neutral body, and add greatly to the members' work load. As a key to the system's productivity and reputation, the staff is worth significant attention in defining roles, recruiting, and motivating. The substantive background, experience, political sense, and acceptability of staff members should be well matched to the political, bargaining, and occupational environment in which they are to operate.

Flexibility of Statute and Operations

A major reason that bargaining can occur well beyond the point that an impasse might be declared comes from the ability to apply tools that can affect the specific obstacles to bargaining. Without flexibility in choice of tools and their application, the point of impasse may remain exactly that. With a wider range of choices, however, a path around the impasse may be found. Interestingly, the most recalcitrant disputes seem to be based on personality or political factors, a set of factors to which a flexible and joint mechanism can permit attention.

Tools to Fit the Problem. The advantages ascribed to the membership and staff can be used to resolve disputes only if the statute permits them to responsibly fashion procedures appropriate to the problems and practices in the jurisdiction. For example, in the Seabury case described in Chapter 5, the parties had been tied up in the LBO process and subsequent litigation for years; there were no other options to break the impasse. Yet the emergence of the JLMC permitted an entirely different approach to the problem, which dealt with the personalities and the local political history. More generally, a flexible statute makes possible a forum where problems can always be brought and new tools applied to resolve them. In addition, a statute that does not prescribe steps or procedures may allow avoidance of superfluous or expensive steps.

Adapting to Change. A flexible structure may also allow adaptation of the mechanism to changing external and internal circumstances. As the JLMC's adjustment after the 1980 rescinding of binding arbitration authority suggests, the capacity to adapt to dramatic external events can be important in maintaining relative labor peace in public safety services. The lack of a viable dispute settlement mechanism at a time when fiscal constraints and employee welfare are in such direct conflict could have had serious consequences for labor peace and the delivery of public services.

Flexibility in the statute also allows changes in practices and emphasis without either reopening political debate to obtain a new statute or causing a major change in the parameters of bargaining or dispute settlement. As the needs of the jurisdiction change or as new concepts or techniques become available, flexibility permits alterations. Further, as a new joint mechanism is formed, all eventualities cannot be adequately predicted or prepared for.

An inability to adjust dispute resolution practices as experience accumulates might have been a serious problem early in the JLMC's existence: Some members initially expected to be intimately involved in mediating each dispute. They soon became disabused of the utility of this approach as the work load and resultant time requirements became apparent. Subsequently, the role and size of the staff expanded and the mechanism evolved in a far different way than had been imagined. The bulk of the mediating is now left to the staff, but the members retain policy control, use peer influence, and serve as another level of intervention as successive impasses are reached. Had their original notion been specified in the statute, adjustments would have been difficult and peer bargaining, one of the most interesting techniques, might not have evolved. This unanticipated development remains a key method of resolving difficult disputes.

Impact of Uncertainty on Settlement. A mechanism's flexibility in applying available tools also may have an impact on the parties' willingness to settle a dispute. In the certain, serially organized process that characterized the steps leading to LBO proceedings, parties could, in some instances, plan a strategy to carry them through that process and effectively prevent settlement at any stage but arbitration. In contrast, when the next step or its probable result is unknown, such planning is not useful, and the calculus may then be in favor of early settlement rather than continued uncertainty.

On the other hand, it could be argued that this form of uncertainty creates resentment and confusion. Probably, such confusion will diminish as Committee practices and policies become better known to the parties. After several years, the parties have had an opportunity to become familiar with the range of Committee procedures, but the wide array of potential tools that it can apply still leaves a degree of uncertainty. Procedural flexibility and the resultant uncertainty are unlikely to have neutral effects and should be analyzed accordingly.

Risks of Flexibility. Certainly delegation of broad authority to a joint mechanism may risk having the process captured by the parties contrary to the public interest. But perhaps the risk to the public interest is not greater than in a mechanism designed by one side only or by legislative staff or attorneys. The breadth of representativeness and the competing interests represented in the mechanism can reduce this risk and encourage balanced actions. Therefore, any joint mechanism must have a proper membership and appointments process. The membership and its appointment process provides not only the ingredients for a variety of tools but also an important aspect of natural and constructive tension. Also, without support for the mechanism and membership, the use of unorthodox or original techniques would be challenged—perhaps successfully. The participation of each side and their internal agreement on membership and on procedures permits the mechanism's flexibility to be used without undue suspicion of political or other influence.

To maintain the flexibility to create and apply tools as necessary and appropriate and to maintain credibility and support among constituents and with the larger political system, it is important to adjust the tools to fit evolving reality. The joint nature of representation and an appointment process that keeps each side's confidence, along with the presence of a strong neutral, can keep the risks of politicization or corruption low, and the possibilities for good results strong, and thus permit the ability to remain flexibly intact.

Neutrality in Many Forms

While the neutral chair will play a major role in lending impartiality to the system, it is the neutrality of the entire institution that is ultimately at stake. Only a mechanism perceived to be neutral in its processes and outcomes will be accepted by both sides for handling disputes; therefore certain of the necessary skills for ensuring neutrality must derive from actors other than the neutral chair. The mixture of levels and types of neutrals (chair, cochair, committee, senior staff, junior staff, outside neutral) provides opportunities for a variety of political, labor relations, and operational skills to be blended in a manner that no single neutral, regardless of stature, could accomplish. Such a variety of neutrals also permits matching individuals' availability and skills to the local circumstances in any given dispute. For example, when the dispute involves an executive-legislative disagreement, a mayor or selectman from a joint committee might be most appropriate as a neutral. If the major problem is inexperienced people at the table, a staff member skilled at subtly teaching bargaining skills might be best. If it's a police scheduling question, who other than a police officer, who also holds the neutral perspective arising from committee membership, could better understand the substance and genesis of the problem and the need to resolve it? In each instance, the knowledge provided by such expert members or staff persons must be perceived by the parties as being applied neutrally if it is to be effective.

Relation to Other Agencies and Outsiders

Frequently more than one agency, board, or commission has some responsibility for labor relations, whether it be over interest disputes, rights disputes, or representation matters. A joint approach would not be maximally effective unless its power to resolve disputes were preeminent among such agencies. Even where it is preeminent, it would have to work smoothly with other agencies if intramural disputes are to be avoided and parties prevented from forum shopping among agencies for tactical or settlement advantages.

Agencies. It would be confusing and disruptive to labor-management relations if the agencies were making the other's job more difficult by pursuing contrary purposes or narrow issues within their own jurisdiction in a manner that frustrated settlement and labor peace. (Chapter 3 briefly describes this range of problems in Massachusetts.) Beyond statutory requirements in establishing relationships with other agencies, it is essential to attain the cooperation of the top administrators; personal contact is critical, as are good staff working relationships. Both types of interaction must be supported by regular communication to minimize personnel working at cross purposes and to maximize the effective use of resources to resolve disputes.

Most of the smooth interaction with other agencies will come with time and in unexpected ways—another example of the need for flexibility in operations as problems and their solutions develop. The statute, however, should be attentive to any matters of agency jurisdiction or cooperation that would otherwise confuse parties in dispute or contribute to elongating disputes.

The Legislature. Another outside group discussed previously is the legislature. Maintaining good relationships there maintains support for the statute. Good relationships with the legislature also help to fund the mechanism from year to year and, less formally, may help receive early notice of political or legislative activities in areas that might affect the mechanism's mission and environment. Appropriate arrangements and efforts to maintain legislative relationships will be important to the stability of the bargaining environment and longevity of the mechanism.

Outside Neutrals. Access to outside neutrals whose skills can be matched to a task requires a flexible statute but also requires that the neutral, members, or staff be aware of the utility and availability of such people. Good judgment must be exercised in matching the person with the problem. Such people can often assist in speeding resolution of disputes in cases where the principals or staff do not have the appropriate expertise or where a particular personality or skill is called for. Availability of such people provides options when a set of committee actors is "used up" and can no longer be effective. The kind of mediative strength—substantive expertise, experience, maturity, or personal acceptability—that can be gained on a hand-picked, part-time, or one-shot basis frequently cannot be obtained for full-time work because other obligations or career interests may lie elsewhere. However, in utilizing such people, it is important not to allow them to work in isolation.

The strength of this tool is multiplied when the outside mediator's skills can be buttressed by the members and staff, who can provide to the outsider a confidential assessment of the situation and its context. A staff member might be assigned to work with the neutral, thus giving a committee more intimate knowledge of the settlement in order to maintain its overview of settlement patterns and to absorb techniques that are used. With freedom to select and by keeping in close touch with the outside neutral, it is more likely that outside work will be consistent with the mechanism's philosophy and general practices and consistent with other settlements over which a committee presides or otherwise is attentive to.

Constituents.   A flexible joint mechanism relies on consensus for its authority and support and must therefore be attentive to opposition. A mechanism that requires flexibility, political acuity, and consensus will not function as a simple result of a statute or authority granted to it. Power flows to a mechanism like this by agreement and support of constituents. Some of this power results from bargaining and persuasion just as its product (collective bargaining settlements) depends on bargaining and persuasion. Thus, to maintain its utility, a joint mechanism must be sensitive to the variety of needs and interests in the community that it serves. Therefore, membership and staff must spend time in their representative and educational roles and perform those aspects of their informal duties that require keeping in touch with parties to a dispute or holding more general discussions about dispute resolution with their peers. The responsibility for the maintenance of these relationships can be divided according to the skills and relationships of different individuals within the membership.

Critical Aspects of Policy and Management

In addition to matters of structure and organization, a dispute resolution agency must have a philosophy, policies, and management procedures that will allow the successful use of that structure and its opportunities. While any joint mechanism will develop its own philosophies, depending on the circumstances, the personalities, and the background of the members and staff, there are a number of dimensions that may be instrumental in successful operations. In general, in a new and flexible structure, it probably would be prudent to start slowly and simply, giving the group and its policies time to conform to local conditions and the talents of the group. Tools should be tested before a large case load is accumulated and expectations raised.

Cost to the Parties

Low cost can encourage parties to seek assistance from an informal joint mechanism, as well as encourage support for the mechanism. In contrast, more formal proceedings such as LBO generally require legal help. For small towns, the ability to settle the problem themselves represents a significant cost savings. The cost factors may be less important in some jurisdictions than in others—or it may even be deemed desirable to impose a cost—but the influence of out-of-pocket costs on settlement-seeking behavior should be considered in setting up a mechanism to encourage resolution. Costs should not be punitive and thereby block parties from seeking a form of assistance that could be helpful. [2]

Quick Action

It is generally useful to maintain momentum by moving quickly at each stage of a case. While there may be good reason to hold action while waiting for an election or other event to pass, the sense of momentum will frequently affect the parties' willingness and ability to settle and may also affect their perception of the neutral's competence and fairness. A limited staff and a voluntary membership may make it difficult to process cases as quickly as interest in progress would dictate. Careful scheduling, increased efficiency of actions (as experience accumulates), more effective membership involvement, and proper staffing can accelerate the time for case handling.

Staff competence affects speed of resolution by their skill, aggressiveness, and attentiveness to detail and nuances. Skilled staff can judge, on a case-by-case basis, whether an impasse is ready to benefit from a hearing or other involvement of the mechanism and its principals. The quality of information and insight they are able to pass on assists action and cuts down on learning time by members or outside neutrals. A good briefing prior to a hearing or useful mediation work between hearings may make the difference between the need for one hearing or the need for several plus the days or weeks of waiting in between. These variables can make an overall difference of several months, especially if it is difficult to schedule hearings. (A smaller case volume might not pose the same problems, however.)

The staff also can save time by its responsiveness and availability to members and to the parties in dispute. Not infrequently, staff will become involved in a dispute that requires large amounts of personal time; and mediation and informal meetings, requiring time, commitment, and adaptability, take place unexpectedly. The membership also plays a role in the speed of handling cases: Members must be willing to spend time in hearings, negotiations, and in dealing informally with parties, or with a case that simply will not move along. This underscores the need to select volunteer members who are willing and able to spend significant amounts of time. Avoiding or settling disputes depends frequently on timing, and the willingness to be available at odd times may be important to expeditious resolution.

Management of Internal Operations

While this study did not focus on the internal management of the JLMC mechanism, it is a sufficiently important subject to merit mention. In a joint mechanism that depends on joint decision making by volunteers, day-to-day management may well slip through the cracks, so attention should be given to management process and staff activities.

Case Tracking. Because of its informal and part-time nature, a joint committee can best establish momentum and keep track of cases and case developments if there is a system through which to do so. The system should be simple, permitting lots of interaction and information exchange among members and staff, and anticipation of problems. A formal system relying on written reports would not fit the style and constraints of labor relations professionals and practical politicians. However, a simple case tracking system that creates group incentives to expeditiously resolve cases and which establishes productive group norms would be desirable.

Meetings and Communications. Regular and frequent meetings of all members and staff permit exchange of information and building of trust without a lot of formality. By dealing with all or most cases at least briefly at each case meeting, responsibilities can be fixed and all members can gain insight on techniques and settlement ranges and also can contribute information gleaned from their background or peer network. The meetings should be short so that interest is maintained and time can be spent working on disputes. Frequent meetings and informal discussions before and after, moreover, contribute to development of relationships and respect within the group. Also needed are working sessions apart from the case meetings where more detailed problem solving may take place, especially if case meetings are public, as a public sector dispute settlement mechanism might be expected to require.

The nature of the information that a joint mechanism can obtain requires discussions wherein specifics are divulged on a "need to know" basis, which if made public, might be harmful to settlement or to a bargaining relationship. The ethics of mediation generally require that this information be kept confidential. These same principles of confidentiality must pertain if a joint mechanism is to capitalize on the relationships and expertise that its membership permits. Thus, there is a necessity to compromise between the public sector tendency to place information in the public domain and the principles of confidentiality that pertain in effective resolution of disputes.

Avoiding Bureaucracy. The informal and frequently confidential nature of the peer network permits the strengths of a joint mechanism to be utilized. Formal requirements concerning reports and meetings might threaten the confidentiality that is a crucial part of negotiations and mediation. Extensive requirements for forms and reports would interfere with and could negate some important strengths that arise from informal and discrete access to members and staff, although there is some danger in extreme informality. The case work load may in some situations suggest stiffer requirements such as waiting times or more uniform reports. However, to remain a problem-solving forum with an eye on improved bargaining relationships and results, and not on forms and process, such temptation is best avoided. Also, to permit the parties to use the joint mechanism without the expense of legal representation, the procedures must be kept simple and undemanding with respect to paperwork, technical requirements, and their preparation.

Supervision. A joint staff poses some difficulties in management because supervision by two bosses is a difficult task under any circumstances. Here, however, the issue is compounded by the need for neutrality, making it difficult to simply elevate one of the senior staff representatives to management of internal administrative operations. Further, control of the administrative mechanism (budget, sending out awards, arranging hearings, etc.) is best not left to the control of one side or the other, lest simple errors or delays be seen in a suspicious light.

The need for neutrality and effectiveness should guide the arrangements. Still, the arrangements will probably require reexamination as any joint mechanism develops and sees more clearly its needs. In any case, the workability of the administrative arrangements is a sufficiently critical aspect of joint dispute resolution that there is a need for deliberate consideration of this aspect. Without prescribing a specific form of administration and management, staff and operational arrangements should conform to a committee's objectives and be able to service those objectives through the skills, relationships, and operating practices that develop. Techniques such as joint mediation, assessing, panel briefings, and other tools will work far more effectively if the internal workings of the group are cooperative and build trust and if assignments are thoughtfully made.

The entire mechanism, as well as its purposes, benefits from the better service rendered by an efficient staff and office and by the better relationships it permits them to maintain with each other (committee to committee, staff to staff, and committee to staff) and with their constituents.

Consistent Treatment of the Parties

The variation in tools and in the personal or constituent relationships that are part of a joint approach leaves open possibilities for unequal treatment of the parties in a dispute or differences in the treatment afforded parties in different disputes. Still, to maintain credibility and to keep the parties' trust, a high degree of consistency is necessary. Good relationships among the committee and staff contribute to equal treatment of parties as an atmosphere of respect for each other's views—and constituents—is maintained. Perceptions of the professionalism of the members, the neutral, and the staff will be determined partly by the parties' views of their treatment at the hands of the collective or single neutral. Operationally, therefore, the institution should keep in close touch with both sides as the situation dictates and move with equivalent dispatch on all cases. In one dispute, management was unforgiving toward the JLMC for failure to keep that side informed as it perceived that the labor side had been well informed and consequently had been influential regarding the outcome. Inadequate contact increases the probability of uncertainty, feelings of being left out, and lack of knowledge about, hence lack of faith in, the fairness of the process or—later— dissatisfaction with settlements. Members must represent constituents fairly and consistently, and no special favors can even seem to be shown.

Using the Power of Arbitration

A conscious decision regarding the use of arbitration is central and should be part of the initial discussions on a proposed statute. Essentially, however, the appeal of a joint mechanism is its capacity to encourage bargaining to satisfy labor's interest in closure and to satisfy management by not engendering undue third-party involvement. Arbitration, therefore, is not the preferred way to resolve disputes. The question of whether and how it should be used is, however, an important matter of policy. As Chapter 7 noted, while the majority of police and fire settlements in Massachusetts since 1978 were made without the use of arbitration, it was employed as a tool.

The relative decline in the use of arbitration is attributable partly to the improvement in the bargaining climate, partly to the availability of other tools, and partly because of the policy to avoid it. If the tool exists, it is tempting to use, especially after a dispute has been resistant to an array of other tools. Interestingly, since December 1980 arbitration has not been an option in Massachusetts, owing to the interpretation of Proposition 2½. Still the JLMC has continued to settle disputes at an equal pace without the availability of arbitration. More extensive use of persuasion with the parties and with the local legislature, especially by peers, seems to have contributed to a continuing capacity to settle most disputes. It could be argued, therefore, that with the presence of a joint dispute settlement mechanism, the power to arbitrate is not necessary—a prospect that is likely in many jurisdictions to delight management and disturb labor.

However, the power to arbitrate may serve a number of purposes worth noting here. Most obviously, by issuing an arbitration award which in fact has been agreed to by each side, a joint committee allows parties to maintain public positions on issues, even while being willing to compromise and settle. Next, it provides the "stick-in-the-closet" common to med-arb: Where neutrals are appointed to med-arb or where staff or members mediate, the parties'

knowledge that the power of arbitration exists may help persuade
parties to review their positions. In the context of a joint committee,
a staff mediator or member can use the threat of arbitration by
informing a party of the probable outcomes of an arbitration proceeding, thus providing information as well as settlement pressure
to a party who might otherwise have gambled on a particular outcome. Thus arbitration provides a tool for dealing with unreasonable
expectations. In Seabury it was this sort of information that helped
persuade the town manager to accept the JLMC settlement proposal.

Most disputes actually arbitrated by the JLMC (not de facto
agreed to) and those otherwise most resistant to settlement have
been cases in which personality or political factors were the major
obstacles. (This view is widely shared by both sides of the JLMC.) In
such instances continued bargaining may not achieve resolution, and
the use of a more interventionist tool may be required. Therefore,
some form of final closure may be an important consideration for
even the most successful and cooperative joint mechanism.

While the availability of arbitration seems helpful, it may not in all
instances be necessary—just as it may not in all instances be detrimental to management's interest. If it is one of a wide selection of
tools used more as a coax to bargaining rather than a substitute for it,
in a general atmosphere of trust it may be a useful tool even in a
system that eschews its use. Ironically, since the power to impose
binding arbitration settlements has been rescinded in Massachusetts, there has been some discussion between labor and management about the desirability of establishing a final closure device.

Consensus

A joint mechanism requires consensus to work. Consensus on procedures, philosophy, and on specific case actions and decisions encourages cooperation and commitment to the mechanism. A system
that encourages parties to accommodate their differences may be
more credible and believable if its own operations reflect consensus.

Consensus will be especially important early in the mechanism's
existence, particularly if its history has been one of bitterness and
mistrust. By seeking early agreement on administrative and similar
matters, unnecessary pique can be avoided that might otherwise
interfere with the sort of personal cooperation necessary for the
group to resolve bargaining problems. With agreement on early and

simple administrative matters, channels and relationships can most easily be built. As consensus seeking involves all members in the process, it can provide to each member a challenge and sense of importance and satisfaction that will be important in maintaining involvement of volunteer members.

When operations and decisions are handled by consensus, the capacity is strengthened to involve the expertise of members. More members are likely to be aware of all of the cases, decisions, and techniques being used, which in turn strengthens their individual and collective capacity to contribute to solutions on other cases or policies. In addition to the improvement in each member's abilities, operation by consensus will help the group develop a common and acceptable philosophy and will make more likely a consistent approach to cases and constituents. Internal agreement on a policy or case outcome makes it more likely that the mechanism will treat all "customers" equally.

Operation by consensus also makes it less likely that particularly aggressive personalities or those with significant outside influence will control the process. To maintain the faith of members and their constituencies in the joint mechanism, all representatives must be seen as having a voice. With an unduly dominant member or faction, disgruntlement can impede the internal cooperation and interest. The same problem may cause external views of the group to suffer.

Consensus decision making prevents the existence of "losers." If, for example, issues were frequently decided by a vote in which the chair voted with one side or the other to produce a majority, the views of the members and of their constituents on such outcomes— and of the neutral—might harm perceptions of neutrality.

Just as it is desirable for parties to a dispute to reach consensus and take responsibility for its resolution, a joint mechanism itself can place responsibility with its own party's representatives and thereby expect a more practical and acceptable result. If, in reaching consensus on a case or policy, each member has been properly attentive to that member's constituents' needs, a committee's actions are much more likely to be acceptable to both parties and to the labor and management community at large. Thus, operation by consensus has value in preserving the neutrality and acceptability—both internally and externally—of decisions and actions by a joint mechanism.

Consensus as an operating policy does not mean that there are no disagreements. It simply means that the resolution of those disagreements includes the views of all parties with a stake in it and that the resolution is generally satisfactory to all. Disputes over substantive questions will and should arise. The two sides of a joint mechanism may reach an impasse, but wherever possible it should be worked out so that the principle of joint problem solving and mutual satisfaction with its outcome is maintained. The process of reaching consensus on a matter may air some issues that would otherwise have festered or remained buried; it may in fact lead to a creative solution of a problem that might otherwise have been swept under the rug. However, operation by consensus requires time, energy, and often risks.

The JLMC has never taken a formal or counted vote on anything, including the disposition of a case. In only one instance has the neutral decided an issue in a peer bargaining situation. The lack of formal voting is a source of pride and cohesion, leading, consequently, to great efforts at mutual accommodation and search for creative solutions. Virtually everything has been worked out by consensus, occasionally maddening those who wish to have the issue resolved more quickly. The principle has been adhered to and respected, probably accounting for the unusual degree of informality in case and other discussions and encouraging the relatively open and trusting relationships that seem to have developed within the group.

A committee's ability to frankly disagree but to reach consensus serves, for members and constituents, as an example of constructive labor-management relationships and problem solving. If there is a central lesson in the Massachusetts experiment, perhaps its own operation by joint effort and accord is most important. A dispute resolution mechanism can best encourage bargaining if its policies and attitudes reflect a desire to increase accommodation and reduce conflict. Such policy must accompany the presence of a flexible tool kit if the mechanism is to realize its goals.

Summary

The concepts and principles underlying the Massachusetts experiment, abstracted in this chapter, reflect ways of handling some of the most difficult issues in resolving public sector disputes and may provide ideas for developing closure mechanisms elsewhere. The factors accounting for the Massachusetts' results are suggestive of some important features in public bargaining and dispute resolution.

To one degree or another, certain minimal conditions must be present to generate a workable system. First there must be mutual interest in development of an alternative system among and within the parties and between them and the relevant political forces. Second, and relatedly, the problem must have definable political, occupational, and geographic boundaries containing labor and management infrastructures capable of generating a practical alternative concept and a process to promote and establish it.

Probably the most critical operational ingredient of a useful joint system for dispute resolution is the membership structure. It provides a range and depth of tools and the capacity to adapt to changes in the bargaining environment and it provides channels to maintain the confidence of the parties and the wider community. As the key to balancing the desire to maximize collective bargaining with the desire to ensure proper attention to sovereignty, joint membership is the key to proper handling of politics and assurance of neutrality. The staff is a critical adjunct and executor of the substantive role of the principals and careful attention must be given to their quality and neutrality of action.

Through the variety of skills and interplay available among members and staff, the form and action of the neutral body can be tailored to resolve even the most stubborn of disputes. Further, possibilities exist for a representative problem-solving mechanism to engage in resolution of wider public policy problems of interest to labor and management. A flexible statute is necessary to permit the membership structure to best formulate policy, adapt to the specific labor-management and political environment and its problems, to effect change and to maintain the trust of the parties and the public.

The operating philosophy of the system will determine whether a joint mechanism can capitalize on the possibilities presented by its structure and membership. A commitment to neutrality, working by consensus, and leaving as much as possible the responsibility for settlement to the parties are operating principles that seem critical to resolving impasses in a manner that promotes stability and improvement in public bargaining and its outcomes and which meets the needs of both parties and the public.

Endnotes

1. Many of the facts and ideas for the references to dispute settlement in education result from participation in a seminar on dispute resolution at a conference of the Massachusetts Teachers Association, sponsored by the Trade Union Program, Harvard University Graduate School of Business Administration, November 1980. My thanks to Joseph P. O'Donnel, Director of the Trade Union Program, for inviting me to participate.
2. For a brief discussion of the impact of costs to the parties, see Kochan *et al.*, *Dispute Resolution under Fact Finding and Arbitration*, pp. 142–43 and 152–54.

Appendix A

"MEMORANDUM OF UNDERSTANDING," SEPTEMBER 19, 1977

This memorandum, agreed to by representatives of the Massachusetts Professional Fire Fighters Association and the Massachusetts League of Cities and Towns, formed the basis of the statute in Appendix B, which created the Joint Labor-Management Committee and empowered it to resolve impasses in municipal police and fire fighter collective bargaining. The memorandum was drawn up by John T. Dunlop, who mediated the parties' differences at their request.

Draft
September 19, 1977

MEMORANDUM OF UNDERSTANDING

The following memorandum of understanding is entered into between the Professional Fire Fighters of Massachusetts, AFL-CIO and the Massachusetts League of Cities and Towns.

I.   PURPOSES

The major purposes of this memorandum are:

(a) to strengthen the collective bargaining process so that it will operate more constructively in the public interest;

(b) to place greater responsibility on the parties to collective agreements and on their state-wide representatives for the determination and resolution of any impasse;

(c) to develop an improved data base relating to wages, benefits and other provisions of agreements that is mutually respected in order to facilitate collective bargaining;

(d) to reduce continuing confrontation, conflict, and potential litigation over the framework for collective bargaining, at least for a period, to permit the responsible parties directly to seek more practical and equitable procedures and solutions;

(e) to develop procedures to achieve higher productivity, safety, and training and to improve the quality of firefighting and management performance and organization in the public interest.

II.   JOINT LABOR-MANAGEMENT COMMITTEE

(1) The parties to this Memorandum of Understanding agree to establish a Joint Labor-Management Committee to effectuate the above purposes and to administer this Memorandum. The Joint Labor-Management Committee shall be comprised of an equal number of labor representatives (drawn from the firefighters and municipal police officer organizations) and representatives of cities and towns, each side named by the organizations signatory to this Memorandum of Understanding. Initially there shall be six representatives on each side. This number can be changed by action of the Joint Labor-Management Committee.

(2) Each side of the Joint Labor-Management Committee shall designate a chairman for that side, and each side shall designate a staff representative.

(3) The two sides of the Joint Labor-Management Committee shall agree upon an Impartial Chairman. It is intended that the Joint Labor-Management Committee shall seek to reach agreement and consensus on all matters which come before it. The Impartial Chairman, however, is authorized to cast a deciding vote on any matter within the scope of this Memorandum.

(4) On matters relating solely to the firefighters, on the labor side of the

Joint Labor-Management Committee, only representatives of their organization shall be represented and on matters relating solely to municipal police officers, only representatives of their organizations shall be represented; on general and common matters both groups shall be represented.

III. IMPASSE RESOLUTION

(1) At its discretion the Joint Labor-Management Committee may consider any dispute over the terms of a collective bargaining agreement involving firefighters or municipal police officers prior to fact finding or after fact finding and prior to final offer arbitration under the laws of the Commonwealth of Massachusetts, Chapter 347. The Committee may meet with the parties, conduct formal or informal conferences, and take other steps to encourage an agreement on the terms of the collective bargaining agreement or on procedures to resolve the dispute. The Committee shall make every effort to encourage the parties to engage in good-faith negotiations to reach a settlement.

(2) In any dispute over the terms of an agreement which the Joint Labor-Management Committee has taken under consideration, the parties to this Memorandum of Understanding intend that the view and judgment of the Committee shall be determinative as to whether a genuine impasse exists in negotiations and the process of collective bargaining have been exhausted, and they intend that the Committee's view and judgment shall be respected by the state board in any determination than an impasse exists.

IV. SCOPE OF ARBITRATION

(1) The parties to this Memorandum of Understanding recognize that aside from procedures for dispute resolution in the event parties to collective bargaining agreements do not reach agreement in direct negotiations, there have been other differences between parties relating to the scope of arbitration. The parties to this Memorandum intend that the Joint Labor-Management Committee shall explore systematically each of these questions in the year ahead seeking agreement in broad principle or in particular disputes.

(2) The parties to the Memorandum are of the view that it may be appropriate for the parties to collective bargaining agreements to discuss and negotiate over such items as the status and definition of supervisors and the definition of management rights. They are not in full agreement, however, as to the limits within which such issues as remain in dispute among the parties shall be determined by arbitration. These questions are often best explored in particular situations. Accordingly, it is agreed that the Committee, in cases which it takes under consideration, may seek to secure agreement or to determine the scope of such issues presented to arbitration.

V.   LEGISLATION AND RELATIONS TO COMMONWEALTH

The parties to this Memorandum of Understanding agree to consult with appropriate executive and legislative authority in the Commonwealth, and to draft appropriate legislation, should that be necessary, to achieve the purposes and establish the procedures and mechanism set forth in this Memorandum. These consultations shall include the cooperative relationships between the agencies established under state law and those specified in this Memorandum.

VI.   OTHER PROVISIONS

(1) The parties to this Memorandum agreed to nominate the members of the Joint Labor-Management Committee specified above and to cooperate fully with the Committee and to accept its determinations.

(2) This Memorandum shall run for a period until June 30, 1979. The parties to the Memorandum shall meet periodically to review the operation of the Memorandum, and they shall meet sixty days prior to the expiration date to review proposals for revision or cancellation.

(3) The effective date of this Memorandum shall be _____.

SIGNATORIES

Appendix B

MASSACHUSETTS GENERAL LAWS, CHAPTER 154, ACTS OF 1979

This chapter of the General Laws authorized the operation of the Joint Labor-Management Committee for Municipal Police and Fire Fighters from July of 1979, when the previous statute authorizing the Committee since January 1978 expired. The differences in the two statutes concern largely the addition in 1979 of a vice-chairman and in the alteration which required parties filing an impasse petition to do so with the Committee. Previously, petitions were filed with the Board of Conciliation and Arbitration.

Subsequently, as of December 1980, the power to impose funding of settlements on local legislatures was excised as part of the passage of Proposition 2½, a tax limitation measure.

Chapter 154.

THE COMMONWEALTH OF MASSACHUSETTS

In the Year One Thousand Nine Hundred and Seventy-nine

AN ACT RELATIVE TO A JOINT LABOR-MANAGEMENT COM-
MITTEE OVERSEEING MUNICIPAL POLICE AND FIRE FIGHTER
COLLECTIVE BARGAINING AND ARBITRATION PROCEEDINGS.

*Be it enacted by the Senate and House of Representatives in General
Court assembled, and by the authority of the same, as follows:*

SECTION 1. Chapter 1078 of the acts of 1973 is hereby amended by
striking out section 4A, inserted by section 1 of chapter 730 of the acts of
1977, and inserting in place thereof the following section:

Section 4A. There shall be in the department of labor and industries, but
not subject to the jurisdiction thereof, a committee to be known as the joint
labor-management committee in this section referred to as the committee.
The committee shall be composed of fourteen members, including a chairman, and a vice-chairman. Twelve committee members shall be appointed
by the governor for a term of one year, as follows: three from nominations
submitted by the Professional Firefighters of Massachusetts, International
Association of Firefighters, AFL-CIO, three from nominations submitted
by the International Brotherhood of Police Officers, NAGE and the Massachusetts Police Association, and six from nominations submitted by the
local government advisory committee established pursuant to executive
order one hundred and twenty-three, dated January thirteenth, nineteen
hundred and seventy-six. Any member of the committee may be removed
by the governor for neglect of duty, malfeasance in office, or upon request
by the nominating body. The chairman and vice-chairman shall be nominated by the committee, and appointed by the governor for a term of one
year. The chairman shall be the chief administrative officer of the committee. The vice-chairman shall assist the chairman and may be authorized by
the chairman to act for him in his absence and shall have the full powers
of the chairman when so authorized and he shall vote only in the absence
of the chairman.

In matters exclusively pertaining to municipal firefighters, committee
members nominated for appointment by professional police officer organizations shall not vote. In matters exclusively pertaining to municipal police
officers, committee members nominated for appointment by professional
firefighter organizations shall not vote. All committee members shall be
eligible to vote on matters of common and general interest. The number of

committee members representing the local government advisory committee and the number of committee members representing the professional firefighter or police organizations entitled to vote on any matter coming before the committee shall be equal. The chairman may cast the deciding vote on any matter relating to a dispute concerning negotiations over the terms and provisions of a collective bargaining agreement, including any decision to take jurisdiction over a dispute.

Members of the committee shall serve without compensation, but shall be entitled to reimbursement, out of any funds available for the purpose, for reasonable travel or other expenses actually incurred in the performance of their committee duties. The chairman and vice-chairman shall be compensated for time spent for the committee business on a per diem basis at a rate to be determined by the secretary of administration and finance. The committee may purchase such supplies and equipment, and may employ such clerical, staff and other personnel who shall not be subject to the provisions of section nine A of chapter thirty or chapter thirty-one of the General Laws, as they deem necessary to the conduct of committee business out of any funds available for the purpose. Members of the committee employed by a municipality shall be granted leave, if on duty, by the municipal employer for those regularly scheduled work hours spent in the performance of committee business.

The committee shall have oversight responsibility for all collective bargaining negotiations involving municipal police officers and firefighters. The committee shall, at its discretion, have jurisdiction in any dispute over the negotiation of the terms of a collective bargaining agreement involving municipal firefighters or police officers; provided, however, that notwithstanding section four of chapter one thousand and seventy-eight of the acts of nineteen hundred and seventy-three to the contrary, the committee may determine whether the proceeding for the prevention of any prohibited practices filed with the labor relations commission shall or shall not prevent arbitration pursuant to this section.

After notification by the committee, the parties to any municipal police and fire negotiations shall file with committee, in such time as the committee orders:

(1) copies of all requests to bargain, and of all bargaining agenda;

(2) notification of impasse in bargaining;

(3) notification of all pending unfair labor practice proceedings between the parties;

(4) copies of any factfinding reports;

(5) notification of any impasse extending beyond completion of factfinding procedures;

(6) copies of any collective bargaining agreements, and any relevant personnel ordinances, by-laws, and rules and regulations; and

(7) such other information as the committee may reasonably require.

Notwithstanding the provisions of the first paragraph of section nine of chapter one hundred and fifty E of the General Laws to the contrary, when either party or the parties acting jointly to a municipal police and fire collective bargaining negotiations believe than an impasse exists in their negotiations, the party or both parties shall petition first the committee for the exercise of jurisdiction and for the determination of the existence of an impasse.

The committee shall forthwith review the petition and shall make a determination within thirty days whether to exercise jurisdiction over the dispute. Subject to the provisions of the eleventh paragraph, if the committee declines to exercise jurisdiction over the dispute or fails to act within thirty days of receipt of the petition on jurisdiction, the petition shall be automatically referred to the board of arbitration and conciliation hereinafter referred to as the board, for disposition in accordance with the provisions of section nine of chapter one hundred and fifty E of the General Laws.

The petition to the committee shall identify the issues in dispute, the parties, the efforts of the parties to resolve the dispute and such other information as may be prescribed in the rules of the committee.

Said board shall not accept any petition from a party to a municipal police and fire negotiation under section nine of chapter one hundred and fifty E of the General Laws if the petition has not been first reviewed in accordance with the provisions of this section by the committee.

The committee or its representative or mediators appointed by it may meet with the parties to a dispute, conduct formal or informal conferences, and take other steps including mediation to encourage the parties to agree on the terms of a collective bargaining agreement or the procedures to resolve the dispute. The committee shall make every effort to encourage the parties to engage in good faith negotiations to reach settlement through negotiations or mediation.

The committee after consultation with the board of arbitration and conciliation may remove at any time from the jurisdiction of the board any dispute in which the board has exercised jurisdiction, and the board shall then take no further action in such dispute. The committee may, at any time, remand to the board any dispute in which the committee has exercised jurisdiction. The board shall assist and cooperate with the committee in its performance of the committee's duties. Disputes over which the committee does not exercise jurisdiction shall be governed by all other applicable provisions of law.

The committee shall have exclusive jurisdiction in matters over which it assumes jurisdiction and shall determine if a genuine impasse exists and if the processes of collective bargaining have been exhausted.

If the committee determines that a genuine impasse exists, and the process of collective bargaining has been exhausted, the committee shall:

(1) specify the issue or issues to be arbitrated; provided, however, that the committee shall not specify for arbitration any issue excluded from arbitration pursuant to section four, and the committee may, however, administer the provisions of said section four relative to firefighter assignments and transfers;

(2) nominate the panel of neutral arbitrators from which the arbitrator is to be selected by the parties; if the parties cannot agree on an arbitrator within a time prescribed by the committee, the committee shall appoint the neutral arbitrator or arbitrators or the committee may appoint the chairman, the vice-chairman or a panel of the committee including the chairman or vice-chairman to arbitrate the dispute;

(3) determine the form of arbitration, conventional arbitration, issue by issue, last best offer, or such other form as the committee deems appropriate; and

(4) determine the procedures to be followed in the arbitration proceeding. Except as provided herein, arbitration proceedings in matters over which the committee assumes jurisdiction, shall be conducted in accordance with the standards, provisions and limitations of said section four. The committee may direct the parties to a dispute to conduct further negotiations concerning issues not specified for arbitration.

In dispute resolution conducted by other than the committee or its members or staff, the parties shall share and pay equally the costs involved in such resolution.

The committee shall have jurisdiction in any particular dispute concerning job titles over which the parties have negotiated, or to remove specific job titles from collective bargaining for individuals performing certain specified management duties.

The committee shall promulgate rules and regulations necessary for the performance and enforcement of the responsibilities and powers set forth herein in this act; provided, however, that said committee file a copy of any regulations or amendments thereto with the clerks of the senate and the house of representatives who, with the approval of the president of the senate and speaker of the house of representatives, shall refer such regulations to an appropriate committee of the general court. Within thirty days after such filing, the appropriate committee of the general court shall hold a hearing on such regulations and shall issue a report and file a copy with the joint labor-management committee. Said joint labor-management committee shall consider such report and make revisions in the regulations as it deems appropriate in view of such report and shall forthwith file a copy of the final regulations with the chairman of the committee of the general court to which the regulations were referred.

The provisions of chapter thirty A of the General Laws, unless otherwise provided, shall apply to the committee.

The committee shall have the power to administer oaths and to require by subpoena the attendance and testimony of witnesses, the production of books, records, and other evidence relative to or pertinent to the issues presented to the committee.

It is hereby declared that the provisions of this act are severable, and if any provisions of this act shall be declared unconstitutional by the valid judgment or decree of any court of competent jurisdiction, such unconstitutionality shall not affect any of the remaining provisions of this act.

SECTION 2. Said chapter 1078 is hereby further amended by striking out section 8, as amended by section 3 of chapter 347 of the acts of 1977, and inserting in place thereof the following section:

Section 8. The provisions of section four of this act shall terminate on June thirtieth, nineteen hundred and eighty-three. Any arbitration proceedings pending on June thirtieth, nineteen hundred and eighty-three shall be completed under the provisions of section four.

Appendix C

"RULES: JOINT LABOR-MANAGEMENT COMMITTEE," JULY 2, 1979

Following are the procedural rules of the Joint Labor-Management Committee which correspond to the statute in Appendix B.

RULES

JOINT LABOR-MANAGEMENT COMMITTEE

Adopted July 2, 1979

The purpose of the Joint Labor-Management Committee is to encourage the parties to collective bargaining disputes involving municipal police officers and fire fighters to agree on the terms of collective bargaining agreements or the procedures to resolve particular disputes. The Committee shall make every effort to encourage the parties to engage in good faith negotiations to reach settlement and a constructive long-term relationship.

I. *The Operations of the Committee*

1. *Types of Meetings.* The Committee may hold two types of meetings: general meetings and case meetings.

(a) General meetings are to be concerned with issues of policy of the Committee, with questions of rules and procedures and the operations of the Committee, and with matters of common interest to both professional police officers including superior officers and to professional fire fighters and the representatives of the cities and towns.

(b) Case meetings are to be concerned with particular disputes and collective bargaining matters.

(c) Each part of the Committee, professional police officers, professional fire fighters and representatives of the cities and towns shall designate a chairman of its group within the Committee in special circumstances and to facilitate consultation and communications.

2. *Voting.* In case type meetings, in matters exclusively pertaining to municipal fire fighters, committee members nominated for appointment by professional police officer organizations shall not vote, and in matters exclusively pertaining to municipal police officers, committee members nominated for appointment by professional fire fighter organizations shall not vote.

3. All Committee members shall be eligible to vote on matters of common and general interest.

4. The number of votes of Committee members representing the local government advisory committee and the number of votes of Committee members representing the professional fire fighter or police organizations entitled to vote on any matter coming before the Committee shall be equal.

5. The Chairman may cast the deciding vote on any matter relating to a dispute concerning negotiations over the terms and provisions of a collective bargaining agreement, including any decision to take jurisdiction over a dispute. The Chairman shall be the chief administrative officer of the Committee. The Vice-Chairman shall assist the Chairman and may be authorized by the Chairman to act for him in his absence and shall have the full powers of the Chairman when so authorized and he shall vote only in the absence of the Chairman.

6. *Open Meeting Law.* The Committee shall comply with the Open Meeting Law of the Commonwealth as amended. That statute provides, Chapter 30, Section 11B (3), that executive sessions may be held "to conduct collective bargaining sessions" including related mediation and such sessions may be closed by the Committee.

7. *Quorum.* A *quorum for a general type meeting* shall consist of one member of the Committee representing the local government advisory committee and one member of the Committee representing the professional fire fighter organizations and one member of the Committee representing the professional police officers organizations and the Chairman or Vice-Chairman. A *quorum for a case type meeting* shall consist of one member of the Committee representing the local government advisory committee and one member of the Committee representing either the professional police organizations or the professional fire fighter organizations, depending upon whether the case concerns professional police officers or professional fire fighters and the Chairman or Vice-Chairman.

8. *Alternate Members.* The Committee expects that its members shall

regularly attend meetings of the Committee. Each part of the Committee shall specify in advance, with the approval of the Committee, alternate members to assure that the work of the Committee may go forward. Alternate members are expected regularly to attend general meetings of the Committee.

9. *Senior Staff.* The Committee shall appoint one full-time senior staff person nominated by the members of the Committee representing the local government advisory committee and one full-time senior staff person nominated by the members of the Committee representing the professional police officer and professional fire fighter organizations. The two senior staff persons shall work together to further the purposes of the Committee. They may be assigned by the Committee through the Chairman to gather facts, to facilitate negotiations, to mediate, and otherwise to encourage agreement between parties.

10. The Committee may specify other staff positions in accordance with law and within the budget. The Committee may also appoint special mediators to handle particular cases. The Chairman shall supervise such staff.

II. *The Involvement of the Committee in Particular Disputes*

1. *Relationships to Agencies.* The Committee shall request the Department of Labor and Industries, the Board of Conciliation and Arbitration and the Labor Relations Commission each to designate a person with whom the Committee shall maintain a flow of information and through whom the Committee shall consult these Agencies on particular cases to assure cooperative relations and consistent activities in the interest of improved collective bargaining and dispute resolution.

2. *Oversight Responsibility.* The Committee shall have oversight responsibility for all collective bargaining negotiations involving municipal police officers and fire fighters.

3. *Petitions to take Jurisdiction.* Should either party or the parties acting jointly to a municipal police and fire collective bargaining negotiations believe that an impasse exists in their negotiations, the party or both parties shall petition first the Committee for the exercise of jurisdiction and for the determination of an impasse. Such petition shall identify the issues in dispute, the parties and the efforts of the parties to resolve the dispute.

The Committee shall forthwith review the petition and shall make a determination within thirty (30) days of the receipt of the petitions whether to exercise jurisdiction over the dispute. If the Committee declines to exercise jurisdiction over the dispute or fails to act within thirty (30) days of receipt of the petition of jurisdiction, the petition shall automatically be referred to the Board of Conciliation and Arbitration for disposition in accordance with its procedures.

The Committee may subsequently at any stage after consultation with the Board of Conciliation and Arbitration remove the dispute from the jurisdiction of the Board and handle the case as if it had retained jurisdiction at the outset. The Committee may, at any time, remand to the Board any dispute in which the Committee has exercised jurisdiction. The Committee's decisions on jurisdiction are to be formally communicated to the Board of Conciliation and Arbitration and to the parties.

4. *Request for Data.* After notification of the Committee, the parties to any municipal police and fire fighter negotiations shall file with the Committee at its offices in Boston, Massachusetts.

(a) Copies of requests to bargain and proposals of each side.

(b) Notification of impasse in bargaining.

(c) Notification of all pending unfair labor practice proceedings between the parties.

(d) Copies of any fact finding reports.

(e) Notification of any impasse extending beyond completion of factfinding procedures, and

(f) Collective bargaining agreements and relevant personnel ordinances, bylaws, and rules and regulations including wage and salary and benefit schedules.

(g) Such other information as the Committee may reasonably require.

5. *The Committee's Jurisdiction in a Dispute.* The Committee may, at its discretion, and on its own initiative, exercise jurisdiction in any dispute over the negotiations of the terms of a collective bargaining agreement involving municipal fire fighters or police officers. The Committee may also exercise jurisdiction in any dispute concerning job titles over which the parties have negotiated or in any dispute over proposals to remove specific job titles from collective bargaining for individuals and performing certain specified management duties.

6. *Dispute Resolution.* The Committee or its representative or mediators appointed by it may meet with the parties to a dispute, conduct formal or informal conferences, and take other steps including mediation to encourage the parties to agree on the terms of a collective bargaining agreement or the procedures to resolve the dispute. The Committee shall make every effort to encourage the parties to engage in good faith negotiations to reach settlement through negotiations or mediation.

7. If the Committee determines a genuine impasse exists, the Committee may order fact finding or appoint a factfinder or the Committee may order arbitration in accordance with this paragraph. The Committee may specify the issue or issues to be arbitrated; (provided, however, that the Committee shall not specify for arbitration any issue excluded in arbitration pursuant to Section 4 of Chapter 1078, the Committee may, however, administer the provisions of said Section 4 relative to fire fighter assignments and transfer). The Committee may also nominate a panel of neutral arbitrators, and if the parties cannot agree on an arbitrator from the panel

within a time prescribed by the Committee, the Committee shall appoint the neutral arbitrator or the panel of arbitrators, and determine the form of arbitration and the procedures to be followed in the arbitration proceedings.

The Committee may designate as arbitrators a panel of the full Committee including the Chairman or Vice-Chairman of the Committee or the Chairman or Vice-Chairman alone. The Committee may for a limited period direct the parties to a dispute to conduct further negotiations concerning issues not specified for arbitration.

8. In dispute resolution conducted by other than the Committee or its members or staff, the parties shall share and pay equally the costs involved in such resolution.

9. The Committee shall have the power to administer oaths and to require by subpoena the attendance and testimony of witnesses, the production of books, records, and other evidence relative to or pertinent to the issues presented by the Committee.

10. Except as provided in Section 4A of the Statute effective July 1, 1979, arbitration proceedings should be conducted in accordance with the standards, provisions and limitations of Chapter 150E of the general laws.

III. *Other Procedural Matters*

1. The Committee may assemble a file of collective bargaining agreements and wage, salary and fringe benefit data and other statistical information to facilitate constructive collective bargaining and dispute resolution.

2. The Committee shall review periodically the operation of these Rules in light of experience and in view of suggestions received from interested parties and appropriate legislative committees.

3. These proposed Procedural Rules shall be filed with the clerks of the Senate and House of Representatives of the Commonwealth of Massachusetts. In accordance with the procedures specified in the statute, the Committee shall subsequently adopt final regulations which shall supersede the Rules of March 1978.

INDEX